CAMBRIDGE TEXTS IN THE
HISTORY OF POLITICAL THOUGHT

ANDREW FLETCHER
Political Works

D1707783

CAMBRIDGE TEXTS IN THE
HISTORY OF POLITICAL THOUGHT

Series editors

RAYMOND GEUSS
Lecturer in Social and Political Sciences, University of Cambridge

QUENTIN SKINNER
Regius Professor of Modern History in the University of Cambridge

Cambridge Texts in the History of Political Thought is now firmly established as the major student textbook series in political theory. It aims to make available to students all the most important texts in the history of Western political thought, from ancient Greece to the early twentieth century. All the familiar classic texts will be included but the series seeks at the same time to enlarge the conventional canon by incorporating an extensive range of less well-known works, many of them never before available in a modern English edition. Wherever possible, texts are published in complete and unabridged form, and translations are specially commissioned for the series. Each volume contains a critical introduction together with chronologies, biographical sketches, a guide to further reading and any necessary glossaries and textual apparatus. When completed, the series will aim to offer an outline of the entire evolution of Western political thought.

For a list of titles published in the series, please see end of book.

ANDREW FLETCHER

Political Works

EDITED BY
JOHN ROBERTSON
St Hugh's College, Oxford

CAMBRIDGE
UNIVERSITY PRESS

PUBLISHED BY THE PRESS SYNDICATE OF THE UNIVERSITY OF CAMBRIDGE
The Pitt Building, Trumpington Street, Cambridge CB2 1RP, United Kingdom

CAMBRIDGE UNIVERSITY PRESS
The Edinburgh Building, Cambridge, CB2 2RU, United Kingdom
40 West 20th Street, New York, NY 10011–4211, USA
10 Stamford Road, Oakleigh, Melbourne 3166, Australia

First published 1997

Printed in the United Kingdom at the University Press, Cambridge

Typeset in Ehrhardt 9.5/12 pt [WV]

A catalogue record for this book is available from the British Library

Library of Congress Cataloguing in Publication data
Fletcher, Andrew, 1655–1716.
Andrew Fletcher: political works/edited by John Robertson.
p.   cm. – (Cambridge texts in the history of political
thought)
Includes index.
ISBN 0 521 43391 6 (hardbound)
1. Scotland – Politics and government – 1689–1745 – Pamphlets.
2. Political science – Scotland.   I. Robertson, John, 1951–   .
II. Title.   III. Series.
DA804.1.F6A25   1997
320'.092–dc21   97–6084 CIP

ISBN 0 521 43391 6 hardback
ISBN 0 521 43994 9 paperback

Contents

Acknowledgements

I would like particularly to thank Sir John Elliott for his comments on the translation and annotation of the *Discourse concerning the Affairs of Spain*, Georgina McLeod for references and other help in tracing Fletcher's movements abroad, and the Modern History Faculty Office in Oxford for assistance in the preparation of the text. More generally I am grateful to all those with whom I have discussed Fletcher over the years: David Armitage, Lord Dacre of Glanton, Istvan Hont, Colin Kidd, Nicholas Phillipson, John Pocock and Blair Worden. My family, as ever, have been a constant support.

Introduction

Andrew Fletcher's *Political Works* comprise six short, precisely argued pamphlets, published between 1697 and 1704. Each was a *pièce d'occasion*, addressed to a particular contemporary issue: the maintenance of a standing army in Britain, the economic predicament of Scotland in the 1690s, the Spanish Succession Crisis, and the crisis in relations between Scotland and England which culminated in the Union of 1707. The pamphlets' individuality is enhanced by their variety of form. Three were 'Discourses', or essays, which combined analysis of the problems addressed with specific proposals to resolve them; and of these one was composed and published in Italian. Another two were in the form of 'Speeches'. One of these was plainly imaginary, and used the rhetorical form in a manner little different from a discourse; the other, however, was a collection of speeches which Fletcher had actually delivered in the Scottish parliament. The final work took a different form again, being written as an 'account of a conversation', or dialogue. To this, the most sophisticated of his chosen forms, Fletcher successfully brought every appearance of realism; but no less evident is his success in using the dialogue form to develop and set off a range of opposing arguments.

Such variety of content and form, allied to an urgent, unadorned style, was (and remains) effective in engaging the reader's appreciation of Fletcher's intelligence and literary quality. But variety can also militate against intellectual coherence. The extent to which the *Political Works* amount to one interconnected set of writings, and were the product of a single, consistent intellectual project, is not automatically clear. In this introduction, therefore, my principal objective is to demonstrate that such a project existed, and that it had a definite intellectual identity. What unifies Fletcher's writings, I shall argue, is an attempt to understand the politics of Europe at the turn of the seventeenth and eighteenth centuries in terms that would do justice to the complexity of its structure – to the circumstances and interests of its many smaller states, whether princely or republican, as well as to those of its few great monarchies. And what gave conceptual coherence to this enquiry was Fletcher's distinctive choice of terms in which to pursue it.

These terms, it will be seen, were derived from Machiavelli. Machiavelli's political works, *The Prince*, the *Discourses on Livy* and *The Art of War*, were composed in Florence between 1513 and 1521. Yet despite an interval of almost two hundred years they remained for Fletcher the pre-eminent source of insight into modern politics. From Machiavelli Fletcher learnt that the wisdom of the ancients, which he revered, lay in recognising politics as a distinct sphere of human activity, with its own values and goals. As the ancients, and more particularly the Romans, further showed, these values and goals must be pursued in this world, and kept apart from any values and goals imposed by a concern for the next world. This was a lesson which had been equally misunderstood by the Scholastic Aristotelians, for whom politics was a branch of ethics, and by the jurists, who treated it as an extension of the study of law. What a Machiavellian politics required was not a general moral 'virtue', but specifically '*virtù*', a manly energy which pursued worldly glory in the face of unpredictable circumstances; not simply a framework of laws, but institutional structures or 'orders' (*ordini*) within which different political interests could be balanced and their energies harnessed to the defence and aggrandisement of the community as a whole. Yet even as Fletcher drew on these concepts, he was, as we shall also see, obliged to modify them in the face of a powerful new force. This force was commerce, whose growing influence Machiavelli had failed to anticipate, and before which even politics would have to bend. Confronted with commerce, Fletcher had to adapt the Machiavellian legacy and develop what might be characterised as a neo-Machiavellian politics. Although others besides Fletcher were thinking along similar lines in the second half of the seventeenth century, in England and in the United Provinces, his *Political*

Works are perhaps the most sophisticated and wide-ranging expression of neo-Machiavellian political thought. Even then, it was a project whose viability Fletcher himself appears to have come to question, in his last and most complex work. It would not be long, as I shall end by noting, before the thinkers of the Enlightenment, not least in Scotland itself, subjected the Machiavellian approach to politics to much more radical criticism for its inappropriateness to the modern world of commerce.

Before developing this account of Fletcher's intellectual significance, however, we should examine what his works may have owed to his life and political experiences.

Andrew Fletcher, discriminating patriot

There is a point of view which regards Fletcher's writings as secondary in importance to the political career that earned him the reputation of 'the Patriot'. On this account, understandably popular in his own country, Andrew Fletcher is almost exclusively a Scot, and specifically the Scot who adamantly and incorruptibly opposed the Union with England in 1707. When viewed in this perspective, Fletcher's writings are important in so far as they clarify and explain his political involvement, and in particular his prominent role in the last Scottish Parliament, from 1703 to 1707. Where his writings do not obviously throw light on his political involvement, however, they tend to be discounted and overlooked.

The problem with this view is not that it is altogether false, but that it is over-simplified to the point of missing most of what makes Fletcher so interesting. Contemporaries, both friends and political opponents, acknowledged the honesty and intransigence with which Fletcher adhered to his principles; and his subsequent reputation as 'the Patriot' – a story in its own right, which has still to be investigated properly – has contributed to the maintenance of a distinct Scottish political identity in opposition to the Union. Nevertheless, the known facts of his life indicate that Andrew Fletcher was a rather more discriminating patriot than his popular reputation would lead us to believe.[1]

[1] The known facts are fewer, and less readily accessible, than a biographer would wish, and it is customary to blame the Earl Marischal's alleged donation of Fletcher's papers to Rousseau, to enable the latter to write his biography, for their

Andrew Fletcher was born the eldest son of Sir Robert, laird of Saltoun, in 1653. The estate, in East Lothian, south-east of Edinburgh, was a good one, although both his father and his grandfather (Lord Innerpeffer, a judge in the Court of Session) were made to pay for their support of the Engagement in favour of Charles I in 1647. Little is known of Andrew Fletcher's early education, except that some part of it was undertaken by Gilbert Burnet, the future Bishop of Salisbury and Whig historian, who was the parish minister during the 1660s. On his father's death in 1665 Andrew Fletcher succeeded as laird; and three years later he left Scotland for London in the company of a governor. There is evidence that he was abroad, moving between London, the Netherlands and Paris, for every year except 1674 until 1678; he may well have been out of Scotland for all ten years, between the ages of 15 and 25.[2] In so doing he not only acquired his higher education outwith Scotland, but set the pattern of the rest of his life.

For Fletcher's way of life was established by travelling. The detailed course of his travels, in so far as it is known, is given in the chronology which follows this introduction. But the general pattern deserves further comment here. Returning to Scotland in 1678, Fletcher was quickly involved in politics, and apparently remained there for four years. By the time he left again, in 1682, he had made himself thoroughly unpopular with the authorities; but not until after he had been condemned as a traitor for his participation in

loss. In fact the Saltoun Papers in the National Library of Scotland contain a good deal of miscellaneous material relating to Andrew Fletcher, including a certain amount of correspondence, his library catalogue, some estate papers, and accounts, bills and receipts. These last, along with his correspondence, have the particular value of enabling Fletcher's movements to be traced. Further letters are to be found in family papers in Scottish archives and in printed collections; and Fletcher's doings were occasionally the subject of official government correspondence now held in the Public Record Office in London. Research in foreign archives may well yield further material. What follows is no more than an outline of the present state of our knowledge. But because of constraints on space in the series in which this edition appears, I will give specific references only when the information is not in the published works on Fletcher's life and thought (for which see the Bibliographical Guide).

[2] The evidence is in the Saltoun Papers, National Library of Scotland (hereafter NLS), ms 16831, ff. 9–56, beginning with a bill dated 14 August 1668 addressed to a Mr John Ferney in London, to pay Mr James Graham, Governor to Mr Fletcher of Saltoun, the sum of £50 sterling, and continuing with bills payable to and receipts signed by Andrew Fletcher, in The Hague, Rotterdam, Paris and London, 1668–78 (except 1674).

Monmouth's Rebellion in 1685 was it essential for him to be in exile. Having escaped to Spain, Fletcher may have travelled there, before making his way back to the United Provinces by 1688. He was able to come home to Scotland in 1689 following William's successful invasion and deposition of James VII and II. But he was away again by 1692, and regularly in London throughout the 1690s.[3] Even after he had been elected a member of the Scottish parliament in 1703 he spent the winter of 1703–4 in London, and this pattern may have been repeated, although the evidence otherwise indicates that he remained in Scotland from 1705 until 1708. Thereafter, however, he was away in every year until his death in 1716, and probably out of the country continuously from 1712, once again moving between London, the United Provinces, Brussels and Paris, with the odd excursion further afield, as to Leipzig in 1709.[4]

In all, Fletcher was out of the country in at least 35 out of the 48 years he lived after first leaving in 1668; and there were three periods in which he seems to have been away continuously for six years or more. Increasingly, and especially after 1708, he may have felt under some pressure to go. Fletcher never married, and in his many absences the running of the estate had devolved on to his younger brother and presumed heir Henry, who with his wife and children lived in the house at Saltoun. But the decision not to settle in Scotland was clearly Andrew's, and its implication is clear. After a while – quite a short while – he became bored by his own country. The world which Andrew Fletcher really enjoyed and chose to spend his time in was one

---

[3] Saltoun Papers: NLS ms 16831 ff. 62–4: various bills for and from Andrew Fletcher in London, dated 1692; and ms 16502 ff. 152–3, 154–5, 167–8, 169–70, 172, covering the years 1694, 1696, 1698, 1699; see also his correspondence with Locke in *The Correspondence of John Locke*, edited by E. S. De Beer, vol. v (Oxford, 1979), pp. 82, 274–5, 303–4, 314: Fletcher to Locke, July [1694], 22 Feb. 1695, 25 Jan. and 3 Feb. 1698.

[4] See the correspondence between Andrew and Henry Fletcher in NLS, Saltoun Papers, mss 16502, 16503; and the correspondence between Andrew, Henry, and Henry's son Andrew, from Paris and London, Oct. 1715 to Sept. 1716, printed in *Letters of Andrew Fletcher of Saltoun and his Family 1715–16*, edited by Irene J. Murray, *Scottish History Society*, Fourth Series, *Miscellany X* (Edinburgh, 1965), pp. 149–64. Also *Letters of Lord Balmerino to Henry Maule, 1710–13, 1721–22*, edited by Clyve Jones, *Scottish History Society*, Fifth Series, vol. VII, *Miscellany XII* (Edinburgh, 1994), pp. 123–38, 151–7, for references to Fletcher in London, Jan.–June 1711, May–June 1713.

beyond Scotland: the world of lodgings and coffee and chocolate houses in Europe's great cities.

In the course of his travels Fletcher developed a range of interests, by no means all confined to politics. He was especially famed for his wide knowledge of the learning of the ancients. He corresponded with John Locke about the Egyptian origins of priestcraft, and with John Wallis, the Oxford mathematician, about the place of music in education among the ancients. Through David Gregory, one of the 'Aberdeen Gregories', who had become Professor of Astronomy at Oxford, he was able to consult both Wren and Hawksmoor about the design of ancient and modern buildings.[5] But Fletcher's greatest interest besides politics was in books themselves. From his earliest travels to his last he was an assiduous and knowledgeable book-buyer; and in his surviving correspondence the purchase and transmission of books are a constant preoccupation. His manuscript catalogue of his books lists, though imperfectly, the collection which he acquired – and which his descendants sold and dispersed, without a modern catalogue, in the 1960s. Far more than a library, this was clearly a collector's collection, which included many rare works and required, over the years, a substantial outlay.[6]

At least as important as his enthusiasm for books and buildings, however, is Fletcher's evident liking for the cities in which he found them. His favourite haunts were London (with a population in 1700 estimated at 575,000), Paris (510,000) and Amsterdam (200,000), respectively the first, second and fourth cities of Europe. (Naples, with some 216,000, was the third.) Together with Brussels and the other towns of the Netherlands which Fletcher frequented, the three northern cities formed an 'urban system' unprecedented in its density and wealth. To those with the requisite means, these cities offered unparalleled opportunities to consume according to taste, whether that taste was in books or in clothes (Fletcher was austere

---

[5] *Correspondence of John Locke*, V, pp. 274–56: Fletcher to Locke, 22 Feb. 1695; and vol. VIII (Oxford, 1989), p. 436: Locke's reply, 1 March 1695. NLS ms 16502 ff. 165–8: John Wallis to Andrew Fletcher, in London, from Oxford 18, 27 August 1698; ff. 208–9: D. Gregory to Andrew Fletcher, London, 21 April 1707.

[6] The 'Catalogue of Books' in Fletcher's own hand is in the Saltoun Papers, NLS ms 17863. Since its dispersion the collection has been reconstructed by Dr Peter Willems, of Wassenaar in the Netherlands; it is to be hoped that he will be able to publish a new catalogue.

at least in his clothes); and while drinking the New World delicacies of coffee or chocolate, to hear news, to engage in conversation and, in London and even more in Amsterdam, to enjoy religious liberty. The irony of an upright country gentleman like Andrew Fletcher indulging such pleasures was a contemporary commonplace, but one nicely caught in his case by John Locke, writing in 1695 to urge Fletcher to leave 'the Witts and the Braveries' of the chocolate house to spend a few days with 'us poore honest country folke' (as he styled himself and Lady Masham) at Oates.[7] Not that Fletcher neglected his own estates: he knew well enough that they were his source of income, and took a definite, if usually distant, interest in Henry's management of the Saltoun lands, advising him firmly on matters from law suits to the planting of trees and crops. But the country's role was to pay for the city: Henry managed an estate burdened with debt to pay for Andrew's passions for books and chocolate houses.[8]

Fletcher's active political career was concentrated into two short periods of his otherwise wandering life. The first occurred immediately after his return to Scotland from the Continent in 1678, and consisted of courageous but ineffective opposition to the measures of Charles II's ministers. Elected a member of the Convention of Estates (an extraordinary meeting of the Scottish parliament) in 1678, Fletcher spoke against the imposition of new taxes to support the maintenance of troops; and in the parliament of 1681 he opposed the Succession Act confirming James, Duke of York as heir apparent. In between he had done what he could in East Lothian to obstruct the government's attempts to use the militia against the Covenanters.

Once abroad, from 1682, Fletcher's reputation aroused the suspicions of the Crown's agents in the Netherlands, but the extent of his involvement in exile politics is by no means clear. Though a kinsman of Argyll, he did not participate in the Earl's landing in the west of Scotland in 1685. He was consulted and trusted by

---

[7] Locke to Fletcher, Oates, 1 March 1695, *Correspondence of John Locke*, VIII, pp. 434–7.
[8] NLS ms 16502, f. 193: [Andrew Fletcher] to [Henry Fletcher], London, 6 Nov. 1703, giving advice on the planting of trees and enclosing of ground; ms 16503, ff. 49–54: correspondence between Andrew and Henry over the latter's tenancy of Saltoun Mill; ms 16504, f. 54: Andrew Fletcher (younger) to Henry Fletcher (his father), 1718, referring to the debts left by his uncle.

Monmouth, but seems to have advised against his expedition. When the Duke went ahead, Fletcher agreed to serve as commander of the cavalry, only to shoot the expedition's most important local contact (and possibly its banker), Thomas Dare, in a quarrel over a horse two days after the landing at Lyme, a crime which could only be expiated by Fletcher's immediate departure. He does not seem to have been involved at all in the planning of William's invasion in 1688; and when he returned to Scotland he could not become a member of the new parliament, since his conviction for treason was not formally lifted until 1690. While still in London early in 1689 he had expressed himself in favour of taking the opportunity to establish a union of parliaments and trade; once back north he had to be content with supporting the efforts of radicals in 'The Club' to persuade parliament to impose additional restrictions on the Crown's powers.

Since the same parliament continued to be summoned throughout William's reign, Fletcher had no further opportunity to participate directly in Scottish politics until the King died. Instead he did what he could in London. In the later 1690s he was known as an associate of the radical Whigs who met at the Grecian Tavern, and contributed his *Discourse of Militias and Standing Armies* (1697) to their paper-war against William's retention of a standing army after the Peace of Ryswick. He also used his connections in London to contribute to the formation of the Company of Scotland, personally subscribing £1000, and acting as an intermediary in the planning of its colony at Darien, near Panama.

With the accession of Anne in 1702, and the obligatory calling of a new parliament, to which he was elected, Fletcher at last had his opportunity. His second and most effective period of political activity lasted from 1703 until 1707. Even before her accession it was clear that Anne would have no direct heir, and the English parliament had accordingly provided in the Act of Settlement (1701) that the succession would pass to the House of Hanover. It was clearly assumed that the Scottish parliament would follow suit, since the only alternative would be to recall the exiled Roman Catholic Stewarts. This would be tantamount to a declaration of war on England, war which Cromwellian experience suggested that England would win. Fletcher's genius was to see that the Scots might still exact a price for their acquiescence. Exploiting the government's reluctance to divert troops from Marlborough's army on the Continent, he urged the Scottish parliament to take the opportunity to secure its own independence under any future shared king. To this end he proposed an Act of Security with 'Limitations' which would restrict the Crown's powers in the event of the same succession in the two kingdoms; and he re-inforced these with a series of carefully written, rhetorically charged speeches, which he published immediately after the close of the session as *Speeches by a Member of the Parliament* (1703). Although his Limitations were never accepted, Fletcher's initiative wrong-footed ministers, and he enjoyed the strong support of a group of young Whig peers, to whom he subsequently addressed the *Account of a Conversation concerning a Right Regulation of Governments* (1704).

But Fletcher's moment was soon over. His independence and intelligence had won him lasting respect, but he was ever more isolated politically. By 1705 relations with his previous supporters had deteriorated to the point that he challenged one of them, the Earl of Roxburgh, to a duel (only narrowly averted); and the bluff behind his attempt to keep open the succession was exposed when he suggested that it be offered to the Prussian Hohenzollerns, who (unlike the Hanoverians) had no connection whatever with the Scottish royal line. In the debates on the Treaty of Union in the last Scottish parliament in 1706–7 the opposition still counted on Fletcher as one of their best speakers; but his temper frequently let him down, obliging him to rely on the intercession of the (pro-Union) Duke of Argyll and the forbearance of the House. With the passage of the Union in 1707 he ceased to have an active political role. His imprisonment in 1708 on suspicion of involvement in a Jacobite plot was a mistake; and although he later kept company in London with crypto-Jacobites like Lockhart of Carnwath and Lord Balmerino, supporting their attempts to have the Union dissolved in 1713, he never succumbed to Jacobitism. During the Rebellion of 1715 he was in Paris, from where he observed wryly that the Pretender's care to ruin his affairs 'convinces everybody who formerly did not believe it that he is of the family'.[9]

Andrew Fletcher's last intelligible words, according to his nephew, called on the Lord to 'have mercy on my poor country that

[9] Fletcher to Andrew, his nephew, Paris, 20 Feb. 1716, 'Letters of Andrew Fletcher', *Scottish History Society, Miscellany X*, pp. 155–6.

is so barbarously oppressed'.[10] These are certainly the sentiments of a patriot; but even in politics Fletcher's patriotism was never simple. The connecting thread of his political career (besides an impolitic temper) was his defence of the independence of parliament from royal and ministerial control; he did not suppose that Scotland's problems would be solved in isolation from the rest of the British monarchy. In politics, and still more in his life as a traveller, bibliophile and aficionado of great cities, Fletcher was a patriot whose horizons were never confined for long by the borders of Scotland itself. It is this discriminating patriotism, I wish to argue, which is reflected in Fletcher's political writings. Far from being of significance only in so far as they throw light on Fletcher's political career, these engaged with the problems of a 'modern' politics in ways which were clearly enhanced by Fletcher's varied experience. All of Fletcher's writings were informed by Scottish concerns, and several explicitly addressed his country's apparently critical predicament in the years immediately before and after 1700. But the interest of what Fletcher wrote lies quite as much in his ability to derive larger issues, and to elaborate a more general vision, from the Scottish case. As he put it at the end of his last work, the *Account of a Conversation*,

> the insuperable difficulty I found of making my country happy by any other way, led me insensibly to the discovery of these things; which, if I mistake not, have no other tendency than to render, not only my own country, but all mankind as happy as the imperfections of human nature will admit. (below p. 214)

What were the things which Fletcher discovered, and set himself to write about?

Andrew Fletcher, neo-Machiavellian

If Fletcher's political activity was concentrated into short periods, his writing was even more so: the six works collected here were all published (and probably written) between 1697 and 1704. It was suggested at the outset that these were unified by Fletcher's

---

[10] Reported by Andrew Fletcher to his father, Henry, in a letter of Saturday [15 Sept.] 1716, from London: 'Letters of Andrew Fletcher', pp. 170–2.

ambition to understand the political prospects of a Europe in which smaller states like Scotland survived uneasily alongside great imperial monarchies, and in which the political agenda seemed increasingly to be set by the needs of commerce. I also suggested that the coherence of this enterprise derived from Fletcher's choice of Machiavellian concepts with which to pursue it. Within this broad framework, however, Fletcher can be seen to have divided his attention and his writings among three issues: arms and citizenship in modern societies, universal monarchy and the advent of a new form of maritime empire, and the choice between incorporating and confederal forms of union between states. Since what was distinctive in Fletcher's thinking about these issues can only be appreciated if his writings are set in the context of previous discussion, I shall briefly outline those contexts, before pointing to ways in which he broke new ground.

The relation between arms-bearing and citizenship was a primary motif of Machiavellian politics. It was the willingness of its citizens to take up arms, Machiavelli had argued, which had made it possible for the early Roman Republic to expand at the expense of its neighbours, creating a great empire; and this willingness had in turn been premised on the agreement to limit land-holding by individual citizens which was enshrined in the Republic's Agrarian Law. On the basis of this example, Machiavelli had made the bearing of arms in a citizens' militia a test of a political community's *virtù* and liberty; conversely, a people who abandoned their defence to paid, mercenary soldiers opened themselves up to political slavery under the arbitrary rule of a tyrant.

What Machiavelli had not attempted to explain, however, was why so many states in modern Europe were failing the test, and had permitted their rulers to acquire professional standing armies. This historical question was first broached in the mid-seventeenth century by English Machiavellians, and in particular by James Harrington, author of *Oceana* (1656). Confronted in England with the puzzle of a standing army which had overthrown a monarchy and established a republic, Harrington sought to explain why the English monarchy had failed to acquire one itself. His answer was that in 'Gothic monarchies', such as England's was before 1500, the sword had been in the hands of the barons and their retainers; but once the Tudors had undermined the barons' power, the balance of property had passed from the nobility to the 'freeholders', while the crown neglected to recognise that it was losing its main military support. From this analysis Harrington concluded that if the new Commonwealth of Oceana (England) was to survive and emulate the imperial achievements of republican Rome, it must transform its army into a militia of freeholders, while at the same time fixing the balance of property in the freeholders' favour by a new Agrarian Law. With the restoration of the monarchy in 1660 Harrington's republican prescriptions became out-dated; but his radical Whig successors continued to use a simplified version of his historical analysis. Opposing the crown's evident wish to maintain a standing army, they now argued that the military power of the barons had been part of England's 'ancient constitution'. A renewal of that 'Gothic liberty', in the form of a county militia, offered the only means of preserving England's immunity from a standing army.

Addressed to the same problem, Fletcher's *Discourse of Government with relation to Militias* (1698) represented a return to the sophisticated level of historical analysis achieved by Harrington, but was by no means a mere repetition of his arguments. (While Machiavelli is referred or alluded to frequently in Fletcher's writings, there is no trace of Harrington.) Fletcher emphasised that the rise of standing armies, and hence of princely power, had been a historical process, not the 'contrivance of ill-designing men'. It had occurred in a world transformed around 1500 by the inventions of printing, the compass and gunpowder, as a result of which there had been 'a total alteration in the way of living'. The new possibilities of luxury consumption had encouraged the nobility to dispense with their retainers, and hence to give up the power of the sword. But the people had been equally disinclined to pick it up, preferring to pay taxes to their princes so that these could raise mercenary troops, with which they then established their arbitrary power. If England had escaped this fate, it was not, in Fletcher's view, because of the excellence of its constitution, but because of its island situation and early loss of continental possessions. This was why the present danger was so great: William's involvement in the Continent's wars gave him the excuse his predecessors had lacked for the maintenance of a large standing army. As England succumbed, moreover, Scotland was being dragged down with it, forced to recruit soldiers and to raise taxes in defence of English (and Dutch) rather than

Scottish interests. Hence, Fletcher argued the need to re-organise both kingdoms' land defences by creating a single militia, divided between several camps. But Fletcher's detailed prescriptions for this force underlined the Machiavellian point that moral and political as well as military benefit was involved. A strict dietary and physical regimen was to be afforced by the exclusion of those notorious sources of temptation and deviance, women and priests; and if the men fell back on their own resources, the 'abusing their own bodies any manner of way' would be punished by death. Little was to be left to chance in the effort to ensure that the militia was 'as great a school of virtue as of military discipline'.

The social foundations of this vision of Scottish citizens in arms were elaborated in the next of Fletcher's writings, the *Two Discourses concerning the Affairs of Scotland* (1698). The immediate inspiration of this work was the acute economic and social crisis facing Scotland in the second half of the 1690s. A series of harvest failures had crippled Scottish agriculture, causing widespread destitution and increased mortality among the poor; and now the Darien expedition, which was widely believed to represent Scotland's one serious hope of independent participation in New World trade, and into which a large portion of Scotland's disposable capital had been sunk, was on the point of departure. At one level, the *Two Discourses* offered a series of prescriptions for remedying the crisis: raising funds for Darien, re-organising poor relief, reforming agriculture. But Fletcher also took the opportunity to explore the changes that would be needed to prevent Scotland being reduced to a condition of economic as well as political dependence within the British monarchy.

In detail, what Fletcher proposed was every bit as draconian as his plan for a militia. The labouring poor of Scotland were to be reduced to a condition of domestic servitude (which Fletcher insisted was not the same as political 'slavery'), and the worst vagrants were to be transported to labour in the Venetian galleys. Meanwhile those who owned land above a certain value would be obliged to dispose of any land which they could not farm directly, and to use the proceeds to buy up to half the rents of smallholders, who would thereby acquire capital to improve their farms. Here too, however, Fletcher was almost certainly as much concerned to make an exemplary statement of Machiavellian principle. Together, the proposals can be seen as the equivalent of an Agrarian Law for Scotland. What Fletcher sought was the removal of existing obstacles to the improvement of agriculture, to enable the poor to be properly supported and employed, and to secure the existence of the class of lesser landholders who were supposed to be the backbone of the militia. Though he was openly critical of the feudal powers of the great lords, Fletcher was not seeking to eliminate inequalities of wealth: under his scheme the rental incomes of former great landowners would still have been substantial. But wealth was a public not a private good: it was not to be consumed at the expense of provision for the poor, and it was best spent, as the ancients had shown, on projects of public benefit, on beautiful buildings, monuments and public works. At least in Fletcher's Scotland the rigours of manly virtue and social subordination would always be tempered by fine architectural prospects.

Fletcher was well aware, however, that the fate of a small kingdom such as Scotland depended on the development of the European states-system as a whole; and in a second set of writings he turned to the threat to that system posed by 'universal monarchy' and the rise of maritime empires. The theme is at the heart of the *Discorso delle cose di Spagna* (1698). Written in Italian, with the imprint 'Napoli' (though almost certainly printed in Edinburgh), the work seems wilfully esoteric. But the reference to Naples is not inexplicable: the third city in Europe, it was the capital of a kingdom whose place within the Spanish monarchy was not dissimilar to Scotland's within the British kingdoms. Moreover it was in Naples that Tommaso Campanella had written the most striking previous account of the Spanish king's prospects of universal monarchy, the *De Monarchia Hispanica* (1640, but written *c.* 1600). The choice of the Italian language for the work has a still more obvious explanation: both in style and in conceptual content, the *Discorso* reads as if it were directly derived from Machiavelli himself. It is the most transparently Machiavellian of all Fletcher's works.

Universal monarchy was not itself a concern of Machiavelli's: he had finished his main political writings before it became clear that the possibility of such a monarchy had been revived by the Emperor Charles V. From the 1520s until the mid-eighteenth century, however, the concept was in widespread use to denote the ambition of one ruler to dominate all the others in Europe and the European world, whether directly, by combining many kingdoms and states under his headship, or indirectly, by establishing political and military hegemony over the rest. Such a universal dominion had been achieved in the ancient world by the Romans; but the greatest monarchies of the modern age seemed set to go 'yet further' (the motto adopted by Charles V), adding the New World to the Old, the empire of the seas to that of the land. Though not even Charles V had actually realised this ambition, his several Spanish successors were thought to have continued to harbour it, before the mantle passed to Louis XIV in the second half of the seventeenth century. After 1667 Louis himself strenuously denied the ambition; but the very real prospect that the French and Spanish monarchies might be united on the death of the ailing Spanish king, Charles II, was quite enough to ensure that the danger of universal monarchy remained vivid in the minds of contemporary observers.

Conceptually, moreover, universal monarchy had come to be closely associated with the doctrine of 'reason of state', with its clear Machiavellian resonances. Giovanni Botero's formative exposition of this doctrine, *Della Ragion di Stato* (1589) had reversed Machiavelli's declared order of preference by putting the preservation of states before expansion. But the doctrine's underlying conception of politics and its purposes owed much to Machiavelli. Botero had sought to explain how Spain might best preserve an already extensive monarchy by control of the sea and the utilisation of the human and economic resources of its parts. In turn these worldly prescriptions had been appropriated by Campanella in the service of a full-blown universal monarchism. By the later seventeenth century a further dimension had been added to the discussion by the recognition that commerce had become a 'reason' of state in its own right, and that a universal monarchy would characteristically seek commercial as well as military and political hegemony.

Fletcher's *Discorso delle cose di Spagna* was a sophisticated commentary on these themes, addressed specifically to the impending Spanish Succession crisis. In the 'Advertisement' which he prefixed to the work he made it clear that it was intended as a warning of the danger facing Europe. But his detailed suggestions for the regeneration of the Spanish monarchy and the re-organisation of its dependent territories were based on an acute analysis of the causes of its present weakness, and of the interests of the other princes of

Europe: if the argument was ironic, it was certainly not fanciful. (Further details of the Spanish Succession crisis, and of the interests at stake, are given in the notes to the *Discourse*.) The argument itself was developed in avowedly Machiavellian terms. Whoever succeeded to the Spanish monarchy was advised to behave as a *principe nuovo*, and to undertake its *rifondazione* by the introduction of a series of new *ordini*. For too long the Spanish had thrown themselves on the mercy of 'Fortune' by relying on the monarchy's 'reputation' rather than its real strengths: wasting the enormous advantage of Spain's situation between the Mediterranean and the Atlantic, its rulers had neglected agriculture, industry and commerce, and had actively encouraged the decline of their population by their religious intolerance. Were a new prince to reverse these policies, however, it was still entirely possible to envisage Spain as the seat of a universal empire. At the same time, Fletcher was able to identify exchanges of territory between the various large and small states of Europe that would strengthen the strategic and political position of the Spanish monarchy relative to others, restoring its former hegemony. This was the more likely were a French prince to succeed to the Spanish throne; but Fletcher made ingenious use of his knowledge of European (and especially Italian) affairs to suggest how other princes might achieve a similar result.

At least by implication, the *Discorso* treated the British monarchy as one of those best placed to frustrate this renewed threat of universal monarchy; and three years later Fletcher made this explicit in the *Speech upon the State of the Nation* (1701). But this work also revealed Fletcher's growing mistrust of William's motives. If the Netherlands and the British kingdoms were to be united, as he suspected William of hoping, the resulting monarchy would itself be ideally placed to command 'the empire of the sea, with an entire monopoly of trade', which was the modern equivalent of a universal monarchy. William's marshalling of Dutch and English interests to frustrate the Scottish Darien venture (whose failure was by now apparent) was obvious evidence to the point. The conclusion this suggested was that if smaller states like Scotland were to preserve their independence in the modern world, it was not enough for them to support larger partners in the struggle against universal monarchy in Europe. They must also attempt to set their relations with those partners on a footing which would provide guarantees for their security, commerce and liberty: they must, in other words, think hard about the forms of union which they were prepared to enter into.

The question of the forms of union appropriate to modern states was the third of the issues on which Fletcher focused, and underlies his last two works, the *Speeches by a Member of the Parliament which began at Edinburgh the 6th of May, 1703* (1703) and the *Account of a Conversation concerning a Right Regulation of Governments for the common Good of Mankind* (1704). The circumstances in which Fletcher delivered the *Speeches*, his most effective direct political intervention, were described above: by exploiting the unsettled succession, he sought to impose formal limitations on the power of the crown, and hence to safeguard the independence of the Scottish parliament. In so doing, however, he was by no means repudiating any form of union with England: the effect of his proposals would have been to reconstitute that union on a new, more explicitly confederal basis. To an extent this was disguised by Fletcher's invocation of the Scottish 'ancient constitution' as the precedent for what he proposed, and by the similarity between his Limitations and the conditions imposed by the Covenanter Parliament on Charles I in 1641. But Fletcher was always vague about what that 'ancient constitution' prescribed, as if aware that it was far less substantial than its English counterpart; and he explicitly denounced the bigotry of the Covenanters, in the clearest statement of the anti-clericalism that pervades all his works. Although he did not treat the Scottish parliament to an explicit lesson in Machiavellian politics, his arguments may be seen as a plea for a *rifondazione* of the Scottish constitution, to match the re-ordering of Scottish society he had recommended in 1698. The outcome of his proposals would have been a stronger, more genuinely independent parliament than the Scots had ever had, with responsibility for appointing ministers and arming the militia within Scotland. With such powers, the parliament should have been on an equal footing with its English counterpart, and thus able to guarantee Scotland's independence within a confederally united British monarchy.

The *Account of a Conversation* took still further this attempt to identify the conditions necessary for an equal, confederal union between the Scots and the English. Written as a dialogue between himself, the pro-Union Earl of Cromarty and two English Tories,

Sir Christopher Musgrave and Sir Edward Seymour, the *Account of a Conversation* was more reflective, and markedly less optimistic, than the *Speeches* had been. It was almost as if Fletcher was already aware that his moment of opportunity had passed. Although no evidence has yet come to light to confirm that a conversation between these participants actually took place, it is almost certainly representative of the sort of encounter which drew Fletcher to London so frequently. At the same time, Fletcher's use of the humanist genre of the dialogue is too artful for the work to be simply the reconstruction of an actual conversation. Even if Fletcher's voice is clearly his own, the dialogue points up the awkwardnesses and ironies of the positions he defends. Conceptually too there are complications, as the Machiavellian themes of his earlier works are now joined by others. Both in form and in content there are several traces of Thomas More's *Utopia* (1516); at other times Fletcher seems close to the concerns which would shortly be explored in Bernard Mandeville's *Fable of the Bees* (1714).

After an introduction devoted to the pleasures and corruptions of London, the conversation proceeds with a vigorous defence by Fletcher of his own and his young supporters' conduct in the preceding Scottish parliament. But Fletcher was evidently keen to move the discussion on to new ground. Anticipating many of the arguments subsequently heard in the Scottish union debate, the case for incorporating union is advanced by Cromarty, with particular emphasis on its economic benefits. In response, Fletcher once more raised the question of a guarantee that the Scots would not simply be treated as a conquered people. The case of Ireland, of which Fletcher was clearly well-informed, provides evidence that they would be. Using Musgrave as a mouthpiece for arguments supporting discrimination against cheaper Irish goods, and silently adapting Sir William Petty's hypothetical argument for the transplantation of Ireland's population to England, Fletcher would demonstrate that the logical outcome of such a policy was the concentration of all resources on London and its hinterland. This, he suggested, was the logic of reason of state applied to trade, and represented the all-too-likely fate of Scotland under an incorporating union. But while Fletcher's disillusionment with trade, 'the golden ball, for which all nations of the world are contending', was now marked, he could give little indication of what other course a country such as

Scotland might pursue, unless it was a policy of strict autarky. To plead, as Fletcher did in response to Musgrave, that there should be 'justice' in trade between nations was to resort to an ideal outwith the Machiavellian lexicon on which Fletcher had previously relied.

Without resolving this problem, Fletcher proceeds instead to offer a visionary sketch of a new political division of Europe. From Ireland to the Balkans, Europe would be divided into a series of roughly equal confederations, each consisting of ten or twelve sovereign cities and their surrounding territories. A number of sources for this plan can be suggested, including French schemes for instituting peace in Europe derived from the so-called *Grand Dessein* of Henry IV, and the models of confederations of sovereign states found in the works of Grotius and Pufendorf. But the closest analogy is to the leagues of city-states formed for defence rather than aggression by the ancient Achaians or Etruscans, and by the modern Swiss, which Machiavelli had discussed in the *Discourses* (Bk II ch. 4). A Machiavellian inspiration is consistent with Fletcher's indifference (in response to a challenge by the ultra-royalist Seymour) as to whether the city-states were republics or principalities: by implication, Fletcher would not have his plan understood simply as an extension of the republican Dutch model of a confederation. Yet what is most remarkable about the proposal – visionary, even utopian, as it was – is its failure to resolve the political problem which was Fletcher's starting-point. For as he proceeds to make clear to his ever more astonished interlocutors, the proposal would entail breaking up the British kingdoms themselves into several smaller units. In other words, it would not even secure the independence (or the sovereignty) of Scotland as a distinct political community.

If this failure has an explanation, it may be that Fletcher's concern with the position of Scotland had been overtaken by another: his preoccupation with the economic power and cultural pre-eminence of Europe's great cities, and of London in particular. For by the end of the conversation it is clear that its beginning, in which the participants first admire the situation and the prospects of London, its civil and religious liberty and its many diversions, then denounce the corruption of its manners, was by no means simply a piece of scene-setting. In itself Musgrave's jeremiad over London's moral corruption does little more than echo the complaints of the contemporary Society for the Reformation of Manners. As the conversation develops, however, it becomes clear that Fletcher's sense of the problem is larger and more interesting. Great cities do threaten to absorb the wealth of whole countries, leaving outlying regions and colonies barren and depopulated; yet at the same time they make possible a much more varied and freer way of life. Ultimately, I suggest, this was the dilemma to which the plan for the division of Europe offered a solution: even more than Scotland's sovereignty, Fletcher's concern was to spread the benefits of the cities from which he himself derived such pleasure. These benefits, moreover, were as much cultural as political: 'so many different seats of government' would not only encourage virtue, but 'tend to the improvement of all arts and sciences; and afford great variety of entertainment to all foreigners and others of a curious and inquisitive genius, as the ancient cities of Greece did' (p. 214). Fletcher almost certainly would not have admitted that the creation of such cities was incompatible with the traditional Machiavellian ideals of armed citizenship and regulated landownership which he had earlier wished to impose on Scotland. Nevertheless, the *Account of a Conversation* had brought him much closer to an admission that there was life in the modern world beyond the reach even of a neo-Machiavellian politics. We have no evidence that Fletcher ever personally encountered Mandeville in a London chocolate house; but it seems likely that he would have appreciated, even if he could not entirely approve, the relish with which Mandeville satirised and celebrated the opportunities offered by the modern city.

After Fletcher: the Enlightenment critique of Machiavelli

The realisation that Machiavelli's way of thinking about politics was ill-adapted to the modern world of commerce and great cities, glimpsed by Fletcher, soon became a commonplace of the Enlightenment. Fletcher himself commanded respect. David Hume referred to him as 'a man of signal probity and fine genius'; when told about him, Rousseau wanted to write his biography. But it seems that his reputation as a patriot, cultivated since the Union by both Tories and Whigs, was already impeding serious engagement with his works. By-passing Fletcher's attempt to develop a neo-Machiavellian politics which would be appropriate to the modern world, Hume went straight for Machiavelli's jugular. 'There is not a word of trade in all Matchiavel', he noted, 'which is strange considering that Florence rose only by trade.'[11] The note formed the basis for the remark in the essay 'Of Civil Liberty' (1741) that neither the ancients nor the Italians had made any mention of commerce. As a result Hume was dismissive of the example of the ancient republics: small in scale, economically restricted, and based on the enforced slavery of the labouring class, these had been the antitheses of a free, commercial society.

Montesquieu took a similar line, criticising the republics of antiquity in the *Esprit des Lois* (1748) as too small, and asserting that the spread of *le doux commerce* had cured Europeans of *Machiavélisme*. Adam Smith, like Hume, was less confident that commerce would dissolve all aggression; but the argument in the *Wealth of Nations* (1776) on behalf of international free trade was also an argument against the reason of state with which Machiavellianism was associated. The 'justice' for which Fletcher had belatedly appealed in matters of trade would be achieved, Smith suggested, by removing all obstacles to free exchange; only in cases of 'the most urgent necessity' (such as a famine) should 'reasons of state' take priority. Even Adam Ferguson, who of all the thinkers of the Scottish Enlightenment most admired the ancients, and who was active in the campaigns of the 1760s and 1780s to re-establish a Scottish militia, acknowledged Montesquieu as the inspiration of his *Essay on the History of Civil Society* (1767), not Machiavelli or Fletcher. Ferguson distrusted commerce much more than most contemporaries; but its importance in shaping the manners of modern society made it impossible to write a work such as the *Essay* in the neo-Machiavellian idiom.

The Enlightenment thinkers had in common with Machiavelli and Fletcher a commitment to the study of human affairs in this world, irrespective of what might happen in the next. But their goal was not worldly political success, understood in terms of a renewal of the values of the ancients. It was the improvement of human existence, measured in economic betterment, personal liberty, and the enlargement of the scope for personal choice of a way of life.

---

[11] 'Hume's early memoranda, 1729–1740', ed. E. C. Mossner, *Journal of the History of Ideas*, 9 (1948), p. 508.

These were not particularly political goals: Rousseau, who admired both Machiavelli and Fletcher, understood the challenge which they represented to the highest ideals of politics. But they were the goals which were drawing contemporary men and women to Europe's rapidly growing cities, and were transforming the old agrarian order. Andrew Fletcher, the discriminating Scots patriot and rigorous neo-Machiavellian, understood this, even as he sought to reaffirm the values of antiquity. The interest and significance of his writings lie in the imaginative intelligence which he brought to the impossible task of reconciling ancient and modern, Machiavelli and Hume.

Chronology of Fletcher's life

The following chronology records Fletcher's movements in as much detail as the evidence presently allows.

1653	born, son of Sir Robert Fletcher of Saltoun and Katherine Bruce
1665	succeeded as laird of Saltoun on the death of his father
1668	left for London, with James Graham as his Governor
1670	in Paris
1671	May: The Hague; June: Rotterdam; October: Paris
1673	Paris
1675	Paris and London
1676–7	Paris
1677–8	London
1678	in Scotland
	June: elected a commissioner (member) for Haddingtonshire (East Lothian) in the Convention of the Estates of Scotland (June–July)
1680	arraigned before the Privy Council of Scotland for obstructing the implementation of the Council's Act to raise a militia in Scotland
1681	elected commissioner for Haddingtonshire in the parliament of Scotland (July): opposed both the Succession and the Test Acts
1682	April: accused before the Privy Council of obstructing the provisioning of troops quartered in East Lothian
	May: left for London

1683	April: in the Netherlands, reportedly travelling with William Carstairs, and frequently in the company of Sir James Dalrymple and other exiles October: Paris
1684	in the Netherlands; December: Brussels
1685	May–June: participated in Monmouth's Rebellion, abandoning it on 13 June; July: landed at Santander, northern Spain; imprisoned but escaped; reputed to have travelled in Spain
1686	January: convicted in his absence of treason in the High Court at Edinburgh: attainted, and his estates forfeit
1686–7	abroad: funds transmitted to him through Amsterdam and Rotterdam, for payment in Geneva, Leipzig and Cleve (which would seem to leave little time for the excursion to fight the Turk in Hungary which he is supposed to have taken)
1688	April–May: Gröningen October: The Hague; preparing to join the invasion of England by William of Orange
1689	January–February: London from March: in Scotland, associated with 'The Club', but not a member of the Convention of Estates
1690	Edinburgh: his estates restored
1691	Saltoun and Edinburgh
1692	London
1694	London
1695	February–March: London; July: Saltoun
1696	in Scotland, subscribed £1000 to the newly formed Company of Scotland
1697	November: London published *A Discourse concerning Militias and Standing Armies* (London)
1698	January–February: London published *A Discourse of Government with relation to Militias* (Edinburgh) [month unknown]; June–July: wrote *Two Discourses concerning the Affairs of Scotland* (Edinburgh) [month of publication unknown]; 19 July: the ships of the Darien expedition sailed from

	Kirkaldy, and the Scottish parliament convened in Edinburgh;
	July: wrote *Discorso delle cose di Spagna* [printed in Edinburgh];
	August: London
1699	February: London; September–December: London
1700	*A Speech upon the State of the Nation* (dated April)
1701	October: Saltoun
1702	January: Edinburgh
1703	May–September: first session of the new Scottish parliament, Fletcher a member for Haddingtonshire, and a frequent speaker;
	June: introduced his Act of Security with Limitations; published *Speeches by a Member of the Parliament which Began at Edinburgh the 6th of May 1703* (Edinburgh);
	November: London
1704	published *An Account of a Conversation concerning a Right Regulation of Governments for the common Good of Mankind. In a Letter to the Marquiss of Montrose, the Earls of Rothes, Roxburg and Haddington, from London the first of December 1703* (Edinburgh, London);
	June: Saltoun
	July–August: second session of the Scottish parliament; Act of Security (without Limitations) accepted by the Crown;
	October: Fletcher reported to be in Holland buying arms in order to give effect to the clause for arming in the Act of Security
1705	in Scotland
	June–September: third session of the Scottish parliament. Limitations again blocked; decision taken to negotiate a union
1706	in Scotland
	October: final session of the Scottish parliament called to debate and vote on the Treaty of Union drafted by Scottish and English negotiators in April–July. Fletcher prominent among opposition speakers
1707	in Scotland
	January: Treaty approved by the Scottish parliament

	28 April: Scottish parliament formally dissolved; 1 May: Act of Union took effect
1708	April–May: imprisoned in Stirling Castle on suspicion of involvement in a Jacobite plot; released without charge; September: left for London and the Continent
1709	Leipzig and The Hague
1710	February–March: London, during Sacheverell's impeachment September: London
1711	January–June: London; August–December: Saltoun
1712	January–May: Saltoun; May: probably to London
1713	until June: London, then Holland; December: London
1714	London
1715	February: London May: The Hague and Leiden; October onwards: Paris
1716	August: left Paris for London, accompanied by his nephew, Andrew Fletcher; 15 September: died in London, having been too ill to travel to Scotland

Bibliographical guide

Fletcher's writings

The works which are securely identified as being by Andrew Fletcher are:

1   *A Discourse concerning Militias and Standing Armies; with relation to the Past and Present Governments of Europe and of England in particular* (London, 1697); revised and re-issued in a second edition as:
    A Discourse of Government with relation to Militia's (Edinburgh, 1698).

2   *Two Discourses concerning the Affairs of Scotland; written in the Year 1698* (Edinburgh, 1698).

3   *Discorso delle cose di Spagna scritto nel mese di Luglio 1698* (Napoli, [i.e. Edinburgh], 1698).

4   *A Speech upon the State of the Nation; in April 1701* (n.p., n.d.); issued in both quarto and octavo versions; the quarto was probably published in 1701, but the octavo may have been later.

5   *Speeches by a Member of the Parliament which began at Edinburgh the 6th of May, 1703* (Edinburgh, 1703).

6   *An Account of a Conversation concerning a Right Regulation of Governments for the common Good of Mankind. In a Letter to the Marquiss of Montrose, the Earls of Rothes, Roxburg and Hadding-ton, from London the first of December, 1703* (Edinburgh, 1704).

Collected editions of these six works were published as *The Political Works of Andrew Fletcher* in London in 1732 and 1737, and in Glasgow in 1749. These reprinted the second (1698) edition of *A*

xxxv

Discourse of Government; and the 1749 edition of the *Political Works* also substituted a translation of 'A Discourse concerning the Affairs of Spain' for the original Italian. A modern edition, *Andrew Fletcher of Saltoun: Selected Political Writings and Speeches*, edited by David Daiches (Scottish Academic Press, Edinburgh, 1979), omitted the *Discourse on Spain* and the *Speech upon the State of the Nation*. The present edition includes all six works, with a new translation of the *Discourse on Spain*.

A number of other pamphlets have been attributed to Andrew Fletcher. A serious case can be made for four in particular:

1   *A Letter to a Member of the Convention of Estates in Scotland. By a Lover of his Religion and Country* (1689)
2   *A Letter from a Gentleman at London to his Friend at Edinburgh, 13 October 1700*
3   *Proposals for the Reformation of Schools and Universities, in order to the better Education of Youth. Humbly offered to the Serious Consideration of the High Court of Parliament* (1704)
4   *State of the Controversy betwixt United and Separate Parliaments* (1706); attributed to Fletcher and reprinted by Sir John Dalrymple in his *Memoirs of Great Britain and Ireland*, vol. II [i.e. III] (Edinburgh, 1788), Appendix III; and again by P. H. Scott, in a Saltire Society pamphlet, New Series, no. 3 (Edinburgh, 1982).

The principal difficulty facing these attributions is the absence of the works in question from the various lists of his own writings made by Fletcher himself at the end of his manuscript library catalogue (now in the National Library of Scotland, ms 17863). The lists indicate numbers of pamphlets either left by Fletcher in Scotland or sent to London in 1708 and again in 1612 [presumably 1712] (i.e. after the publication of all of the attributed works). The fullest list, headed 'Left in the Green Drawer of my Cabinet Sept. 1708' includes all the writings later collected in the *Political Works*, and also '12 Letters'; (it also indicates their state, whether bound, stitched or in quires, suggesting that Fletcher may have acted as his own publisher, keeping the printed stock): NLS, ms 17863, ff. 87v–88v, 94r, 96r–v. There is no further evidence as to which work the '12 Letters' might be: the likeliest candidate is perhaps *A Letter from a Gentleman at London to his Friend at Edinburgh*, since there is a (printed) copy of it in the Saltoun papers, NLS ms 17498,

f. 72. The pamphlet urges the Scottish parliament to concentrate on disbanding the standing army, instead of continuing to assert Scotland's right to Darien.

An excellent scholarly bibliography of Fletcher's writings was prepared by Robert A. Scott Macfie, *A Bibliography of Andrew Fletcher of Saltoun, Publications of the Edinburgh Bibliographical Society*, vol. IV, (1901). But as Macfie himself then noted, 'much remains undone': he did not have the evidence of the library catalogue, and a good deal of correspondence and other manuscript material has come to light since he compiled his bibliography.

Fletcher's life

There is a good short life by G. W. T. Omond, *Fletcher of Saltoun*, in the Famous Scots Series (Edinburgh, 1897); the greater length of W. C. Mackenzie, *Andrew Fletcher of Saltoun. His Life and Times* (Edinburgh, 1935), reflects the inclusion of much more on the times rather than any additional information on the life. Since then biographers may have been deterred by the supposition that Fletcher's papers were lost when the Earl Marischal handed them to Rousseau to enable him to write the life (indeed an unwise move, if true). Nigel Tranter has stepped into the breach, with the fictionalised *The Patriot* (London, 1982, paperback re-issue 1994); evocative on the atmosphere in the Scottish parliament, less successful in its attempt to generate romantic interest and on Fletcher's travels. But there is now a growing body of manuscript material, and almost certainly more to be uncovered, in Britain and abroad: when a new biography is written, it would do well to adopt the European perspective of a work such as John Stoye's *Marsigli's Europe 1680–1730. The Life and Times of Luigi Ferdinando Marsigli, Soldier and Virtuoso* (New Haven and London, 1994).

Fletcher's thought

The first scholar to appreciate the interest of Fletcher's thought in a wider context was Caroline Robbins in her study of later seventeenth- and eighteenth-century republicanism in England,

Scotland and Ireland, *The Eighteenth-Century Commonwealthman* (Cambridge, Mass., 1959, repr. New York, 1968), esp. ch. 6, 'The case of Scotland'. Noting her insights, John G. A. Pocock developed an exciting and influential account of Fletcher's intellectual originality in 'Machiavelli, Harrington and English political ideologies in the eighteenth century' in his *Politics, Language and Time* (London, 1972), and more amply in *The Machiavellian Moment: Florentine Political Thought and the Atlantic Republican Tradition* (Princeton, 1975), ch. 8: 'Neo-Machiavellian political economy'. Almost contemporaneously, Nicholas Phillipson realised the transformative effect which Fletcher had on Scottish political debate in the 1690s and 1700s: 'Culture and society in the eighteenth-century province: the case of Edinburgh and the Scottish Enlightenment', in Lawrence Stone (ed.), *The University in Society* (Princeton, 1974), II, pp. 407–48. He has reiterated the point in various essays, including 'Politics, politeness and the anglicisation of early eighteenth-century Scottish culture', in Roger A. Mason (ed.), *Scotland and England 1286–1815* (Edinburgh, 1987). These insights were developed and qualified by John Robertson in 'The Scottish Enlightenment at the limits of the civic tradition', in Istvan Hont and Michael Ignatieff (eds.), *Wealth and Virtue. The Shaping of Political Economy in the Scottish Enlightenment* (Cambridge, 1983), and in *The Militia Issue and the Scottish Enlightenment* (Edinburgh, 1985), ch. 2, 'The challenge of Andrew Fletcher'; and by Istvan Hont, in 'Free trade and the economic limits to national politics: neo-Machiavellian political economy reconsidered', in John Dunn (ed.), *The Economic Limits to Modern Politics* (Cambridge, 1990), which offers a particularly acute account of Fletcher's thinking in the setting of the debate over Irish trade. Further assessment of Fletcher's place in the republican canon is to be found in Blair Worden, 'English Republicanism', in J. H. Burns with Mark Goldie (eds.), *The Cambridge History of Political Thought 1450–1700* (Cambridge, 1991). Colin Kidd, *Subverting Scotland's Past. Scottish Whig historians and the creation of an Anglo-British identity 1689–c.1830* (Cambridge, 1993), adds suggestive remarks on Fletcher's social thinking. Among Japanese scholars, Shigemi Muramatsu has written perceptively on Fletcher's economic thought: in English, see his 'Some types of national interest in the Anglo-Scottish Union

of 1707. Scotland's responses to England's political arithmetic',
Journal of Economics, Kumamoto Gakuen University, vol. 3, (1996).

Fletcher and the Union

The best general account of the making of the Union of 1707 is that
of William Ferguson, *Scotland's Relations with England: a survey to
1707* (Edinburgh, 1977), with perceptive remarks on Fletcher's role.
T. C. Smout, 'The road to Union', in Geoffrey Holmes (ed.), *Britain after the Glorious Revolution 1689–1714* (London, 1969), high-
lighted Fletcher's early declaration in favour of a union of parlia-
ments and trade in 1689. Christopher A. Whatley, *'Bought and Sold
for English Gold': Explaining the Union of 1707* (Glasgow: Economic
and Social History Society of Scotland pamphlet, 1994), is a level-
headed stock-taking of recent scholarship on most aspects of the
Union. Wider perspectives are explored by Mark Goldie, 'Diver-
gence and Union: Scotland and England 1660–1707', in Brendan
Bradshaw and John Morrill (eds.), *The British Problem c.1534–1707*
(London, 1996); and by John Robertson, 'Union, state and empire:
the Union of 1707 in its European setting', in Lawrence Stone (ed.),
An Imperial State at War: Britain from 1689 to 1815 (London, 1994),
giving pride of place to Fletcher's analysis.

An attempted full-length treatment of Fletcher's part in the
Union is P. H. Scott's *Andrew Fletcher and the Treaty of Union*
(Edinburgh, 1992); but despite endorsement by a professor of Scottish history as 'impeccably researched', the book is, alas, anything
but. The range and character of Fletcher's thinking about union are
explored by John Robertson, 'Andrew Fletcher's vision of Union',
in Mason (ed.), *Scotland and England 1286–1815*. But understanding of his role in the Union debate has been significantly enlarged
by several contributors to John Robertson (ed.), *A Union for Empire.
Political Thought and the British Union of 1707* (Cambridge, 1995),
which demonstrates the debate's intellectual quality and wider significance: on Fletcher see especially the chapters by Robertson, on
concepts of empire and union and on the course of the Union
debate, by David Armitage on Darien, and by Laurence Dickey on
Defoe. There are further suggestive remarks on Fletcher's contri-
bution to the debates in the last Scottish parliament in 1706 in

Douglas Duncan, 'Introduction' to *History of the Union of Scotland and England, by Sir John Clerk of Penicuik*, Scottish History Society, Fifth Series, vol. 6, (Edinburgh, 1993 [1995]). For an early indication of the fruits of new research under way by the New Zealand scholar Bridget McPhail, see 'Scotland's sovereignty asserted: the debate over the Anglo-Scottish Union of 1707', *Parergon*, 11, 2 (1993), pp. 27–44.

Fletcher and the Scottish Enlightenment

Fletcher's intellectual legacy to the Scottish Enlightenment is a central theme of works mentioned above by Phillipson, 'Culture and society in the eighteenth-century province', and Robertson, 'The Scottish Enlightenment at the limits of the civic tradition', and *The Scottish Enlightenment and the Militia Issue*; see also Nicholas Phillipson, 'The Scottish Enlightenment', in R. Porter and M. Teich (eds.), *The Enlightenment in National Context* (Cambridge, 1981). Uninhibited by problems of evidence, George Davie placed Hume's supposed response to the challenge of Fletcher at the centre of his *The Scottish Enlightenment* (Historical Association Pamphlet, G99, 1981; reprinted in *The Scottish Enlightenment and other Essays*, Edinburgh, 1991). An equally imaginary but rather less convincing variation on this theme is Alasdair MacIntyre's attempt, in *Whose Justice? Which Rationality?* (London, 1988), to use a work insecurely attributed to Fletcher (the *Proposals for the Reformation of Schools and Universities*) as an Aristotelian stick with which to beat the sceptical, anglicising Hume. Among several works in Japanese which set Fletcher's texts alongside those of the Enlightenment is Hideo Tanaka's *A Study of the History of the Scottish Enlightenment: Civilised Society and Constitution* (Nagoya, 1991).

Biographical notes

ALBERT, archduke of Austria (1559–1621). Youngest brother of the Emperor Rudolph and nephew of Philip II of Spain; married Philip's youngest daughter Isabella (*qv*). Philip made them joint rulers of the Netherlands (in practice, of the mainly southern Netherlands which remained under Spanish control following the secession of the seven northern provinces) in 1598.

ALVA (or Alba), Fernandez Alvarez de Toledo, duke of (1507–82). Castilian nobleman and servant of both Charles V and Philip II; sent by the latter to the Netherlands as governor in 1567 to suppress the revolt which had recently broken out: his use of military force and harsh measures against heresy successfully ensured that the revolt would continue; withdrawn in 1573.

ANJOU. Philip, duke of: see PHILIP V, king of Spain.

ANNE (1665–1714), queen of England, Scotland and Ireland (1702–7); queen of Great Britain and Ireland (1707–14).

BEAUCAIRE, de Peguillon, François (1514–91). Bishop of Metz, a Gallican and adherent of the Guises, having been tutor to the cardinal of Lorraine; author of *Rerum Gallicarum Commentarii* (1625), a history of France from 1461 to 1580.

BELHAVEN, John Hamilton, 2nd baron (1656–1708). Lesser Scottish nobleman; friend and neighbour of Fletcher's in East Lothian, and a strenuous opponent of the Court and the Union from 1703 to 1707; his lament for the passing of 'Mother Caledonia' was the most memorable speech in the last Scottish parliament.

BENTINCK, William, earl of Portland (1649–1709). Dutch nobleman, longest-serving adviser to William of Orange; created earl of Portland in 1689, and subsequently active in foreign negotiations on William's behalf, preparing for the Treaty of Ryswick (1697) and the Partition Treaties (1698–9).

BERRY, Charles, duke of (1685–1714). Grandson of Louis XIV by his eldest son, the dauphin: briefly considered by Louis as the Bourbon candidate for the Spanish succession before his older brother Philip of Anjou was chosen instead.

CHARLES, duke of Burgundy, known as 'the Bold' (1433–77). During his short reign 1467–77, he asserted the independence of the duchy of Burgundy from the kingdom of France, and sought recognition as a king in his own right, only for his hopes to be dashed by defeat at the hands of the Swiss in 1477.

CHARLES V (1500–58), duke of Burgundy 1506–55; as Charles I, king of Spain (properly, of Castile, Aragon, Sicily, Naples, etc. as individual kingdoms) 1516–56; as Charles V, Holy Roman Emperor 1519–56.

CHARLES I (1600–49), king of England, Scotland and Ireland 1625–49.

CHARLES II (1630–85), king of England, Scotland and Ireland 1660–85.

CHARLES II (1661–1700), king of Spain (i.e. of Castile, Aragon, Sicily, Naples, etc.) 1665–1700. Sickly and without heirs, he lived far longer than expected, postponing the inevitable crisis over who should succeed him.

CHARLES, archduke of Austria (1685–1740): second son of Emperor Leopold I, and the principal Habsburg candidate for the Spanish succession after the death of Prince Joseph Ferdinand of Bavaria. Was to claim the title 'King of Spain' after the allies had captured Barcelona in 1705, and added the kingdom of Naples in 1707. On becoming emperor as Charles VI in 1711, he was obliged to drop his claim on Spain.

COLVIN (or Colvill), William (d. 1675): Minister, and Principal of Edinburgh University 1652–3 and again from 1662. Author of sermons and a treatise of moral philosophy, *Philosophia Moralis Christiana* (1670).

COMMINES, Philippe de (1447–1511). Served Charles, duke of Burgundy (*qv*) before switching sides in 1472 to become an adviser to Louis XI of France: author of acerbically hard-headed *Memoirs* of Louis' reign.

CROMARTY, George Mackenzie, 1st earl of (1630–1714). Scottish peer, as a result of persistence in office under Charles II, James VII, William and Anne: created Lord Tarbat (a Lord of Session) in 1661, and earl of Cromarty in 1703. An Episcopalian, with a long-standing interest in prophecy, he was a vigorous and intelligent advocate of the Union on entirely secular economic and political grounds.

CROMWELL, Oliver (1599–1658). Parliamentarian officer 1642–8; regicide 1649; commander-in-chief in Ireland 1649–51 and against the Scots 1650–51, decisively defeating both; Lord Protector of England, Ireland and Scotland 1653–8.

DALRYMPLE, Sir James, 1st viscount Stair (1619–95). Scottish lawyer and politician: twice Lord President of the Court of Session 1676–81, 1690–5; author of the *Institutions of the Law of Scotland* (1681), subsequently revered as the bible of Scots Law. A presbyterian who went into exile in the 1680s, but only after ensuring that his son would take over both his estates and his political career: he was happiest when able to support the Crown.

DALRYMPLE, Sir John, 1st earl of Stair (1648–1707). Son of Sir James, and even more successful in serving apparently incompatible masters. Briefly imprisoned in 1682–3, but appointed by James VII as Lord Advocate in 1686 and Lord Justice Clerk in 1688. Reappointed as Lord Advocate after the Revolution, and served William as joint Secretary of State 1691–5, in which guise he was widely held responsible for the massacre of Glencoe in 1692. Created earl in 1703: supported the Act of Union.

EDWARD I (1239–1307), king of England 1272–1307. Asserted a claim to lordship over Scotland, treating the king of Scotland as his vassal: frequently invaded Scotland.

EDWARD II (1284–1327), king of England 1307–27. Reasserted the claim to lordship over Scotland: defeated by Robert Bruce and the Scots at Bannockburn 1314.

EDWARD III (1312–77), king of England 1327–77. Restarted the wars with Scotland in 1332, and began the Hundred Years' War with the king of France.

EDWARD VI (1537–53), king of England and Ireland 1547–53.

ELIZABETH I (1533–1603), queen of England and Ireland 1558–1603. Supported the Scottish Protestant rebels in driving Mary Queen of Scots (*qv*) from her throne.

FERDINAND II (1452–1516), king of Aragon 1479–1516; also of Sicily from 1468, and from 1506 effectively ruler of Castile following the death of Isabella, his wife, in 1504.

GODOLPHIN, Sidney, 1st earl of (1645–1712). Minister to Charles II, James II, William III and Anne, by whom he was appointed Lord Treasurer in 1702. Though a Tory, he gradually distanced himself from the high church wing of the party; an active proponent of the Union.

HADDINGTON, Thomas Hamilton, 6th earl of (1680–1735). Scottish noble, brother of John, earl of Rothes (*qv*). Supported Fletcher in the 1703 parliament, and was an addressee of the *Account of a Conversation*. With Rothes subsequently became a leader of the Whig *Squadrone volante*, and thus a supporter of the Act of Union.

HENRY VII (1457–1509), king of England 1485–1509. The marriage of his daughter Margaret to James IV of Scotland in 1503 established the dynastic connection between the Tudors and the Stewarts which would enable James VI of Scotland to succeed Queen Elizabeth of England in 1603.

HENRY VIII (1491–1547), king of England 1509–47, and of Ireland 1541–7.

ISABELLA, Infanta (1566–1633). Daughter of Philip II and Elizabeth of Valois; married the archduke Albert of Austria (*qv*); joint ruler with him in the Netherlands 1598–1621, and thereafter on her own until her death.

JAMES VI AND I (1566–1625), king of Scotland as James VI 1567–1625, king of England and Ireland (or, as he proclaimed himself, king of Britain) as James I 1603–25.

JAMES VII AND II (1633–1701), king of England and Ireland as James II and of Scotland as James VII 1685–88. Before becoming king he had acted as High Commissioner in Scotland in 1679 and 1680–2, setting up court in Holyrood Palace. But by then he had converted to Catholicism, for which, and for his consequent 'tyranny', he was overthrown in 1688.

DON JOHN (Juan José) (1629–79). Illegitimate son of Philip IV of Spain who made several attempts to gain power during the reign of his enfeebled half-brother Charles II (*qv*), finally succeeding in 1677–9.

LOUIS XI (1423–83), king of France 1461–83. Successfully maintained the integrity of the kingdom against the threat of Burgundian secession.

LOUIS XIV (1638–1715), king of France 1643–1715. As the most powerful king in later seventeenth-century Europe, widely believed (including, briefly, by himself) to be an aspirant to Universal Monarchy.

MACHIAVELLI, Niccolò (1469–1527). Committed servant of the Florentine republic as second chancellor between 1498 and 1512, when the return of the Medici family to power in the city forced him into exile. While in office wrote a number of shorter works of political commentary; out of office wrote *The Prince* (*c.* 1513), the *Discourses on Livy* (*c.* 1519), and *The Art of War* (published 1521). Partially restored to favour when commissioned by Giuliano de' Medici to write the *History of Florence* in 1520. His works were to provide Andrew Fletcher with his most constant source of intellectual inspiration.

MARY Tudor (1516–58), queen of England and Ireland (1553–8). Married Philip II in 1554.

MARY of Guise, also of Lorraine (1515–60). Married James V of Scotland in 1537; Regent on behalf of their daughter, Mary, Queen of Scots 1554–9.

MARY Stewart (1542–87), Queen of Scots 1542–67. Married the dauphin of France in 1558, and became queen to François II, king of France 1559–60; ruled Scotland only from 1559–67, when she was forced to abdicate; fled to England in 1568, whereupon she was imprisoned by Elizabeth, who finally ordered her execution in 1587.

MEDINACELI, Luis de La Cerda, 9th duke of Medinaceli (1660–1711). Castilian grandee, succeeded to the title on the death of his father, the 8th duke, in 1691; viceroy of Naples 1695–1700, where he was a patron of the arts and learning. Died under suspicion of treason against Philip V, after an indifferent military career during the war of the Spanish Succession.

MONMOUTH, James Scott, duke of (1649–85). Natural son of Charles II by Lucy Walter; married Anne Scott, countess of Buccleuch in 1663 and took the surname Scott. Sent to Scotland in 1679 to suppress the Covenanter Rising in that year; but soon after was banished to Holland. Banished again in 1684 after alleged involvement in the Rye House Plot; returned in 1685 (accompanied by Fletcher) to launch a rebellion against James II. Captured and executed.

MONTROSE, James Graham, 1st marquis of (1611–50). Signatory to the National Covenant in 1638, but went over to Charles I in 1641; raised a mixed Irish–Highland force for Charles, and successfully harried the Covenanter armies 1644–5, before escaping to the Continent. Active again 1649–50 before capture and execution.

MONTROSE, James Graham, 4th marquis of (*c.* 1682–1742). Descendant of the 1st marquis; one of the young nobles who supported Fletcher in the 1703 parliament, and to whom he addressed the *Account of a Conversation*. By 1705 was an adherent of the court. Created duke in 1707 as a reward for his support of the Act of Union.

MUSGRAVE, Sir Christopher (1632?–1704). Long-standing member of parliament for seats in the north-west, including Carlisle (1661–90) and Westmoreland (1690–5, 1700–1, 1702–4). A Tory of 'country' leanings (though his virtue was not altogether immune to ministerial temptations in the 1690s); he was a leading defender of English economic interests against Irish competition.

PATERSON, William (1658–1719). Proposed the institution of a Bank of England in 1691, and was one of its first directors on its establishment in 1694. Projector of the Darien Scheme, and director of the Company of Scotland which implemented it, participating in the first expedition to Darien in 1698–9. Actively involved in pamphleteering on behalf of the Act of Union, and in advising on its economic and financial terms.

PHILIP II (1527–98), king of Spain on the same basis as his father, Charles V (*qv*), whom he succeeded in 1556.

PHILIP V (1683–1746), king of Spain 1700–46. Previously duke of Anjou, second son of the dauphin, and grandson of Louis XIV, who preferred him to his brother the duke of Berry (*qv*) as the Bourbon candidate for the Spanish succession. Gained the throne following Charles II's designation of him as sole heir in his will in 1700.

QUEENSBERRY, James Douglas, 2nd duke of (1662–1711). Scottish peer who enjoyed more of William's trust than most of his kind and was thus a particular target of Fletcher's invective. As earl of Drumlanrig, deserted James II in the face of William's army in November 1688. Succeeded his father as 2nd duke in 1695, and was at the centre of the Scottish ministry from 1696. Commissioner to the Scottish parliament in 1703 and 1706, when he led the effort to enact the Treaty of Union.

ROTHES, John Hamilton, 8th earl of (1679–1722). Elder brother of Thomas, earl of Haddington (*qv*), and with him a supporter of Fletcher in 1703 and an addressee of the *Account of a Conversation*. Likewise became a member of the *Squadrone volante*, and a supporter of Union in 1706–7.

ROXBURGH, John Ker, 5th earl of (*c.* 1680–1741). Another young noble who supported Fletcher in 1703, and to whom Fletcher addressed the *Account of a Conversation*. Subsequently a leader of the *Squadrone volante*, and in 1705 almost fought a duel with Fletcher, after the latter thought he had been accused of ill manners. Supported the Union, and like Montrose (*qv*), was created duke immediately afterwards.

SEYMOUR, Edward, duke of Somerset (*c.* 1506–52). Protector during the regency for Edward VI 1547–9; subjected the Scots to a 'rough wooing' in the 1540s, culminating in a clear victory over them at Pinkie, near Musselborough, in 1547.

SEYMOUR, Sir Edward (1633–1708). A descendant of Protector Somerset. Tory and Anglican high churchman; a member of parliament from 1661 for various west-country constituencies, and speaker of the House of Commons 1673–9. Opposed James once he had openly turned against the Church of England, and supported the Revolution; but quickly fell out with William. An incurable Scotophobe, he was portrayed by Fletcher as a literal little Englander, happy to think of England being concentrated in London and the country surrounding it.

TEMPLE, Sir William (1628–99). Diplomat, scholar and author of works on Ireland, the United Provinces, the origin and nature of government, and ancient and modern learning.

WILLIAM III (1650–1702). As William of Orange, statdholder of Holland 1672–1702, and captain-general of the army and navy of the United Provinces; following his successful invasion in 1688, became in addition king of England, Scotland and Ireland 1689–1702.

A note on the text and the edition

The text used is that of the first edition of the collection *The Politi-cal Works of Andrew Fletcher, Esq.*, published in London in 1732, with the exception of the *Discourse concerning the Affairs of Spain*, which I have translated from the Italian *Discorso delle cose di Spagna* printed in the 1732 edition of the *Political Works*.

In transcribing the works in English from the 1732 text I have modernised the use of the apostrophe and have added capitals after a period, but have otherwise retained the original punctuation and spelling.

The task of translating the *Discorso delle cose di Spagna* into English is complicated by the artificiality of Fletcher's original com-position of it in Italian. I have not tried to recreate what Fletcher's English might have been beneath the Italian; and I have generally put literalness before elegance. I have usually retained the original punctuation, in particular the use of semi-colons to break up long sentences, even when they do not determine a main clause.

There are no footnotes in the original text; all the footnotes to this text are editorial. In annotating the text I have been chiefly concerned to identify Fletcher's allusions and references, to eluci-date technical or colloquial terms, and to identify places which are now unfamiliar. Where it serves to illuminate the text, I have given a limited amount of background historical information: this seemed particularly desirable in the case of the *Discourse on Spain*, whose argument presupposes knowledge of the intricacies of the Spanish Sucession crisis. Occasionally I have added an interpretative gloss to an argument of Fletcher's that seems cryptic or obscure.

A
DISCOURSE
of
GOVERNMENT
With relation to
MILITIA'S.

Edinburgh;
Printed in the Year MDCXCVIII.

THE
POLITICAL WORKS
of
ANDREW FLETCHER, Esq;

London, Re-printed:
And Sold by A. Bettesworth and
C. Hitch, in *Pater-noster-Row*; and
J. Clarke, under the *Royal Exchange*.
MDCCXXXII

Advertisement

Mr. Fletcher never wrote for a party; and his writings therefore ought to last: being scarce, they are collected with that regard which is due to his great judgement and sincerity.

Fletcher's texts are followed by a list of variants. The text of the 1732 edition of the *Political Works* reproduces the texts of the original pamphlets, with only minor changes of spelling and punctuation, which it would be excessive to list. But two sets of variants are important enough to be recorded. The first of these relates specifically to the 1698 *Discourse of Government with relation to Militias*, of which an earlier, shorter version was published in 1697 as *A Discourse concerning Militias and Standing Armies; with relation to the Past and Present Governments of Europe and of England in particular*. By listing the variants it is possible to see how Fletcher adapted the earlier text to include the case of Scotland, and to offer his own plan for a British militia.

A second significant set of variants derives from the manuscript emendations to a bound copy of the first four pamphlets printed in the *Political Works*: the *Discourses of Government, Scotland*, and *Spain*, and the *Speech on the State of the Nation*. The copy, which is simply entitled *Discourses*, is now in the National Library of Scotland, to which it was presented by R. A. S. Macfie, Fletcher's bibliographer. The title pages of each of the three discourses bear the signature of David Fletcher, Andrew Fletcher's nephew. The emendations are in a hand similar but not clearly identical to that of Andrew Fletcher; facing the title page of the *Discourse of Government* is a note: 'The corrections inserted are copied from the author'. Circumstantial and internal evidence both make this credible. David Fletcher died aged seventeen in 1718, only two years after his uncle, and he is unlikely himself to have been responsible for emendations as precise and detailed as these are. As will be seen, they alter the details of Fletcher's proposals for a militia and for agricultural reform in Scotland, and correct some of his speculations on the fate of the parts of the Spanish monarchy. There is no indication as to what prompted the alterations, or when they were made; but it seems most likely that they date from the later part of Fletcher's life, and represent his own afterthoughts, rather than a response to criticism by others.

There is not perhaps in humane affairs any thing so unaccountable as the indignity and cruelty with which the far greater part of mankind suffer themselves to be used under pretence of government. For some men falsly persuading themselves that bad governments are advantageous to them, as most conducing to gratify their ambition, avarice and luxury, set themselves with the utmost art and violence to procure their establishment: and by such men almost the whole world has been trampled under foot, and subjected to tyranny, for want of understanding by what means and methods they were enslaved. For though mankind take great care and pains to instruct themselves in other arts and sciences, yet very few apply themselves to consider the nature of government, an enquiry so useful and necessary both to magistrate and people. Nay, in most countries the arts of state being altogether directed either to enslave the people, or to keep them under slavery; it is become almost every where a crime to reason about matters of government. But if men would bestow a small part of the time and application which they throw away upon curious but useless studies, or endless gaming, in perusing those excellent rules and examples of government which the antients have left us, they would soon be enabled to discover all such abuses and corruptions as tend to the ruin of publick societies. 'Tis therefore very strange that they should think study and knowledge necessary in every thing they go about, except in the noblest and most useful of all applications, the art of government.

Now if any man in compassion to the miseries of a people should endeavour to disabuse them in any thing relating to government, he will certainly incur the displeasure, and perhaps be pursued by the rage of those, who think they find their account in the oppression of the world; but will hardly succeed in his endeavours to undeceive the multitude. For the generality of all ranks of men are cheated by words and names; and provided the antient terms and outward forms of any government be retained, let the nature of it be never so much altered, they continue to dream that they shall still enjoy their former liberty, and are not to be awakened till it prove too late. Of this there are many remarkable examples in history; but that particular instance which I have chosen to insist on, as most suitable to my purpose, is, the alteration of government which happened in most countries of Europe about the year 1500. And 'tis worth observation, that though this change was fatal to their liberty, yet it was not introduced by the contrivance of ill-designing men; nor were the mischievous consequences perceived, unless perhaps by a few wise men, who, if they saw it, wanted power to prevent it.

Two hundred years being already passed since this alteration began, Europe has felt the effects of it by sad experience; and the true causes of the change are now become more visible.

To lay open this matter in its full extent, it will be necessary to look farther back, and examine the original and constitution of those governments that were established in Europe about the year 400, and continued till this alteration.

When the Goths, Vandals, and other warlike nations, had at different times, and under different leaders, overrun the western parts of the Roman empire, they introduced the following form of government into all the nations they subdued. The general of the army became king of the conquered country; and the conquest being absolute, he divided the lands amongst the great officers of his army, afterwards called barons; who again parcelled out their several territories in smaller portions to the inferiour soldiers that had followed them in the wars, and who then became their vassals, enjoying those lands for military service. The king reserved to himself some demesnes for the maintenance of his court and attendance. When this was done, there was no longer any standing army kept on foot, but every man went to live upon his own lands; and when the defence of the country required an army, the king summoned the barons to his standard, who came attended with their vassals. Thus were the armies of Europe composed for about eleven hundred years; and this constitution of government put the sword into the hands of the subject, because the vassals depended more immediately on the barons than on the king, which effectually secured the freedom of those governments. For the barons could not make use of their power to destroy those limited monarchies, without destroying their own grandeur; nor could the king invade their privileges, having no other forces than the vassals of his own demesnes to rely upon for his support in such an attempt.

I lay no great stress on any other limitations of those monarchies; nor do I think any so essential to the liberties of the people, as that which placed the sword in the hands of the subject. And since in our time most princes of Europe are in possession of the sword, by standing mercenary forces kept up in time of peace, absolutely depending upon them, I say that all such governments are changed from monarchies to tyrannies. Nor can the power of granting or refusing money, though vested in the subject, be a sufficient security for liberty, where a standing mercenary army is kept up in time of peace: for he that is armed, is always master of the purse of him that is unarmed. And not only that government is tyrannical, which is tyrannically exercised; but all governments are tyrannical, which have not in their constitution a sufficient security against the arbitrary power of the prince.

I do not deny that these limited monarchies, during the greatness of the barons, had some defects: I know few governments free from them. But after all, there was a balance that kept those governments steady, and an effectual provision against the encroachments of the crown. I do less pretend that the present governments can be restored to the constitution before mentioned. The following discourse will shew the impossibility of it. My design in the first place is, to explain the nature of the past and present governments of Europe, and to disabuse those who think them the same, because they are called by the same names; and who ignorantly clamour against such as would preserve that liberty which is yet left.

In order to this, and for a further and clearer illustration of the matter, I shall deduce from their original, the causes, occasions, and the complication of those many unforeseen accidents; which falling out much about the same time, produced so great a change. And it will at first sight seem very strange, when I shall name the restoration of learning, the invention of printing, of the needle and of gunpowder, as the chief of them; things in themselves so excellent, and which, the last only excepted, might have proved of infinite advantage to the world, if their remote influence upon government had been obviated by suitable remedies.[1] Such odd consequences,

---

[1] Printing, the compass needle and gunpowder were three inventions unknown to the ancient world: they therefore served as symbols of the advent of the modern world out of the intervening Dark Ages. The best-known discussion of their significance was that by Francis Bacon, in the *Novum Organum* (1620), transl. as *The New Organon*, Book I, aphorism no. 129: in J. Spedding, R. L. Ellis and D. D. Heath, *The Works of Francis Bacon* (London 1857–8), vol. I: *Philosophical Works*, pp. 221–3, and IV, p. 114. But Bacon was not the first to have seen the inventions' significance: see e.g. Hieronimo Cardano, *De Subtilitate* (1554), Lib. xvii, 'De artibus artificiosque rebus'.

and of such a different nature, accompany extraordinary inventions of any kind.

Constantinople being taken by Mahomet the second, in the year 1453, many learned Greeks fled over into Italy; where the favourable reception they found from the popes, princes, and republicks of that country, soon introduced amongst the better sort of men, the study of the Greek tongue, and of the antient authors in that language.[2] About the same time likewise some learned men began to restore the purity of the Latin tongue. But that which most contributed to the advancement of all kind of learning, and especially the study of the antients, was the art of printing; which was brought to a great degree of perfection a few years after. By this means their books became common, and their arts generally understood and admired. But as mankind from a natural propension to pleasure, is always ready to chuse out of every thing what may most gratify that vicious appetite; so the arts which the Italians first applied themselves to improve, were principally those that had been subservient to the luxury of the antients in the most corrupt ages, of which they had many monuments still remaining. Italy was presently filled with architects, painters and sculptors; and a prodigious expence was made in buildings, pictures, and statues. Thus the Italians began to come off from their frugal and military way of living, and addicted themselves to the pursuit of refined and expensive pleasures, as much as the wars of those times would permit. This infection spread itself by degrees into the neighbouring nations. But these things alone had not been sufficient to work so great a change in government, if a preceding invention, brought into common use about that time, had not produced more new and extraordinary effects than any had ever done before; which probably may have many consequences yet unforeseen, and a farther influence upon the manners of men, as long as the world lasts; I mean, the invention of the needle, by the help of which navigation was greatly improved, a passage opened by sea to the East Indies, and a new world discovered. By this means the luxury of Asia and America was added to that of the antients; and all ages, and all countries concurred to

---

[2] The capture of Constantinople by the Ottomans in 1453, which brought to an end the Byzantine Empire, was at this time regarded as inaugurating the Renaissance, as Byzantine scholars fled into exile in Italy, carrying with them copies of ancient texts previously unknown in the West.

sink Europe into an abyss of pleasures; which were rendered the more expensive by a perpetual change of the fashions in clothes, equipage and furniture of houses.

These things brought a total alteration in the way of living, upon which all government depends. 'Tis true, knowledge being mightily increased, and a great curiosity and nicety in every thing introduced, men imagined themselves to be gainers in all points, by changing from their frugal and military way of living, which I must confess had some mixture of rudeness and ignorance in it, though not inseparable from it. But at the same time they did not consider the unspeakable evils that are altogether inseparable from an expensive way of living.

To touch upon all these, though slightly, would carry me too far from my subject: I shall therefore content myself to apply what has been said, to the immediate design of this discourse.

The far greater share of all those expences fell upon the barons; for they were the persons most able to make them, and their dignity seemed to challenge whatever might distinguish them from other men. This plunged them on a sudden into so great debts, that if they did not sell, or otherwise alienate their lands, they found themselves at least obliged to turn the military service their vassals owed them, into money; partly by way of rent, and partly by way of lease, or fine, for payment of their creditors. And by this means the vassal having his lands no longer at so easy a rate as before, could no more be obliged to military service, and so became a tenant. Thus the armies, which in preceding times had been always composed of such men as these, ceased of course, and the sword fell out of the hands of the barons. But there being always a necessity to provide for the defence of every country, princes were afterwards allowed to raise armies of volunteers and mercenaries. And great sums were given by diets and parliaments for their maintenance, to be levied upon the people grown rich by trade, and dispirited for want of military exercise. Such forces were at first only raised for present exigencies, and continued no longer on foot than the occasions lasted. But princes soon found pretences to make them perpetual, the chief of which was the garisoning frontier towns and fortresses; the methods of war being altered to the tedious and chargeable way of sieges, principally by the invention of gunpowder. The officers and soldiers of these mercenary armies depending for their subsistence and preferment, as immediately upon the prince, as the former militias did upon the barons, the power of the sword was transferred from the subject to the king, and war grew a constant trade to live by. Nay, many of the barons themselves being reduced to poverty by their expensive way of living, took commands in those mercenary troops; and being still continued hereditary members of diets, and other assemblies of state, after the loss of their vassals, whom they formerly represented, they were now the readiest of all others to load the people with heavy taxes, which were employed to encrease the prince's military power, by guards, armies, and citadels, beyond bounds or remedy.

Some princes with much impatience pressed on to arbitrary power before things were ripe, as the kings of France and Charles duke of Burgundy. Philip de Commines says of the latter,

> That having made a truce with the King of France he called an assembly of the estates of his country, and remonstrated to them the prejudice he had sustained by not having standing troops as that king had; that if five hundred men had been in garison upon their frontier, the king of France would never have undertaken that war; and having represented the mischiefs that were ready to fall upon them for want of such a force, he earnestly pressed them to grant such a sum as would maintain eight hundred lances. At length they gave him a hundred and twenty thousand crowns more than his ordinary revenue, (from which tax Burgundy was exempted). But his subjects were for many reasons under great apprehensions of falling into the subjection to which they saw the kingdom of France already reduced by means of such troops. And truly their apprehensions were not ill-grounded; for when he had got together five or six hundred men at arms, he presently had a mind to more, and with them disturbed the peace of all his neighbours: he augmented the tax from one hundred and twenty to five hundred thousand crowns, and increased the numbers of those men at arms, by whom his subjects were greatly opprest.[3]

---

[3] Philippe de Commines, *Les Memoires, contenans l'Histoire des Roys Louys XI et Charles VIII, depuis l'an 1464 jusques en 1498*, revues et corrigez sur divers manuscrits, augmenter de plusieurs traitez, par Denys Godefroy (The Hague, 1682), Livre III, ch. iii, p. 144, (an edition listed by Fletcher in his library catalogue: NLS, mss 17863 f. 9r). The translation appears to be his own. The paragraph in which this and the following quotation are contained was added in 1698.

Francis de Beaucaire bishop of Metz in his history of France speaking of the same affair, says,

> That the foresaid states could not be induced to maintain mercenary forces, being sensible of the difficulties into which the commonalty of France had brought themselves by the like concession; that princes might increase their forces at pleasure, and sometimes (even when they had obtained money) pay them ill, to the vexation and destruction of the poor people; and likewise that kings and princes not contented with their antient patrimony, were always ready under this pretext to break in upon the properties of all men, and to raise what money they pleased. That nevertheless they gave him a hundred and twenty thousand crowns yearly, which he soon increased to five hundred thousand: but that Burgundy (which was the antient dominion of that family) retained its antient liberty, and could by no means be obliged to pay any part of this new tax.[4]

'Tis true, Philip de Commines subjoins to the forecited passage, that he believes standing forces may be well employed under a wise king or prince; but that if he be not so, or leaves his children young, the use that he or their governours make of them, is not always profitable either for the king or his subjects. If this addition be his own, and not rather an insertion added by the president of the parliament of Paris, who published, and, as the foresaid Francis de Beaucaire says he was credibly informed, corrupted his memoirs, yet experience shews him to be mistaken:[5] for the example of his master Lewis the eleventh, whom upon many occasions he calls a wise prince, and those of most princes under whom standing forces were first allowed, demonstrates, that they are more dangerous under a wise prince than any other: and reason tells us, that if they are the only proper instruments to introduce arbitrary power, as shall be made plain, a cunning and able prince, who by the world is called a wise one, is more capable of using them to that end than a weak prince, or governours during a minority; and that a wise

---

[4] Francisco Belcario Peguilione (François Beaucaire de Peguillon), *Rerum Gallicarum Commentarii ab anno MCCCCLXI (1461) ad annum MDLXXX (1580)*, (Lyons, 1625), Book II, para xxv, anno 1470, p. 43; the translation is Fletcher's.

[5] Beaucaire, *Rerum Gallicarum Commentarii*, Book VII, para x, anno 1495, pp. 188–9, suggests that Commines' manuscript may have been altered and 'mutilated' by Jean Selua of the Parlement of Paris.

prince having once procured them to be established, they will maintain themselves under any.

I am not ignorant that before this change, subsidies were often given by diets, states and parliaments, and some raised by the edicts of princes for maintaining wars; but these were small, and no way sufficient to subsist such numerous armies as those of the barons' militia. There were likewise mercenary troops sometimes entertained by princes who aimed at arbitrary power, and by some commonwealths in time of war for their own defence; but these were only strangers, or in very small numbers, and held no proportion with those vast armies of mercenaries which this change has fix'd upon Europe to her affliction and ruin.

What I have said hitherto has been always with regard to one or other, and often to most countries in Europe. What follows will have a more particular regard to Britain; where, though the power of the barons be ceased, yet no mercenary troops are yet established. The reason of which is, that England had before this great alteration lost all her conquests in France, the town of Calais only excepted; and that also was taken by the French before the change was thorowly made.[6] So that the Kings of England had no pretence to keep up standing forces, either to defend conquests abroad, or to garison a frontier towards France, since the sea was now become the only frontier between those two countries.

Neither could the frontier towards Scotland afford any colour to those princes for raising such forces, since the Kings of Scotland had none; and that Scotland was not able to give money for the subsisting any considerable number. 'Tis true, the example of France, with which country Scotland had constant correspondence, and some French counsellors about Mary of Guise, Queen dowager and regent of Scotland, induced her to propose a tax for the subsisting of mercenary soldiers to be employed for the defence of the frontier of Scotland; and to ease, as was pretended, the barons of that trouble.[7] But in that honourable and wise remonstrance, which

---

[6] Calais was lost to France in 1558; the principal possessions of the king of England in France, including Normandy and Aquitaine, had been lost by the end of the Hundred Years' War, in the mid-fifteenth century.

[7] Mary of Guise, also known as Mary of Lorraine, was regent on behalf of her daughter, the infant Mary Queen of Scots, between 1554 and 1559: Fletcher refers to the opposition aroused by her proposal to raise new taxes in 1555. This and the following paragraph were added in 1698.

was made by three hundred of the lesser barons (as much dissatisfied with the lords, who by their silence betrayed the publick liberty,
as with the Regent her self) she was told, that their forefathers had
defended themselves and their fortunes against the English, when
that nation was much more powerful than they were at that time,
and had made frequent incursions into their country: that they
themselves had not so far degenerated from their ancestors, to
refuse, when occasion requir'd, to hazard their lives and fortunes in
the service of their country: that as to the hiring of mercenary
soldiers, it was a thing of great danger to put the liberty of Scotland
into the hands of men, who are of no fortunes, nor have any hopes
but in the publick calamity; who for money would attempt any
thing; whose excessive avarice opportunity would inflame to a desire
of all manner of innovations, and whose faith would follow the
wheel of fortune. That though these men should be more mindful
of the duty they owe to their country, than of their own particular
interest, was it to be supposed, that mercenaries would fight more
bravely for the defence of other men's fortunes, than the possessors
would do for themselves or their own; or that a little money should
excite their ignoble minds to a higher pitch of honour than that
with which the barons are inspired, when they fight for the preservation of their fortunes, wives and children, religion and liberty:
that most men did suspect and apprehend, that this new way of
making war, might be not only useless, but dangerous to the nation;
since the English, if they should imitate the example, might, without any great trouble to their people, raise far greater sums for the
maintenance of mercenary soldiers, than Scotland could, and by this
means not only spoil and lay open the frontier, but penetrate into
the bowels of the kingdom: and that it was in the militia of the
barons their ancestors had placed their chief trust, for the defence
of themselves against a greater power.[8]

By these powerful reasons being made sensible of her error, the
Queen desisted from her demands. Her daughter Queen Mary,
who, as the great historian says, look'd upon the moderate govern-

---

[8] Fletcher's account of the Remonstrance of the 300 Barons is virtually a translation
of Buchanan's, in *Rerum Scoticarum Historia* (Edinburgh, 1643), Book XVI, pp.
562–3; a contemporary translation, slightly different from Fletcher's, is *The History of Scotland* (London, 1690), Book XVI [vol. II], pp. 117–18. Fletcher owned
several editions of Buchanan's *Historia*.

ment of a limited kingdom, to be disgraceful to monarchs, and upon the slavery of the people, as the freedom of kings, resolved to have guards about her person;[9] but could not fall upon a way to compass them: for she could find no pretext, unless it were the empty show of magnificence which belongs to a court, and the example of foreign princes; for the former kings had always trusted themselves to the faith of the barons. At length upon a false and ridiculous pretence, of an intention in a certain nobleman to seize her person, she assumed them; but they were soon abolished. Nor had her son King James any other guards whilst he was King of Scotland only, than forty gentlemen: and that King declares in the act of parliament, by which they are established, that he will not burden his people by any tax or imposition for their maintenance.

Henry the seventh, King of England, seems to have perceived sooner, and understood better the alteration before-mentioned, than any prince of his time, and obtained several laws to favour and facilitate it. But his successors were altogether improper to second him: for Henry the eighth was an unthinking prince. The reigns of Edward the sixth, and Queen Mary, were short; and Queen Elizabeth loved her people too well to attempt it. King James, who succeeded her, was a stranger in England, and of no interest abroad. King Charles the first did indeed endeavour to make himself absolute, though somewhat preposterously; for he attempted to seize the purse, before he was master of the sword. But very wise men have been of opinion, that if he had been possessed of as numerous guards as those which were afterwards raised, and constantly kept up by King Charles the second, he might easily have succeeded in his enterprize. For we see that in those struggles which the country party had with King Charles the second, and in those endeavours they used to bring about that revolution which was afterwards compassed by a foreign power, the chief and insuperable difficulty they met with, was from those guards.[10] And though King James the

---

[9] The 'great historian' is Buchanan: Fletcher paraphrases Buchanan's account of Mary Queen of Scots' attempt to secure a personal guard in *Rerum Scoticarum Historia*, Book XVII, pp. 609–10; translation in *History*, Book XVII [vol. II], pp. 160–1.

[10] The 'Country Party' was the name given to and taken by independent members of parliament and their supporters who criticised the policies of the King's ministers from the 1670s onwards. One of the principal targets of their criticism was the troop of guards maintained by Charles II after the disbandment of the New

second had provoked these nations to the last degree, and made his own game as hard as possible, not only by invading our civil liberties, but likewise by endeavouring to change the established religion for another which the people abhorred, whereby he lost their affections, and even those of a great part of his army: yet notwithstanding all this mismanagement, Britain stood in need of a foreign force to save it; and how dangerous a remedy that is, the histories of all ages can witness. 'Tis true, this circumstance was favourable, that a prince who had married the next heir to these kingdoms, was at the head of our deliverance:[11] yet did it engage us in a long and expensive war. And now that we are much impoverished, and England by means of her former riches and present poverty, fallen into all the corruptions which those great enemies of virtue, want, and excess of riches can produce; that there are such numbers of mercenary forces on foot at home and abroad; that the greatest part of the officers have no other way to subsist; that they are commanded by a wise and active King, who has at his disposal the formidable land and sea forces of a neighbouring nation, the great rival of our trade;[12] a King, who by blood, relation, other particular ties, and common interest, has the house of Austria, most of the princes of Germany, and potentates of the North, for his friends and allies; who can, whatever interest he join with, do what he thinks fit in Europe; I say, if a mercenary standing army be kept up, (the first of that kind, except those of the usurper Cromwel, and the late King James, that Britain has seen for thirteen hundred years) I desire to know where the security of the British liberties lies, unless in the good will and pleasure of the King: I desire to know, what real security can be had against standing armies of mercenaries,

Model Army at the Restoration: the Country Party regarded these as the nucleus of a standing army. The Country Party was also deeply suspicious of the financial system which enabled the Crown to maintain the soldiers.

The 'revolution compassed by a foreign power' was the Revolution of 1688, in which James II was overthrown by William of Orange, at the head of a large Dutch (and North German) army.

[11] William of Orange had married Mary Stuart, elder daughter of Charles II; in default of James II having a male heir (which he did, but too late), she was next in line to succeed.

[12] The forces of the United Provinces; although William of Orange was not head of state, he was Captain-General and Admiral-General of the republic's land and sea forces.

backed by the corruption of both nations, the tendency of the way of living, the genius of the age, and the example of the world.

Having shewn the difference between the past and present government of Britain, how precarious our liberties are, and how from having the best security for them we are in hazard of having none at all; 'tis to be hoped that those who are for a standing army, and losing no occasion of advancing and extending the prerogative, from a mistaken opinion that they establish the antient government of these nations, will see what sort of patriots they are.

But we are told, that only standing mercenary forces can defend Britain from the perpetual standing armies of France. However frivolous this assertion be, as indeed no good argument can be brought to support it, either from reason or experience, as shall be proved hereafter; yet allowing it to be good, what security can the nations have that these standing forces shall not at some time or other be made use of to suppress the liberties of the people, though not in this king's time, to whom we owe their preservation? For I hope there is no man so weak to think, that keeping up the army for a year, or for any longer time than the parliaments of both nations shall have engaged the publick faith to make good all deficiences of funds granted for their maintenance, is not the keeping them up for ever. 'Tis a pitiful shift in the undertakers for a standing army, to say, we are not for a standing army; we are only for an army from year to year, or till the militia be made useful. For Britain cannot be in any hazard from France; at least till that kingdom, so much exhausted by war and persecution, shall have a breathing space to recover. Before that time our militias will be in order; and in the mean time the fleet. Besides, no prince ever surrendered so great countries and so many strong places, I shall not say, in order to make a new war; but as these men will have it, to continue the same. The French King is old and diseased, and was never willing to hazard much by any bold attempt. If he, or the dauphin, upon his decease, may be suspected of any farther design, it must be upon the Spanish monarchy, in case of the death of that King.[13]

---

[13] The French King referred to is Louis XIV; the Spanish monarch whose death was imminently expected was Charles II. For a fuller account of the problem of

And if it be objected, that we shall stand in need of an army, in such a conjuncture; I answer, that our part in that, or in any other foreign war, will be best managed by sea, as shall be shewn hereafter.

Let us then see if mercenary armies be not exactly calculated to enslave a nation. Which I think may be easily proved, if we consider that such troops are generally composed of men who make a trade of war; and having little or no patrimony, or spent what they once had, enter into that employment in hopes of its continuance during life, not at all thinking how to make themselves capable of any other. By which means heavy and perpetual taxes must be entailed for ever upon the people for their subsistence; and since all their relations stand engaged to support their interest, let all men judge, if this will not prove a very united and formidable party in a nation.

But the undertakers must pardon me if I tell them, that no well-constituted government ever suffered any such men in it, whose interest leads them to imbroil the state in war, and are a useless and insupportable burden in time of peace. Venice or Holland are neither of them examples to prove the contrary; for had not their situation been different from that of other countries, their liberty had not continued to this time. And they suffer no forces to remain within those inaccessible places, which are the chief seats of their power.[14] Carthage, that had not those advantages of situation, and yet used mercenary forces, was brought to the brink of ruin by them in a time of peace, beaten in three wars, and at last subdued by the Romans.[15] If ever any government stood in need of such a sort of

the Spanish Succession and those involved, see note 2 to the *Discourse concerning the Affairs of Spain* (p. 85).

[14] Venice and Holland were the two most successful modern republics, and – as Fletcher tacitly concedes – both had employed professional armed forces. Fifteenth- and sixteenth-century Venice hired mercenary commanders in much the same way as other Italian states, but maintained tighter systems of political control; from the late sixteenth and throughout the seventeenth centuries the Dutch republic defended itself with professional armies which contained sizeable contingents of foreigners; here too, however, command was successfully integrated into the political structures of the republic.

[15] The three Punic Wars between Rome and Carthage were, first, 264–241 BC, at the end of which Rome secured Sicily as its province; second, 218–202 BC, during which Hannibal invaded Italy and won a string of great victories, but was gradually worn down by the delaying tactics of Fabius, until the Romans won a decisive victory in North Africa; third, 151–146 BC, at the end of which Carthage was

men, 'twas that of antient Rome, because they were engaged in perpetual war. The argument can never be so strong in any other case. But the Romans well knowing such men and liberty to be incompatible, and yet being under a necessity of having armies constantly on foot, made frequent changes of the men that served in them; who, when they had been some time in the army, were permitted to return to their possessions, trades, or other employments. And to shew how true a judgment that wise state made of this matter, it is sufficient to observe, that those who subverted that government, the greatest that ever was amongst men, found themselves obliged to continue the same soldiers always in constant pay and service.[16]

If during the late war we had followed so wise a course as that of Rome, there had been thrice as many trained men in the nations as at present there are; no difficulties about recruits, nor debates about keeping up armies in time of peace, because some men resolve to live by arms in time of peace, whether it be for the good of the nations or not. And since such was the practice of Rome, I hope no man will have the confidence to say, that this method was not as effectual for war as any other. If it be objected, that Rome had perpetual wars, and therefore that might be a good practice among them, which would not be so with us; I confess I cannot see the consequence; for if Rome had perpetual wars, the Romans ought still to have continued the same men in their armies, that they might, according to the notion of these men, render their troops more useful. And if we did change our men during a war, we should have more men that would understand something of it. If any man say, not so much as if they continued in the army: I answer, that many of those who continue in the army, are afterwards swept away by the war, and live not to be of use in time of peace; that those who escape the war, being fewer than in the other case, are soon consumed: and that mercenary standing forces in time of peace, if

over-run and the city demolished, the area becoming the Roman province of Africa.

[16] Fletcher almost certainly has in mind Marius and Sulla, Roman consuls early in the 1st century BC, whose rivalry led them to maintain soldiers beyond their normal term; and Julius Caesar, the principal beneficiary of the resulting disorder, whose own soldiers supported his coup against the republic.

not employed to do mischief, soon become like those of Holland in '72, fit only to lose forty strong places in forty days.[17]

There is another thing which I would not mention if it were not absolutely necessary to my present purpose; and that is, the usual manners of those who are engaged in mercenary armies. I speak now of officers in other parts of Europe, and not of those in our armies, allowing them to be the best; and if they will have it so, quite different from all others. I will not apply to them any part of what I shall say concerning the rest. They themselves best know how far anything of that nature may be applicable to them. I say then, most princes of Europe having put themselves upon the foot of keeping up forces, rather numerous than well entertained, can give but small allowance to officers, and that likewise is for the most part very ill paid, in order to render them the more necessitous and depending; and yet they permit them to live in all that extravagancy which mutual example and emulation prompts them to. By which means the officers become insensibly engaged in numberless frauds, oppressions and cruelties, the colonels against the captains, and the captains against the inferiour soldiers; and all of them against all persons with whom they have any kind of business. So that there is hardly any sort of men who are less men of honour than the officers of mercenary forces: and indeed honour has now no other signification amongst them than courage. Besides, most men that enter into those armies, whether officers or soldiers, as if they were obliged to shew themselves new creatures, and perfectly regenerate, if before they were modest or sober, immediately turn themselves to all manner of debauchery and wickedness, committing all kind of injustice and barbarity against poor and defenceless people. Now though the natural temper of our men be more just and honest than that of the French, or of any other people, yet may it not be feared, that such bad manners may prove contagious? And if such manners do not fit men to enslave a nation, devils only must do it. On the other hand, if it should happen that the officers of standing armies in Britain should live with greater regularity and modesty than was ever yet seen in that sort of men, it might very probably fall out, that being quartered in all parts of the country, some of them might

---

[17] A reference to the invasion of the United Provinces by Louis XIV in 1672, when the French initially made rapid gains; strictly speaking, however, the gains were in the eastern provinces of the Union, and they did not penetrate Holland itself.

be returned members of parliament for divers of the electing boroughs; and of what consequence that would be, I leave all men to judge. So that whatever be the conduct of a mercenary army, we can never be secure as long as any such force is kept up in Britain.

But the undertakers for a standing army will say; will you turn so many gentlemen to starve, who have faithfully served the government? This question I allow to be founded upon some reason. For it ought to be acknowledged in justice to our soldiery, that on all occasions, and in all actions, both officers and soldiers have done their part; and therefore I think it may be reasonable, that all officers and soldiers of above forty years, in consideration of their unfitness to apply themselves at that age to any other employment, should be recommended to the bounty of both parliaments.

I confess I do not see by what rules of good policy any mercenary forces have been connived at either in Scotland, England, or Ireland. Sure, 'tis allowing the dispensing power in the most essential point of the constitution of government in these nations.[18]

Scotland and England are nations that were formerly very jealous of liberty; of which there are many remarkable instances in the histories of these countries. And we may hope that the late revolution having given such a blow to arbitrary power in these kingdoms, they will be very careful to preserve their rights and privileges. And sure it is not very suitable to these, that any standing forces be kept up in Britain: or that there should be any Scots, English, or Irish regiments maintained in Ireland, or any where abroad; or regiments of any nation at the charge of England. I shall not say how readily the regiments that were in the service of Holland came over against the duke of Monmouth: he was a rebel, and did not succeed. But we all know with what expedition the Irish mercenary forces were brought into Britain to oppose his present majesty in that glorious enterprize for our deliverance.[19]

---

[18] The Crown's dispensing power (a prerogative power to dispense subjects from the law) had been declared contrary to law by both the English and the Scottish parliaments in 1689. Fletcher's contention is that the maintenance of standing forces since then has virtually restored the dispensing power to the Crown.

[19] There were three English and three Scottish regiments in the Anglo-Dutch Brigade: originally formed in 1585, to assist the revolt against Spain, the Brigade was reformed in 1674 after the Third Anglo-Dutch War. The regiments recruited in Britain, and technically formed part of the English and Scottish armies, on permanent loan to the United Provinces. The Brigade had been recalled to fight

The subjects formerly had a real security for their liberty, by having the sword in their own hands. That security, which is the greatest of all others, is lost; and not only so, but the sword is put into the hand of the king by his power over the militia. All this is not enough; but we must have in both kingdoms standing armies of mercenaries, who for the most part have no other way to subsist, and consequently are capable to execute any commands: and yet every man must think his liberties as safe as ever, under pain of being thought disaffected to the monarchy. But sure it must not be the antient limited and legal monarchies of Scotland, and England, that these gentlemen mean. It must be a French fashion of monarchy, where the king has power to do what he pleases, and the people no security for anything they possess. We have quitted our antient security, and put the militia into the power of the king. The only remaining security we have is, that no standing armies were ever yet allowed in time of peace, the parliament of England having so often and so expresly declared them to be contrary to law: and that of Scotland having not only declared them to be a grievance, but made the keeping them up an article in the forfeiture of the late King James.[20] If a standing army be allowed, what difference will there be between the government we shall then live under, and any kind of government under a good prince? Of which there have been some in the most despotick tyrannies. If these be limited and not absolute monarchies, then, as there are conditions, so there ought to be securities on both sides. The barons never pretended that their militias should be constantly on foot, and together in bodies in times of peace. 'Tis evident that would have subverted the constitution, and made every one of them a petty tyrant. And 'tis as

Monmouth's rebel invasion in 1685 (an invasion which itself set out from the Netherlands, and in which Fletcher had of course been a leading participant), but had only arrived after the decisive battle of Sedgemoor.

The army in Ireland was effectively catholicised by the duke of Tyrconnell during the reign of James II, and units were brought over to England in 1688 in an unavailing attempt to shore up James's regime.

[20] The levying and keeping a standing army in peace without consent of parliament was declared contrary to law by the English Parliament in the Bill of Rights (1689), and by the Scottish Convention of Estates in the Claim of Right, on 11 April 1689, and was also included in the supplementary Articles of Grievances voted by the Estates on 13 April: *The Eighteenth-Century Constitution*, ed. E. N. Williams (Cambridge, 1960), pp. 26–33; *A Source Book of Scottish History, vol. III: 1567–1707*, ed. W. C. Dickinson and G. Donaldson (Edinburgh, 1954), pp. 200–8.

evident, that standing forces are the fittest instruments to make a tyrant. Whoever is for making the king's power too great or too little, is an enemy to the monarchy. But to give him standing armies, puts his power beyond controul, and consequently makes him absolute. If the people had any other real security for their liberty than that there be no standing armies in time of peace, there might be some colour to demand them. But if that only remaining security be taken away from the people, we have destroyed these monarchies.

'Tis pretended, we are in hazard of being invaded by a powerful enemy; shall we therefore destroy our government? What is it then that we would defend? Is it our persons, by the ruin of our government? In what then shall we be gainers? In saving our lives by the loss of our liberties? If our pleasures and luxury make us live like brutes, it seems we must not pretend to reason any better than they. I would fain know, if there be any other way of making a prince absolute, than by allowing him a standing army: if by it all princes have not been made absolute; if without it, any. Whether our enemies shall conquer us is uncertain; but whether standing armies will enslave us, neither reason nor experience will suffer us to doubt. 'Tis therefore evident, that no pretence of danger from abroad can be an argument to keep up standing armies, or any mercenary forces.

Let us now consider whether we may not be able to defend ourselves by well-regulated militias against any foreign force, though never so formidable: that these nations may be free from the fears of invasion from abroad, as well as from the danger of slavery at home.

After the barons had lost the military service of their vassals, militias of some kind or other were established in most parts of Europe. But the prince having every where the power of naming and preferring the officers of these militias, they could be no balance in government as the former were. And he that will consider what has been said in this discourse, will easily perceive that the essential quality requisite to such a militia, as might fully answer the ends of the former, must be, that the officers should be named and preferred, as well as they and the soldiers paid, by the people that set them out. So that if princes look upon the present militias as not capable of defending a nation against foreign armies; the people have little reason to entrust them with the defence of their liberties.

And though upon the dissolution of that antient militia under the barons, which made these nations so great and glorious, by setting up militias generally through Europe, the sword came not into the hands of the commons, which was the only thing could have continued the former balance of government, but was every-where put into the hands of the king: nevertheless ambitious princes, who aimed at absolute power, thinking they could never use it effectually to that end, unless it were weilded by mercenaries, and men that had no other interest in the commonwealth than their pay, have still endeavoured by all means to discredit militias, and render them burdensome to the people, by never suffering them to be upon any right, or so much as tolerable foot, and all to persuade the necessity of standing forces. And indeed they have succeeded too well in this design: for the greatest part of the world has been fool'd into an opinion, that a militia cannot be made serviceable. I shall not say 'twas only militias could conquer the world; and that princes to have succeeded fully in the design before-mentioned, must have destroyed all the history and memory of antient governments, where the accounts of so many excellent models of militia are yet extant. I know the prejudice and ignorance of the world concerning the art of war, as it was practised by the antients; though what remains of that knowledge in their writings be sufficient to give a mean opinion of the modern discipline. For this reason I shall examine, by what has passed of late years in these nations, whether experience have convinced us, that officers bred in foreign wars, be so far preferable to others who have been under no other discipline than that of an ordinary and ill-regulated militia; and if the commonalty of both kingdoms, at their first entrance upon service, be not as capable of a resolute military action, as any standing forces. This doubt will be fully resolved, by considering the actions of the marquis of Montrose, which may be compared, all circumstances considered, with those of Caesar, as well for the military skill, as the bad tendency of them; though the marquis had never served abroad, nor seen any action, before the six victories, which, with numbers much inferiour to those of his enemies, he obtained in one year; and the most considerable of them were chiefly gained by the assistance of the tenants and vassals of the family of Gordon.[21] The battle of Naseby

---

[21] James Graham, marquis of Montrose, signed the National Covenant (1638) in protest against Charles I, but in 1644 began a year-long rising on Charles' behalf in Scotland. His forces were a mixture of Irish and Highlanders, the latter raised

will be a farther illustration of this matter, which is generally thought to have been the deciding action of the late civil war. The number of forces was equal on both sides; nor was there any advantage in the ground, or extraordinary accident that happened during the fight, which could be of considerable importance to either. In the army of the parliament, nine only of the officers had served abroad, and most of the soldiers were prentices drawn out of London but two months before. In the king's army there were above a thousand officers that had served in foreign parts: yet was that army routed and broken by those new-raised prentices; who were observed to be obedient to command, and brave in fight; not only in that action, but on all occasions during that active campaign.[22] The people of these nations are not a dastardly crew, like those born in misery under oppression and slavery, who must have time to rub off that fear, cowardice and stupidity which they bring from home. And though officers seem to stand in more need of experience than private soldiers; yet in that battle it was seen, that the sobriety and principle of the officers on the one side, prevailed over the experience of those on the other.

'Tis well known that divers regiments of our army, lately in Flanders, have never been once in action, and not one half of them above thrice, nor any of them five times during the whole war. Oh, but they have been under discipline, and accustomed to obey! And so may men in militias. We have had to do with an enemy, who, though abounding in numbers of excellent officers, yet durst never fight us without a visible advantage. Is that enemy like to invade us, when he must be unavoidably necessitated to put all to hazard in ten days, or starve?[23]

A good militia is of such importance to a nation, that it is the chief part of the constitution of any free government. For though as to other things, the constitution be never so slight, a good militia will always preserve the publick liberty. But in the best constitution that ever was, as to all other parts of government, if the militia be

from the family connections of the Gordons and the Grahams. This discussion of his actions was added to the 1698 edition of the pamphlet.

[22] The Battle of Naseby in 1645 was the greatest of all Parliament's victories against the forces of Charles I.

[23] The following eight paragraphs, in which Fletcher sets out a model of a militia for England and Scotland, were added in 1698. They replaced three paragraphs in the original 1697 edition of the pamphlet in which Fletcher excused himself from offering such a model. See the List of Variants.

not upon a right foot, the liberty of that people must perish. The militia of antient Rome, the best that ever was in any government, made her mistress of the world: but standing armies enslaved that great people, and their excellent militia and freedom perished together. The Lacedemonians continued eight hundred years free, and in great honour, because they had a good militia. The Swisses at this day are the freest, happiest, and the people of all Europe who can best defend themselves, because they have the best militia.[24]

I have shewn that liberty in the monarchical governments of Europe, subsisted so long as the militia of the barons was on foot: and that on the decay of their militia, (which though it was none of the best, so was it none of the worst) standing forces and tyranny have been every-where introduced, unless in Britain and Ireland; which by reason of their situation, having the sea for frontier, and a powerful fleet to protect them, could afford no pretence for such forces. And though any militia, however slightly constituted, be sufficient for that reason to defend us; yet all improvements in the constitution of militias, being further securities for the liberty of the people, I think we ought to endeavour the amendment of them, and till that can take place, to make the present militias useful in the former and ordinary methods.

That the whole free people of any nation ought to be exercised to arms, not only the example of our ancestors, as appears by the acts of parliament made in both kingdoms to that purpose, and that of the wisest governments among the antients; but the advantage of chusing out of great numbers, seems clearly to demonstrate. For in countries where husbandry, trade, manufactures, and other mechanical arts are carried on, even in time of war, the impediments of men are so many and so various, that unless the whole people be exercised, no considerable numbers of men can be drawn out, without disturbing those employments, which are the vitals of the political body. Besides, that upon great defeats, and under extreme calamities, from which no government was ever exempted, every nation stands in need of all the people, as the antients sometimes did of

---

[24] The Lacedaemonians were the ancient Spartans; the Swiss formed a confederation of self-governed cantons, known as the Eidgenossenschaft, or Helvetic League. The League traced its origins to the thirteenth century; its independence was recognised by the Habsburgs early in the sixteenth century, although it remained formally a member of the Empire until 1648. Each canton raised its own militia.

their slaves. And I cannot see, why arms should be denied to any man who is not a slave, since they are the only true badges of liberty; and ought never, but in times of utmost necessity, to be put into the hands of mercenaries or slaves: neither can I understand why any man that has arms, should not be taught the use of them.

By the constitution of the present militia in both nations, there is but a small number of the men able to bear arms exercised; and men of quality and estate are allowed to send any wretched servant in their place: so that they themselves are become mean, by being disused to handle arms; and will not learn the use of them, because they are ashamed of their ignorance: by which means the militias being composed only of servants, these nations seem altogether unfit to defend themselves, and standing forces to be necessary.[25] Now can it be supposed that a few servants will fight for the defence of their masters' estates, if their masters only look on? Or that some inconsiderate freeholders, as for the most part those who command the militia are, should, at the head of those servants, expose their lives for men of more plentiful estates, without being assisted by them? No bodies of military men can be of any force or value, unless many persons of quality or education be among them; and such men should blush to think of excusing themselves from serving their country, at least for some years, in a military capacity, if they consider that every Roman was obliged to spend fifteen years of his life in their armies. Is it not a shame that any man who possesses an estate, and is at the same time healthful and young, should not fit himself by all means for the defence of that, and his country, rather than to pay taxes to maintain a mercenary, who though he may defend him during a war, will be sure to insult and enslave him in time of peace. Men must not think that any country can be in a constant posture of defence, without some trouble and charge; but certainly 'tis better to undergo this, and to preserve our liberty with honour, than to be subjected to heavy taxes, and yet have it insolently ravished from us, to our present oppression, and the last-

---

[25] The present militias in England and Scotland were those established respectively by Act of Parliament in 1660 and by Act of the Estates in 1663. Although the Scottish Act gave the Crown even more latitude in the use and deployment of the militia, the Acts were broadly similar: both were selective, making provision for a ballot to choose those obliged to serve, but both also permitted substitution, whereby a man ballotted to serve could provide another to take his place.

ing misery of our posterity. But it will be said, where are the men to be found who shall exercise all this people in so many several places at once? For the nobility and gentry know nothing of the matter; and to hire so many soldiers of fortune, as they call them, will be chargeable, and may be dangerous, these men being all mercenaries, and always the same men, in the same trusts: besides that the employing such men would not be suitable to the design, of breeding the men of quality and estate to command, as well as the others to obey.

To obviate these difficulties; and because the want of a good model of militia, and a right method for training people in time of peace, so as they need not apprehend any war, though never so sudden, is at this day the bane of the liberty of Europe, I shall propose one, accommodated to the invincible difficulty of bringing men of quality and estate, or men of any rank, who have passed the time of youth, to the use of arms; and new, because though we have many excellent models of militia, delivered to us by antient authors, with respect to the use of them in time of war, yet they give us but little information concerning the methods by which they trained their whole people for war in time of peace; so that if the model which I shall propose, have not the authority of the antients to recommend it, yet perhaps by a severe discipline, and a right method of disposing the minds of men, as well as forming their bodies, for military and virtuous actions, it may have some resemblance of their excellent institutions.[26]

What I would offer is, that four camps be formed, one in Scotland, and three in England; into which all the young men of the respective countries should enter, on the first day of the two and twentieth year of their age; and remain there the space of two years, if they be of fortunes sufficient to maintain themselves; but if they are not, then to remain a year only, at the expence of the publick.[27]

---

[26] If Fletcher's proposal had no ancient precedent, it had a contemporary parallel in John Toland's *The Militia Reform'd: or, an Easy Scheme of Furnishing England with a Constant land-Force, capable to prevent or to subdue any foreign power; and to maintain perpetual quiet at home, without endangering the Public Liberty* (London, 1698; 2nd edn 1699). Toland proposed that there be four annual camps, three in the provinces and one in the capital.

[27] Manuscript emendations to David Fletcher's copy of this work suggest that Fletcher was later minded to alter his proposal: see the List of Variants. According to these emendations, Fletcher would have multiplied the number of camps by

In this camp they should be taught the use of all sorts of arms, with the necessary evolutions; as also wrestling, leaping, swimming, and the like exercises. He whose condition would permit him to buy and maintain a horse, should be obliged so to do, and be taught to vault, to ride, and to manage his own horse. This camp should seldom remain above eight days in one place, but remove from heath to heath; not only upon the account of cleanliness and health, but to teach the youth to fortify a camp, to march, and to accustom them (respect being always had to those of a weak constitution) to carry as much in their march as ever any Roman soldier did; that is to say, their tents, provision, arms, armour, their utensils, and the palisadoes of their camp. They should be taught to forage, and be obliged to use the countrymen with all justice in their bargains, for that and all other things they stand in need of from them. The food of every man within the camp should be the same; for bread they should have only wheat, which they are to be obliged to grind with hand-mills; they should have some salt, and a certain number of beeves allowed them at certain times of the year.[28] Their drink should be water, sometimes tempered with a proportion of brandy, and at other times with vinegar. Their cloaths should be plain, coarse, and of a fashion fitted in every thing for the fatigue of a camp. For all these things those who could, should pay; and those who could not, should be defray'd by the publick, as has been said. The camp should be sometimes divided into two parts, which should remove from each other many miles, and should break up again at the same time, in order to meet upon some mountainous, marshy, woody, or in a word, cross ground; that not only their diligence, patience, and suffering in marches, but their skill in seizing of grounds, posting bodies of horse and foot, and advancing

breaking Scotland up into six districts for the purpose, England into twenty-eight and Ireland into sixteen. He would also have lowered the age of service to eighteen, and have modified the period of training to two months every summer, diminishing at intervals as a man grew older. The multiplication of the number of camps parallels (but does not exactly match) the political division of the three kingdoms envisaged in the *Account of a Conversation*.

[28] Fletcher's prescriptions for the diet of militia-men are striking: in Scotland, at least, the vast majority of the people ate no wheat, but a great deal of oatmeal. Beeves (the plural of beef) might include flesh other than that of cattle. See the splendid scholarship of A. J. S. Gibson and T. C. Smout, *Prices, Food and Wages in Scotland 1550–1780* (Cambridge, 1995), ch. 7 'Food', esp. pp. 234–6, and p. 253: Table on the diet of Scottish Soldiers *c.* 1689.

towards each other; their chusing a camp, and drawing out of it in order to a battel, might be seen, as well as what orders of battel they would form upon the variety of different grounds. The persons of quality or estate should likewise be instructed in fortification, gunnery, and all things belonging to the duty of an ingineer: and forts should be sometimes built by the whole camp, where all the arts of attacking and defending places should be practised. The youth having been taught to read at schools, should be obliged to read at spare hours some excellent histories, but chiefly those in which military actions are best described; with the books that have been best written concerning the military art. Speeches exhorting to military and virtuous actions should be often composed, and pronounced publickly by such of the youth as were, by education and natural talents, qualified for it. There being none but military men allowed within the camp, and no churchmen being of that number,[29] such of the youth as may be fit to exhort the rest to all christian and moral duties, chiefly to humility, modesty, charity, and the pardoning of private injuries, should be chosen to do it every sunday, and the rest of that day spent in reading books, and in conversation directed to the same end. And all this under so severe and rigorous orders, attended with so exact an execution by reward and punishment, that no officer within the camp should have the power of pardoning the one, or withholding the other. The rewards should be all honorary, and contrived to suit the nature of the different good qualities and degrees in which any of the youth had shewn, either his modesty, obedience, patience in suffering, temperance, diligence, address, invention, judgment, temper, or valour. The punishments should be much more rigorous than those inflicted for the same crimes by the law of the land. And there should be punishments for some things, not liable to any by the common law, immodest and insolent words or actions, gaming, and the like. No woman should be suffered to come within the camp, and the crimes of abusing their own bodies any manner of way,

---

[29] Fletcher's curt exclusion of chaplains from the militia, and of all clergy from service, is in line with the sentiment expressed in his letter to John Locke of 22 February 1695: 'If you ask me what I am doing I shal tell you that I am tracing pristcraft from its first original in Aegypt. Wheir I find lickways many other monsters but none so abominable.' *The Correspondence of John Locke*, edited E. S. De Beer, vol. v (Oxford, 1979), no. 1851, p. 275.

punished with death. All these things to be judged by their own councils of war; and those councils to have for rule, certain articles drawn up and approved by the respective parliaments. The officers and masters, for instructing and teaching the youth, in all the exercises above-mentioned, should upon the first establishment of such a camp, be the most expert men in those disciplines; and brought by encouragements from all places of Europe; due care being taken that they should not infect the youth with foreign manners. But afterwards they ought to consist of such men of quality or fortune as should be chosen for that end, out of those who had formerly past two years in the camp, and since that time had improved themselves in the wars; who upon their return should be obliged to serve two years in that station. As for the numbers of those officers, or masters; their several duties; that of the camp-master-general, and of the commissaries; the times and manner of exercise, with divers other particulars of less consideration, and yet necessary to be determined, in order to put such a design in execution, for brevity's sake I omit them, as easy to be resolved. But certainly it were no hard matter, for men that had passed through such a discipline as that of the camp I have described, to retain it after they should return to their several homes; if the people of every town and village, together with those of the adjacent habitations, were obliged to meet fifty times in the year, on such days as should be found most convenient; and exercise four hours every time: for all men being instructed in what they are to do; and the men of quality and estate most knowing, and expert of all others, the exercise might be performed in great perfection. There might also be yearly in the summer time, a camp of some thousands of the nearest neighbours brought and kept together for a week to do those exercises, which cannot be performed in any other place: every man of a certain estate being obliged to keep a horse fit for the war. By this means it would be easy upon any occasion, though never so small (as for example, the keeping of the peace, and putting the laws in execution where force is necessary) or never so great and sudden (as upon account of invasions and conspiracies) to bring together such numbers of officers and soldiers as the exigence required, according to the practice of antient Rome; which in this particular might be imitated by us without difficulty: and if such a method were once established, there would be no necessity of keeping up a militia formed into regiments of foot and horse in time of peace. Now if this militia should stand in need of any farther improvement (because no militias seem comparable to those exercised in actual war; as that of the barons by their constant feuds; and that of Rome, and some other antient commonwealths, by their perpetual wars) a certain small number of forces might be employed in any foreign country where there should be action; a fourth part of which might be changed every year; that all those who had in this manner acquired experience, might be dispersed among the several regiments of any army, that the defence of these countries should at any time call for; which would serve to confirm and give assurance to the rest. Such a militia would be of no great expence to these nations; for the mean cloathing and provisions for those who could not maintain themselves, being given only for one year, would amount to little; and no other expence would be needful, except for their arms, a small train of artillery for each camp, and what is to be given for the encouragement of the first officers and masters.

A militia upon such a foot, would have none of the infinite and insuperable difficulties there are, to bring a few men who live at a great distance from one another, frequently together to exercise; at which consequently they must be from home every time several days: of finding such a number of masters, as are necessary to train so many thousands of people ignorant of all exercise, in so many different places, and for the most part at the same time: it would have none of those innumerable incumbrances, and unnecessary expences, with which a militia formed into regiments of foot and horse in time of peace is attended. In such a camp the youth would not only be taught the exercise of a musket with a few evolutions, which is all that men in ordinary militias pretend to, and is the least part of the duty of a soldier; but besides a great many exercises to strengthen and dispose the body for fight, they would learn to fence, to ride, and manage a horse for the war; to forage and live in a camp; to fortify, attack, and defend any place; and what is no less necessary, to undergo the greatest toils, and to give obedience to the severest orders. Such a militia, by sending beyond seas certain proportions of it, and relieving them from time to time, would enable us to assist our allies more powerfully than by standing armies we could ever do. Such a camp would take away the great difficulty of bringing men of all conditions, who have passed the time of their youth, to apply themselves to the use and exercise of arms; and beginning with them early, when like wax they may be moulded into any shape, would dispose them to place their greatest honour in the performance of those exercises, and inspire them with the fires of military glory, to which that age is so enclined; which impression being made upon their youth, would last as long as life. Such a camp would be as great a school of virtue as of military discipline: in which the youth would learn to stand in need of few things; to be content with that small allowance which nature requires; to suffer, as well as to act; to be modest, as well as brave; to be as much ashamed of doing anything insolent or injurious, as of turning their back upon an enemy; they would learn to forgive injuries done to themselves, but to embrace with joy the occasions of dying to revenge those done to their country: and virtue imbibed in younger years would cast a flavour to the utmost periods of life. In a word, they would learn greater and better things than the military art, and more necessary too, if anything can be more necessary than the defence of our country. Such a militia might not only defend a people living in an island, but even such as are placed in the midst of the most warlike nations of the world.

Now till such a militia may be brought to some perfection, our present militia is not only sufficient to defend us; but considering the circumstances of the French affairs, especially with relation to Spain, Britain cannot justly apprehend an invasion, if the fleet of England, to which Scotland furnished during the late war seven or eight thousand seamen, were in such order as it ought to be. And it can never be the interest of these nations to take any other share in preserving the balance of Europe, than what may be performed by our fleet. By which means our money will be spent amongst ourselves; our trade preserved to support the charge of the navy; our enemies totally driven out of the sea, and great numbers of their forces diverted from opposing the armies of our allies abroad, to the defence of their own coasts.

If this method had been taken in the late war, I presume it would have proved, not only more advantageous to us, but also more serviceable to our allies than that which was followed. And 'tis in vain to say, that at this rate we shall have no allies at all: for the weaker party on the continent must be contented to accept our assistance in the manner we think fit to give it, or inevitably perish.

But if we send any forces beyond the seas to join those of our allies, they ought to be part of our militia, as has been said, and not standing forces; otherwise, at the end of every war, the present struggle will recur, and at one time or other these nations will be betrayed, and a standing army established: so that nothing can save us from following the fate of all the other kingdoms in Europe, but putting our trust altogether in our fleet and militias, and having no other forces than these. The sea is the only empire which can naturally belong to us. Conquest is not our interest, much less to consume our people and treasure in conquering for others.

To conclude;[30] if we seriously consider the happy condition of these nations, who have lived so long under the blessings of liberty, we cannot but be affected with the most tender compassion to think that the Scots, who have for so many ages, with such resolution, defended their liberty against the Picts, Britons, Romans, Saxons, Danes, Irish, Normans, and English, as well as against the violence and tyranny of so many of their own princes; that the English, who, whatever revolutions their country has been subject to, have still maintained their rights and liberties against all attempts; who possess a country, every where cultivated and improved by the industry of rich husbandmen; her rivers and harbours filled with ships; her cities, towns, and villages, enriched with manufactures; where men of vast estates live in secure possession of them, and whose merchants live in as great splendor as the nobility of other nations: that Scotland which has a gentry born to excel in arts and arms: that England which has a commonalty, not only surpassing all those of that degree which the world can now boast of, but also those of all former ages, in courage, honesty, good sense, industry, and generosity of temper; in whose very looks there are such visible marks of a free and liberal education; which advantages cannot be imputed to the climate, or to any other cause, but the freedom of the government under which they live: I say, it cannot but make the hearts of all honest men bleed to think, that in their days the felicity and liberties of such countries must come to a period, if the parliaments do not prevent it, and his majesty be not prevailed upon to lay aside

---

[30] The concluding peroration incorporates references to Scotland absent from the original 1697 edition of the pamphlet, developing a powerful comparative analysis of the significance of the threat represented by standing armies to each country. See the List of Variants.

the thoughts of mercenary armies, which, if once established, will inevitably produce those fatal consequences that have always attended such forces in the other kingdoms of Europe; violation of property, decay of trade, oppression of the country by heavy taxes and quarters, the utmost misery and slavery of the poorer sort, the ruin of the nobility by their expences in court and army, deceit and treachery in all ranks of men, occasioned by want and necessity. Then shall we see the gentry of Scotland, ignorant through want of education, and cowardly by being oppressed; then shall we see the once happy commonalty of England become base and abject, by being continually exposed to the brutal insolence of the soldiers; the women debauched by their lust; ugly and nasty through poverty, and the want of things necessary to preserve their natural beauty. Then shall we see that great city, the pride and glory, not only of our island, but of the world, subjected to the excessive impositions Paris now lies under, and reduced to a pedling trade, serving only to foment the luxury of a court. Then will Britain know what obligations she has to those who are for mercenary armies.

TWO
DISCOURSES
Concerning the
AFFAIRS
OF
SCOTLAND;

Written in the Year 1698.

Edinburgh, 1698.

The first discourse

No inclination is so honourable, nor has any thing been so much esteemed in all nations, and ages, as the love of that country and society in which every man is born. And those who have placed their greatest satisfaction in doing good, have accounted themselves happy, or unfortunate, according to the success of their endeavours to serve the interest of their country. For nothing can be more powerful in the minds of men, than a natural inclination and duty concurring in the same disposition.

Nature in most men prevails over reason; reason in some prevails over nature: but when these two are joined, and a violent natural inclination finds itself owned by reason, required by duty, encouraged by the highest praises, and excited by the most illustrious examples, sure that force must be irresistible. Constrained by so great a force, and the circumstances of my affairs not allowing me to be otherwise serviceable to my country, I have in the following discourse given my opinion concerning divers matters of importance, which probably may be debated in the approaching session of parliament.[1] I shall be very well satisfied, if any thing I say do afford a hint that may be improved by men of better judgment to the publick good. I hope I shall not be blamed, for giving my opinion in matters of publick concernment; since 'tis the right and duty of every man to write or speak his mind freely in all things that may come before any parliament; to the end that they who represent the nation in that assembly, may be truly informed of the sentiments of those they represent. Besides, we are now no more under those tyrannical reigns in which it was a crime to speak of publick affairs, or to say that the king had received bad counsel in any thing. If in this discourse I argue against some things, which perhaps may not be proposed in the ensuing session of parliament; they are neverthe-

---

[1] The seventh session of the first (and only) parliament called by King William began on 19 July 1698, the previous session having been adjourned on 8 December 1696; commissions for the new session were issued on 24 June 1698: *The Acts of the Parliaments of Scotland, vol. X: 1696–1701* (London, 1833), pp. 115–16. Fletcher was not himself a member of the parliament, which may explain his reference to his circumstances not allowing him to serve his country other than by writing. He was clearly writing in expectation of the new session, which suggests that the work was composed in late June and early July; it may have been published by the start of the new session on 19 July.

less such as persons in publick trust have in their conversation given just cause to think they were designed.

'Tis probable that the parliament, before they proceed to any other business, will take into consideration a transaction, which having passed since the last session, may, if it be not abolished, import no less than the infringing the freedom of this and all subsequent parliaments; I mean, the farming of the customs to the state of burroughs.[2]

Corruption is so entirely disowned by all men, that I may be allowed to say, when I name it, that I name the blackest of crimes; and when I name any guilty of it, I name a very odious criminal. But corruption is more or less dangerous in proportion to the stations in which corrupt men are placed. When a private man receives any advantage to betray a trust, one, or a few persons may suffer; if a judge be corrupted, the oppression is extended to greater numbers: but when legislators are bribed, or (which is all one) are under any particular ingagement, that may influence them in their legislative capacity, much more when an entire state of parliament is brought under those circumstances, then it is that we must expect injustice to be established by a law, and all those consequences, which will inevitably follow the subversion of a constitution, I mean, standing armies, oppressive taxes, slavery; whilst the outward form only of the antient government remains to give them authority. I confess I have been often struck with astonishment, and could never make an end of admiring the folly and stupidity of men living under some modern governments, who will exclaim against a judge that takes bribes, and never rest till he be punished, or at least removed; and yet at the same time suffer great numbers of those who have the legislative authority, to receive the constant bribes of places and pensions to betray them. But we shall have less to say for ourselves, if we suffer the votes of the whole state of burroughs to be at once influenced by the farming of the customs. For in other places the impudence of bribery has gone no farther than to attack single persons; but to endeavour at once to bribe a whole state of parliament, is an attempt of which it seems we only are capable.

---

[2] The Crown and its ministers used the prospect of granting the Customs' Farm (the administration of customs in return for a fixed sum) to the burghs themselves as a bait to secure their votes for the ministry in the parliament.

Yet to shew how far I am from suspecting any man of the least bad design, without a cause, I shall say, that as I know this business of the farm above-mentioned was first moved without any design to influence the votes of the burroughs in parliament; so I am willing to believe that few of those who have since acted in this affair had any such design. But if any man, after due consideration of the evil consequences which must follow, and are inseparable from such a farm, shall still persist in endeavouring to continue it, he cannot but be an enemy to the liberties of his country.

This is so bold an attempt, and so inconsistent with the freedom of parliament, that till it be removed 'tis to be presumed they will not proceed to any other business: but this obstruction once taken away, we may hope they will begin with that affair which presses most, and in which the nation is so universally concerned, I mean that of the African and Indian company.[3]

I know some will exclaim against this method, and propose that the business of the army may be first taken into consideration, as of more general concernment to the nation whether it stand or be disbanded. They will not fail to say, that before all other things the king's business (as their stile runs) ought to be done. To this I answer, that he who makes a distinction between the business of the king and that of the country, is a true friend to neither. And if

---

[3] 'The African and Indian Company', or Company of Scotland trading to Africa and the Indies, had been established by an Act of the Scottish parliament on 26 June 1695, which was approved by William partly to deflect the odium arising from the Massacre of Glencoe in 1692 (see below, fn 23). This company was originally conceived as a means for Scots to circumvent the monopoly of the London East India Company; and half of its capital was intended to be (and quickly was) subscribed by English merchants, likewise keen to break the East India Company monopoly. Following protests by the English parliament, the English subscribers were forced to withdraw, obliging the Company to look for funds elsewhere; and in 1696–7 William's representatives in Hamburg and other Hanse towns did everything they could to frustrate the efforts of the Scots to secure investment there. By mid-1696 the directors of the Scottish Company were taking an interest in William Paterson's suggestion (which was not originally an object of the Company) that the Scots should establish a colony on the Isthmus of Darien, in Panama; and by the spring of 1698 preparations were well-advanced for an expedition to that end. The expedition sailed from Edinburgh on 14 July 1698 (and, definitively, from Kirkcaldy on 19 July), just as the new session of parliament began. Fletcher subscribed £1000 to the Company, and had been directly involved in the preparations for the expedition to Darien. See G. P. Insh, *The Company of Scotland Trading to Africa and the Indies* (London and New York, 1932).

it be consider'd, that the ships of the company are sailed; that Scotland has now a greater venture at sea than at any time since we have been a nation; that the accidents and misfortunes to which an enterprize of this nature is subject, are so many and so various, either by the loss of ships from the ordinary hazards of the sea, or hurricanes; by sickness of the men, who for the most part are neither accustomed to such long voyages, nor to climates so different from their own; by the death of one or more of those to whom the conduct of this affair is principally entrusted; by being disappointed of fresh provisions when those they carry with them are spent; by being attacked at sea or at land, before they have fortified a place for themselves, or a thousand other accidents, (for all things are extremely difficult to the first undertakers) I say, if it be considered, that provisions, or the smallest things necessary, falling short but by a few days, have often been the ruin of the greatest undertakings, and chiefly of those of this kind; there cannot be any more urgent affair than that of providing incessantly a supply for the necessities of so many men as are on board those ships, who may be brought under extraordinary sufferings by a delay, whilst our standing forces are living at ease. Especially since the nation has so great a concern in this enterprize, that I may well say all our hopes of ever being any other than a poor and inconsiderable people are imbarked with them.

The reputation and power of this nation was formerly very considerable as long as armies were composed of those numerous militias of the barons. Our ancestors have often seen sixty, eighty, or a hundred thousand men under their ensigns, which then might well bear the motto, That none should provoke them unpunished.[4] Since that time, the face of things is quite changed throughout all Europe; and the former militias being altogether decayed, and no good ones any where established, every country is obliged to defend itself in time of war, and maintain its reputation by the force of money; that is, by mercenary troops, either of their own, or of other countries both by sea and land. But such a vast expence the riches of no country is able to support without a great trade. In this great alteration our case has been singularly bad and unfortunate: for partly

---

[4] 'Nemo me impune lacessit' was the motto incorporated into the royal arms of Scotland by 1617.

through our own fault, and partly by the removal of our kings into another country, this nation, of all those who possess good ports, and lie conveniently for trade and fishing, has been the only part of Europe which did not apply itself to commerce; and possessing a barren country, in less than an age we are sunk to so low a condition as to be despised by all our neighbours, and made uncapable to repel an injury, if any should be offered: so that now our motto may be inverted, and all may not only provoke, but safely trample upon us. To recover from such a condition, what would not any people do? What toils would they refuse? To what hazards would they not expose themselves? But if the means by which they are to recover, are not only just and honourable, but such as with restoring honour and safety to the nation, may give encouragement to that excellent, though now suppressed and almost extinguished spirit of our people, and gratify every man in the eases and pleasures of life: is it not strange that there should be found men amongst us capable to oppose those things; especially at a time, when, I may say, by no contrivance of any man, but by an unforeseen and unexpected change of the genius of this nation, all their thoughts and inclinations, as if united and directed by a higher power, seem to be turned upon trade, and to conspire together for its advancement, which is the only means to recover us from our present miserable and despicable condition? For hitherto our convenient situation and good harbours, our rich seas and lakes have been unprofitable to us; no care has been taken to set the poor at work; and multitudes of families, for want of employment by trade and manufactures, go yearly out of the kingdom without any intention to return. In such a state and condition of this nation, it seems these men find their account better, than if our country were filled with people and riches, our firths covered with ships, and they should see everywhere the marks of what good government and trade are able to produce.

But I shall be told, that I go upon a mistake; and that no Scotsman is an enemy to the African company: that those who approach his majesty, know most of his mind, and are most entrusted by him in the government of this nation; and such as are influenced by them, would only have the parliament to consider the streights and difficulties his majesty would be put to, if he should in an extraordinary manner encourage this trade, by reason, that being King of

England, and Stadtholder of the United Provinces, our interest in this point may come to interfere with that of those nations.[5] The people of those countries solicit, each in favour of their own companies: will not these men so much as advise the king to distribute impartial justice, and to let every one have the proportionable reward of his industry? O but we have an immunity from customs for many years, which neither the English nor Dutch enjoy. I shall not say, that when the English nation shall come to a perfect knowledge of their interest, they will be convinced that riches in Scotland will be beneficial to England, since the seat of the monarchy is there. I need not say that the English and Dutch are free people, and may surely procure for themselves as great advantages as Scotland: but that Scotland offered to both nations a share in that advantage which they had obtained for themselves only; and to England an equal share. I know the parliament of England took the thing warmly at first; but when upon due consideration they found that we had not given them the least just ground of offence, but on the contrary, made them the fairest offer we could; it was then let fall, and has not been mentioned in the last session. So that what these gentlemen alledge of his majesty's difficulties to satisfy the English in this point is false, unless by the English they mean those who having for many years oppressed the English colonies in America, are afraid that if any settlement should be made in that part of the world by us, under a free constitution, the English planters removing to it, might occasion a strict inquiry into their crimes, and their punishment for them.[6]

I do not hear that the Dutch have presented any memorial to his majesty against our company, and cannot imagine in what terms any such address, either from them, or the English, can run. Should it be, that his majesty ought not to protect us in our just rights and privileges? That he should break the laws, and violate his oath by our destruction? Or undermine us as the court did the fishing

---

[5] William soon regretted having approved the Act instituting the Company of Scotland in 1695, and claimed to have been misled by his ministers. Both English and Dutch interests were against it; increasingly important, however, was the provocation which the Darien scheme offered to Spain, whose dying king, Charles II, William was anxious not to offend.

[6] The several English colonies in North America had been established on a variety of constitutional terms, and the reign of James II in particular had seen an attempt to assert stronger royal authority over the colonists through their governors.

company in King Charles's time, and frustrate this second as well as that first great attempt to make the nation considerable?[7] That there have been underhand dealings (though without his majesty's knowledge, as we ought to believe) the affair of Hamborough does sufficiently demonstrate; and likewise that his majesty's ministers abroad, paid by the Crown of England, are no more to be looked upon as ministers for the Crown of Scotland.[8] Since we are separate kingdoms, and have separate ministers at home, we ought to have separate ministers abroad; especially in an affair wherein we may have a separate interest from England, which must always be in matters of trade, though never so inconsiderable. Neither ought we to have separate ministers only upon the account of trade, but upon all occasions, wherein the honour or interest of the nation is concerned. That we have not had them formerly, since we were under one king with England, was, I suppose, to save charges, and because we trusted to the impartiality of such as we judged to be the ministers of the King of Great Britain: but now we are undeceived, and sure the nation could never have bestowed money better, than in having a minister at the late treaty of peace, who might have obtained the re-establishment of the nation in the privileges they had in France, which was totally neglected: and notwithstanding the great and unproportionable numbers of sea and land soldiers that we were obliged to furnish for the support of the war, yet not one tittle of advantage was procured to us by the peace.[9]

[7] Both Charles I and Charles II had sought to encourage fishing, in Scotland as well as England, by means of an association or company. Charles I encouraged the formation of the Association for Fishing in 1632, and Charles II revived it as the Royal Fishery in 1661. Neither venture was successful: the Royal Fishery failed to raise the funds it sought, and fishing was severely disrupted by the Dutch Wars in the mid-1660s and early 1670s. The Scottish Company was defunct by the early 1670s, and was formally dissolved by Act of Parliament in 1690. See J. R. Elder, *The Royal Fishery Companies of the Seventeenth Century* (Glasgow, 1912).

[8] Envoys to foreign courts and consuls or residents in foreign ports were appointed by the English Crown, and there was no separate representation of the Scottish Crown. Fletcher's point is that the envoys could not therefore be relied upon to forward Scottish interests: 'the affair of Hamborough' (Hamburg) refers to the blocking of the Scots' attempts to secure investment for their company by the English resident, Sir Paul Rycault.

[9] The peace was that of Ryswick, agreed in September 1697, which ended the so-called Nine Years' War.

Now these gentlemen, at the same time, would persuade us to pay almost as many forces in time of peace, as we did in time of war; and like Pharoah's tax-masters would have us make brick without allowing us straw. And all, that these forces, and the regiments, which to the consuming of our people, we recruit in Holland, in case of any rupture abroad upon the account of the English or Dutch trade, may be employed in their defence.

To obviate then part of so many shameful things, 'tis my opinion, that in place of laying a land tax upon the kingdom for maintaining forces to defend the English and Dutch trade, we should raise one for the carrying on of our own: and (since the nation is so generally concerned in this Indian trade, that the ruin of it, which, God forbid, may very probably draw along with it that of the whole trade of the kingdom, and a perpetual discouragement from ever attempting any thing considerable hereafter) that a twelve-months' cess should be levied for the support of it;[10] and that whatsoever may be the product of that money, by the trade of the company, shall go to the easing of the nation from publick burdens, whenever they shall make a dividend of clear profit. For 'tis but reasonable that, since the company has been unjustly hindered of that supply of money which they expected, and might have had from strangers, they should have recourse for redress to the parliament, who if they shall think fit to take such a resolution, the company will be able immediately to procure an advance of money upon the credit of the cess.

It will be also fit, that the company petition the parliament to address his majesty, that the three small frigats, lately built at the expence of this nation, may be appointed for a convoy to the next ships they shall send out.

The parliament having provided for this pressing affair, will (no doubt) proceed to the business of the forces, and to consider whether a standing army shall be kept up in time of peace, as in time of war; for the arguments used to continue them for a year, may be improved to keep them up for ever; especially since we have at this time a stronger argument against them, than I hope shall ever

---

[10] The cess was the Scottish Land Tax: first raised by the Covenanting Parliament in 1645, it had been revived by Charles II in 1665, and an Act of 1667 appointed Commissioners of Supply to collect it.

be alledged hereafter; I mean that of the nation's being exhausted of money by a three years scarcity next to a famine: but how long this may continue God only knows.[11]

A long and tedious war, which has cost this nation much blood, is at length ended in a peace. Our expence of treasure has been inconsiderable by reason of our poverty through want of trade; yet have we contributed our part, if the smallness of our stock be considered. But in the loss of our people, which is an expence of blood and riches too, we have paid a treble proportion. Seven or eight thousand of our seamen were on board the English fleet, and two or three thousand in that of Holland: we had twenty battalions of foot, and six squadrons of dragoons here and in Flanders. Besides, I am credibly informed, that every fifth man in the English forces was either of this nation, or Scots-Irish, who are a people of the same blood with us. All these, by a modest computation, may amount to thirty thousand men.[12] This I only mention to answer the reproaches of those who vilify us as an inconsiderable people, and set a mean value on the share we have borne in this war. I am unwilling to speak of the returns that have been made to us for our assistance, by refusing to our soldiers the donative given to those who had served no better than they, and by pressing our seamen, contrary to the law of nations. Now though resenting the last of these during the war, would have marked us out for disaffection and Jacobitism; yet we ought to hope it may be mentioned at this time without offence. But some will say, that the blessings of peace are so great, that not only the calamities of war, but even affronts and injuries from our neighbours, ought to be forgot and drowned in the joys, which the hopes of ease, tranquillity and plenty must

[11] Scotland suffered severe harvest failures in 1695, 1696 and 1698; Fletcher's judgement that they resulted in dearth or scarcity rather than in outright famine should be set against his much more alarmed, and alarmist, estimates of vagrancy later in the *Second Discourse*. Although the 1697 harvest was not so bad, the effects of the earlier failures of 1695 and 1696 ensured that the scarcity had been felt for 'three years' by early 1698; the provisioning trade and poor relief system had been unable to cope. Mortality varied by place and time; but at least in certain areas may have ranged between 5 and 15 per cent of the population. See M. Flinn (ed.), *Scottish Population History from the Seventeenth Century to the 1930s* (Cambridge, 1977), pp. 164–86.

[12] Fletcher's estimates of Scots serving in the British army are apparently accepted: John Childs, *The British Army of William III 1689–1702* (Manchester, 1987), p. 15.

needs produce. And indeed I should be contented, that all resentments were sacrificed to such charming hopes, if they had any real foundation. But we have a peace, and yet must not reap any benefit by it; a poor country is to maintain almost as many forces as they did in time of war; a nation endeavouring to set up manufactures, and to advance trade, must still see their people consumed, by continuing on foot mercenary forces.

I shall not insist upon the arguments that may be brought against standing forces, nor go about to shew how inconsistent they are with liberty. I shall not mention the examples of almost all the nations of Europe, who by keeping up such forces in time of peace are become slaves. This has been fully made out by divers treatises which have been lately published, and are in the hands of most men.[13] Perhaps also it will be said, that I am not to insist upon the point of right in this case, since there is no article in our claim of right to declare the keeping up of a standing army in time of peace, without consent of parliament, to be against law. Yet those who are of that opinion should consider, that the estates of this kingdom have made the keeping up of a standing army, in time of peace, without consent of parliament, an article in the forfaulture of the late King James.[14] But it seems we must use more modest arguments than such as naturally arise from the hazard our liberty may run, by allowing standing forces, or from any right we have to pretend that 'tis against the constitution of our government to impose them upon us, and be obliged to bring all our reasons from our necessities and inability to maintain any. Indeed, as this is the most modest, so surely 'tis the strongest argument; for such forces are

---

[13] As in his own *Discourse of Government*, and in the works of the English anti-army writers, John Trenchard, John Toland and others.

[14] It is not clear what distinction Fletcher was drawing here, since the Claim of Right pronounced the keeping on foot of a standing army in time of peace by James VII, without consent of parliament, to have been one of the ways in which he had invaded 'the fundamental constitution of the kingdom', altering it from 'a legal limited monarchy, to an arbitrary despotic power', and further declared all these invasions of the constitution to have been 'utterly and directly contrary to the known laws, statutes and freedoms of this realm'. On these grounds James was then held to have 'forefaulted' the right to the throne: *Source Book of Scottish History*, III, pp. 201–3. His point may be that the Claim of Right's declaration of the illegality of keeping up a standing army in peacetime without consent of parliament was not embodied in a subsequent statute, as were other grievances declared in 1689.

not to be maintained, without increasing the poverty of this country, and reducing it at length to utter desolation. 'Tis hard if the charges of a government should be the same in time of peace, or even come near the expence that was perhaps requisite to be made in time of war; such a nation can never hope to be in a flourishing state. Now as our condition will not permit us to keep up these forces, so I can see no reason why we should do it if we could. There is no pretence for them, except only to keep a few wretched Highlanders in order; which might be easily done by a due execution of our old laws made for that purpose, without the help of any fort or garison. We are at a great distance from any other enemy, and cannot justly fear an invasion from beyond so great a sea as must be passed to come at us. And though during the late war we were sometimes under the apprehensions of such an invasion, yet the enemy was not so imprudent to put it to the hazard.

But some will say, that the late King James has still many partizans in this nation, that we have always been, and still are a divided people, and that there are many ill men amongst us: they have also the confidence still to tell us of an invasion upon Scotland by the French King; who to cover this probable design, has delivered up such vast countries, and places of such great importance. Why do they not also say, that as a man every day after he is born, is nearer to his end, so are we every day after the peace nearer to a war? The party of the late King James was always insignificant, and is now become a jest. If the government will encourage good men, they will need no standing forces to secure themselves from the bad. For of what use can any militia be supposed to be, that is not fit to preserve the quiet of a country remote from enemies in time of peace?

Those of the presbyterian persuasion should, I think, be the last of all men to establish an army; for whatever they may promise to themselves, 'tis certain that either upon his majesty's death, or upon alterations of measures, and changes of dispositions in the minds of the members of future parliaments, it will be always a sure rod for the backs of those who have so many enemies. But men are blind in prosperity, forgetting adversity and the vicissitudes of human affairs. And it were but reasonable that those of that persuasion, who in the late King James's reign made so false a step as was like to have proved fatal to our liberties, should now think of making some amends, and shewing that they have profited by their error, and are not (as they express themselves) time-servers.[15]

But to discover the true reason why standing forces are designed to be kept up in this nation in time of peace, we need only look back on the use that was made of them during the late war. For after the reduction of the Highlands they served only for a seminary to the forces of this nation that were with his majesty in Flanders, the best of their men being drawn out yearly for recruiting those forces. This also proves that his majesty knew very well, that there was no hazard from the invasions I mentioned before: for if there had been any real danger of that kind, he would not have weakened the forces in this kingdom so considerably. I am very far from disapproving his majesty's conduct in that affair; I do on the contrary highly commend his wisdom in it, and think it to have been the best use that could be made of forces in this country, whilst the war continued. But must we in time of peace be taxed beyond measure to maintain forces, which upon occasion are to serve for the defence of two of the richest nations in the world; nations that have manifested their unwillingness to let us into the least co-partnership with them in trade, from which all our riches, if ever we have any, must arise? This is to load a poor nation with taxes, and to oppress them with soldiers in order to procure plenty and riches to other countries, of which they are not to have the least share. Rich and opulent nations are to enjoy the benefits of the peace, and we are to suffer, that they may enjoy them with security.

Therefore I am of opinion, that since we can expect no advantages from our neighbours or allies, we do ourselves right, by refusing to maintain any standing forces for their behoof, because we need none for our own defence, and that our militia may be sufficient on all occasions where force is necessary. Eighty-four thou-

---

[15] Likely targets of this remark were the Dalrymples, Sir James, 1st Viscount Stair, and his son, Sir John, Master of Stair. While the first had resigned as Lord President of the Court of Session in 1681 and gone into exile in the United Provinces, his son had remained to serve King James as Lord Advocate. After 1688 Sir James was reinstated as Lord President following the murder of his successor, Sir George Lockhart, while Sir John was re-appointed Lord Advocate, and in 1691 became joint Secretary of State. The elder Stair had sought to refute the charge of being a time-server in *An Apology for Sir James Dalrymple of Stair, President of the Session, by himself* (1690), an answer to the personal attack on him in the anonymous *The late proceedings of the Parliament of Scotland stated and vindicated* (1689).

sand pounds, which is the sum proposed for the yearly maintenance of standing forces, is as much money to us, as two millions five hundred and twenty thousand pounds is to England, since we cannot pretend to above the thirtieth part of their wealth.[16] And yet that nation allows but three hundred and fifty thousand pounds for the forces they keep on foot; of which sum twelve thousand pounds is more than the thirtieth part. If it be said that England allows more for their fleet than for their land forces; I answer, it ought to be considered that England with all its riches maintains only five millions and half of people, and that Scotland upon a thirtieth part maintains a million and half. Eighty-four thousand pounds laid out yearly in husbandry, manufactures and trade, may do great things in Scotland, and not only maintain (though in a different way of living) all those officers and soldiers, of which these forces are designed to consist, but also vastly enrich this nation; whereas great numbers of soldiers produce nothing but beggary in any place. People employed in manufactures, husbandry and trade, make consumption as well as soldiers, and their labour and industry is an overplus of wealth to the nation, whilst soldiers consume twice as much as they pay for, and live idle.

'Tis not the least misfortune of this country, that the younger sons of the nobility and gentry have in all times had their inclinations debauched to an idle, for the most part criminal, and almost always unprofitable sort of life; I mean that of a soldier of fortune. Their talents might have been much better employed in trade and husbandry to the improvement of their country, and increase of their patrimony. Let us begin to come off from such ruinous ways of living; and if we design to carry on a great trade, let us employ men capable to manage it. From all these considerations I say, that the keeping up of any standing forces in time of peace is not only useless, but destructive to the well-being of this nation.

If it be objected, that this would take away even the ordinary guards; I answer, that whilst we had a king residing in Scotland, he had no other guard than forty gentlemen; and now when we have no king amongst us, we must have a squadron of horse and two battalions of foot, with the title of guards. But I would know what

---

[16] Fletcher's figures are presumably in sterling, since the sum would otherwise have to be adjusted to allow for the lower value of the Scots pound. (A sum of 12 Scots Pounds was roughly equal to £1 sterling in the seventeenth century.)

guards they are we must keep up. Are they those who yielded up the rank of the nation and dignity of a crown, if it have any preheminence above a commonwealth? I am far from pleading for mutiny against a general, or disobedience to a king; but when the meanest officer thinks himself injured in his rank, he demands his pass, and will serve no more; neither is he blamed by any prince for so doing. If the officers of that body would have done as much for the honour of their country, sure they would have merited his majesty's esteem, and deserved rewards from the nation. But how they can pretend to be kept up after an action that our ancestors would have thought to deserve not only breaking, but a decimation to precede it, I cannot imagine. I know there are many brave gentlemen among them who were much grieved at the thing, but they had a bad example from the then commanding officer; and 'tis to be feared that his advancement to the place of the greatest military trust and importance in the kingdom, may by his majesty's enemies be imputed to that action.[17]

But after all we are told, that if we will keep up standing forces we shall have an act of habeas corpus. This would be a wise bargain: here is a price for our liberty; sure we may expect an immense sum, and a security without exception. No, no, but you shall have an act of parliament for the freedom of your persons, though there be never so many standing forces in the kingdom; that is, we shall have the law on our side, and another shall have the force, and then let nature work. If there be no danger that standing forces should violate the law, there is no danger from them.

There is no pretence to speak of a cess or land-tax for maintaining forces, before the business of the army be taken into consideration; and one would think, if the army be disbanded, it should not be mentioned at all. Yet 'tis certain that such men as would recommend themselves by a pretended loyalty, will not fail to tell us, that we ought to be at the least as liberal to his present majesty,

---

[17] The allusion was to no less a figure than the duke of Queensberry, who as earl of Drumlanrig (the title of the eldest son and heir of the duke) had been among the officers who deserted James in the face of the invading army of William in November 1688; at the time Drumlanrig was lieutenant-colonel of Dundee's regiment, which was particularly hateful to Scottish presbyterians. After the Revolution Drumlanrig commanded the Scots Guards, and held on to this post when he succeeded his father as 2nd duke of Queensberry in 1695. By 1698 Queensberry was a key figure in William's Scottish ministry.

who has redeemed us from popery and slavery, as we were to King James, who would have brought us under both: and though they now pretend that a cess for life will not be so much as mentioned in the approaching session, we know very well their conduct in that affair will be regulated upon the disposition they find in the parliament to grant or refuse it; and that if they conceive any hopes of obtaining so considerable a jewel to the crown, they will be sure to bring in that affair when least expected.[18]

The giving his majesty a land-tax during life, and so great a one as that granted to the late King James, with the revenue already settled on him for the same term, makes it impossible for the subject to give more, and consequently is of all those affairs that can come before any parliament the greatest, and of the highest importance; since it tends to the making parliaments less necessary, and consequently to the abolishing them, with the antient constitution of government in this nation.

Those who have the honour to advise his present majesty, if they be true lovers of the monarchy, ought to have a care of treading in the former footsteps, and above all shun to advise him to desire those things of the parliament which King James desired and obtained. It were their duty by all means, to endeavour a fair understanding and a continual good correspondence between king and people, which certainly is the only true support of monarchy. Now there are no occasions of entertaining and encreasing that confidence, and those mutual good offices that should, like regular tides, ebb and flow between king and people, greater than those of parliaments. Endeavours to take away the frequency of parliaments, are endeavours to take away those frequent good offices between king and people. The king stands in need of money, the people of good laws, which their representatives and his great council offer to him, that they may have his sanction, and that he may provide for their due execution. Money may be given at once, for a long time, or for ever; but good laws cannot be so enacted, the occasion and necessity of them discovering itself only from time to time: and if the one go without the other, the mutual good offices, and consequently the mutual confidence between king and people ceases.

---

[18] In the event the court proposed that the cess to maintain the forces be for two years only, and this was accepted: *Acts of the Parliament of Scotland*, x, p. 126.

It may be farther considered, that the king has the power of calling parliaments; and that by giving him for life all that we can give, we shall make parliaments unnecessary to him. If any man suggest that it is a crime to suspect that so good and just a prince as his present majesty is, will not always do what is for the good of his people; I answer, that I have all the deference, respect and esteem for his majesty that any subject ought to have; but it were a fulsome piece of flattery for any man to say, that he cannot be influenced by bad counsel, or that he is not subject to those frailties of mistake and prejudice, from which no mortal was ever free, and princes always most subject to through the suggestions and bad offices of men about them.

But let us suppose that his present majesty will never make the least bad use of this tax, who shall secure us his successor will not? If it be said that 'tis only for his present majesty this tax is desired, and that it is in the power of the parliament to refuse it to the successor; I say, with what probability will it, and with what face can it be refused to him? These men desire it for his present majesty because King James had it, though he made bad use of it; the successor shall desire it because his present majesty had it, and made good use of it; I think his argument is stronger. So that though this be said to be only for the life of his present majesty, yet upon the matter it is for ever. And then I need not tell you the consequence, our parliaments shall be abolished, our kings shall become tyrants, and we, of subjects, slaves.

But if we look more nearly into this demand, I doubt not it will appear very gross. During the late war, land-taxes were only demanded from year to year, and we gave them chearfully, in hopes that a few years would put an end to that charge. When we had undoubted reasons to believe there would be a peace, they were demanded to be given for two years; and now God has blessed us with it, if they be demanded during his majesty's life, will not this look as if we were to have a standing army during the same time?

A land-tax during his majesty's life, is a French taille for that time. And we ought not to forget that we are beginning, to the great advantage of the nation, to make some small progress in trade; but if it be not incouraged, and much more if it be nipt in the bud, there is an end of all our hopes. One of the greatest things in trade, is to encourage exportation; and 'tis known that the greatest commodity of this kingdom is corn: if there be a land-tax on those whose chief riches consist in corn, they cannot sell so cheap to the merchant, that he can make any profit by exporting it.

As for the arguments of those who are for this tax, I need answer none of them; they are, to save the trouble and expence of frequent parliaments; and because the nation did trust King James with this tax, who made bad use of it, (a modest and a sensible argument!) are they not afraid it should be said, that those who advise the King to ask the same trust King James had, may advise him likewise to the same things, for which King James demanded it? Sure I am, that many who plead for this now, are the same persons who did the like for King James: and as for the expence occasioned by frequent parliaments, I believe there is neither shire nor borough but will find persons very willing to represent them, without putting them to any charge. I know 'tis commonly said in this kingdom, that parliaments do more hurt than good; but it is because they are never called unless to impose money: will it mend the matter to lay on at once, and for life, as much as the nation is able to pay? We were getting some good laws for our money, but then we shall be excluded from that benefit.

In a word, our forefathers had two securities for their liberties and properties, they had both the sword and the purse: the sword antiently was in the hand of the subject, because the armies then were composed of the vassals who depended on the barons. That security is gone; shall we throw the other after it, and thereby, I may very well say, dissolve the constitution, and the monarchy? For a government is not only a tyranny, when tyrannically exercised; but also when there is no sufficient caution in the constitution that it may not be exercised tyrannically.

When the parliament has put an end to the affairs before-mentioned, it were to be wished that this being the first session since the conclusion of the peace, and after so long a war, they would pass some act to ease the minds, and take away the fears and apprehensions of many men who are still obnoxious to the law, of whom the greater part are abroad; and all of them both at home and abroad, for want of an act of indemnity, made desperate, and only fitted to involve others in the same uneasy and distracting circumstances under which they themselves live.[19] But acts of indemnity are the worst and most pernicious of all laws to the well being of any government, unless the most notorious offenders be first punished; and in such cases only incouragements to new transgressions, destroying the real security of all government, and effect of all laws, by giving an entire impunity to the attempts against both. So that there seems to be an absolute necessity, both of making an example of the notorious enemies to the liberties of this country, and giving a general pardon to the rest; if we will either secure the government for the future from endeavours to introduce arbitrary power, cut up the party of the late King James by the roots, or quiet the minds of the people, and remove the animosities that may remain in a nation wherein two or more parties have been inflamed against each other, to the ruin of the publick liberty, and extinguish the memory of those factions for ever.

When 'tis confessed and acknowledged, that there have been bold attempts and treacherous practices to destroy the religion, overturn the constitution of government, and suppress the liberty of a nation, and yet no example made of the advisers, and those who have been eminently subservient to such designs; such a people has as much laid the foundation of their own ruin, as if they had declared that those who shall hereafter ingage themselves in the like attempts, need fear no punishment. Upon a revolution followed by a war, circumstances of affairs may be such, that till the war be at an end, 'tis not fit to punish great offenders. But there was no reason, nor any well-grounded political consideration, why immediately upon the late revolution, the most notorious of those offenders should not have been punished; by which means we should have been delivered from our worst men, who have since been very bad instruments in affairs, and have terrified the rest by their example: we might then have quieted the minds of the people by an indemnity; brought the nation to a settlement, and prevented the war which ensued in this country. Yet (because in matters of prudence men

---

[19] Fletcher's proposal of a general Act of Indemnity, accompanied by measures to punish the most notorious offenders, was presumably aimed at Jacobite exiles. It was not taken up in the ensuing session of parliament. It may have reflected Fletcher's frustration at the slowness with which he himself had been indemnified after 1689.

are of different sentiments) though it should be granted, that during the war it was not fit to make any examples, what pretence can there be now of exempting from punishment those who have been notoriously criminal, both under the late reigns, and under this? Which when it is done, what conjuncture of time can be so proper for applying the healing remedy of an act of indemnity and oblivion to the rest, as the present, by reason of the peace?

Before the revolution, the court had been in a formed conspiracy against the religion and liberties of this nation; nor was there any art to introduce arbitrary power, or subvert our religion, for which the late reigns wanted willing instruments; and many endeavoured to signalize themselves in the ruin of their country. Yet no man has been made an example, to deter others from the like crimes. It will I know be thought hard to mention the punishing of offences committed so many years ago, when many of the offenders are dead; and some men will judge it fitter to bury all in a general act of oblivion. To this I answer, that having been highly to blame for neglecting hitherto to punish the enemies of our liberty, this ought to oblige us the rather to make an example of those who are still living. And to convince us of this necessity, we need only to consider what crimes those men would not have punished, nor the least example made of any that have been guilty of them; and whether the suffering them to pass unpunished, will not bring a guilt upon the nation which may not easily be expiated. Publick and private injuries are of a very different nature; and though we are commanded to forgive the last, yet those who have power and right, are required, under the greatest penalties, to punish the other, especially where the crimes are enormous. But if the parliament should follow the advice of those men, they are not to punish any violent proceedings, illegal and arbitrary imprisonments, fines, banishments, and murders under pretext of law, that were set on foot, encouraged, and committed by those evil counsellors mentioned in his majesty's declaration, in order to alter the religion and government of this nation, and in place of them to introduce popery and slavery.[20] They are not to punish those who to recommend them-

---

[20] Fletcher refers to the Declaration of 10 October 1688 in which William had justified his imminent invasion of England as necessary to maintain the Protestant religion, the laws and liberties of those kingdoms, and the right to the succession of his consort, Mary, and to remove the 'evil counsellors' who had overturned

selves to the late kings, by their interest, power, and credit in the parliament, got to be enacted most cruel and unchristian laws, for persecuting a great part of this nation upon the account of their religious opinions, which they could not quit without violating their consciences: they are not to punish those privy counsellors who went further than those very laws would allow them, in a thousand arbitrary and illegal proceedings, issuing out orders to invade such as dissented from them only in religious matters, with an army composed for the most part of barbarous Highlanders, who hunted them from hill to hill, to force them to take arms, that they might have a pretext to destroy them utterly.[21] They are not to punish those who gave orders to impose illegal and unwarrantable oaths upon all persons, even on silly women that might be found travelling in the ordinary road, and to shoot them immediately dead, if they should refuse the same. Nor are they to punish those who put them in execution. Do presbyterians in particular imagine, that if they neglect their duty in punishing these men, they will avoid the guilt of the innocent blood shed in those times? Are such things to be pardoned as private injuries? The making our courts of justice, particularly that of the session, to be the instruments of subjecting all men to arbitrary power, are things to be passed over in silence, and no account to be taken of them. Those who advised and drew a proclamation, declaring the late King James his absolute power in express terms, are not to be questioned for it.[22] If the parliament pass over these things without making any example of the offenders, they make a precedent for abolishing the punishment of all enormous crimes for ever, since there never can be greater than these. Shall there be no examples made of criminals for enormities of such a general influence and concernment, in a nation where a poor man for stealing a little food, is for example's sake (let what I say be

'the religion, laws and liberties of those realms': printed in Williams (ed.), *The Eighteenth-Century Constitution*, pp. 10–16.

[21] The reference is to the policy of James VII's ministers of using Highland troops, the so-called 'Highland Host', against the Presbyterian dissenters, or Covenanters.

[22] It is not clear which proclamation Fletcher had in mind. It may have been the proclamations of 1687 and 1688 granting Indulgence to those who did not conform to the established church. Both referred to 'our sovereign authority, prerogative royal and absolute power', as the basis for the king's decision to suspend the laws against such non-conformists; and both specifically exempted the most radical presbyterians, the 'field conventiclers' from the Indulgence. *Register of the Privy Council of Scotland*, 3rd Series, vol. XIII: *1686–1689* (1932), pp. 156–8, 227–30.

considered is for example's sake) punished with death? If there can be no stop put to the least of crimes, but by the punishment of some of those that are guilty; can there be any remedy against the abettors of arbitrary power, if no example be made of them? Can that government be said to be secure, where there is no punishment, but rewards for conspiracies against its constitution? 'Tis true that it may be fit to overlook some crimes, wherein extraordinary numbers of men are concerned, but not extraordinary crimes, nor the most guilty of the criminals.

It was thought fit to forbear the punishment of the evil counsellors mentioned in his majesty's declaration for some time; that forbearance has lasted to this day; and we have so little hopes of seeing any discouragement put upon those who shall promote arbitrary government in time to come, by an exemplary punishment of the most notorious offenders under the late reigns, that notwithstanding many new provocations, and reiterated treasons under this, they have not only hitherto escaped punishment, but have been also encouraged. For not long after the revolution, the most considerable of them (I do not speak of those who took arms) entered into new conspiracies against their country, to betray it again to the late King James, and took the oaths to this King, that they might have the better opportunity to bring back the other. Yet after all this his majesty was advised to put some of them into the most important places of trust in the kingdom. What are we then to expect, if we shall not now proceed to make some examples, but that they, and men of the like principles, will insinuate themselves into all the places of trust; and have the power as well as the will to throw us into prisons, and by their pernicious counsels to betray his present majesty into the same misfortunes that were brought upon the late King? Is it not enough, that the punishment of those who endeavoured to enslave us under the late reigns, has been delayed till now? Because they have renewed the same practices under this, must it still be delayed, to the end that (as they have already done in the affair of Glenco) they may continue to give his majesty the same bad counsel with which the late kings were poisoned?[23] Now, to

---

[23] 'The affair of Glenco' was the notorious massacre, on 13 February 1692, of some 40 members of the Clan MacDonald of Glencoe under its chief, Ian MacIan, by a party of Campbells, acting on government orders. It was generally believed that ultimate responsibility for the atrocity lay with Sir John Dalrymple, Master of

pardon them we have this encouragement, that having passed over former crimes, we embolden them to commit new, and to give fresh wounds to that country which has already so often bled under their hands.

When the greatest offenders are punished, an act of indemnity will be as necessary to the well-being of this nation as peace itself, since there can be no ease or quiet without it. But so little hopes have we of this, that whilst the evil counsellors, against whom his majesty did so justly declare, live at ease, an act (as we are told) is to be brought into the parliament for banishing during pleasure many thousands of inconsiderable people who cannot be charged with crimes any way comparable to theirs; and some of them free of the least appearance of any. What construction would the advisers of these things have even those who are best affected to the government put upon them? One might reasonably think that such things may be fit to keep up the party of the late King James, and fright the nation into a belief of the necessity of continuing a standing army, that they may be fit to lead men of estates, or those who have any thing to lose, into snares both at home and abroad (particularly in France, where the late King James is still suffered) by pretending correspondence or conversation with such as may be obnoxious to the law: but no man can suspect the worst of counsellors of such designs. And therefore I confess I am at a stand; for such vast numbers of people were never yet banished for crimes of state: nor does the multitude ever suffer for them, except only in barbarous countries. If it be said that ill men may have designs against his majesty's life, and therefore ought to be banished; I answer, nothing is more likely to draw on such a mischief, than extraordinary severities used against them. For nothing does so much fit a man for such an attempt, as despair; against which no distance of place can long protect.

My opinion therefore is, that an act of indemnity (excepting only assassins and other notorious criminals, whom we cannot at present reach) is more suitable to our present condition, than an act of banishment: and that to procure the nation so great a blessing, the parliament should proceed, without delay, to the punishing of the

Stair, who had served James before successfully switching to William (and on whom see above, fn 15). Others thought to have maintained covert links with King James included Queensberry.

greatest criminals, both of this and the last reigns without which an oblivion will be one of the greatest injuries that can be done to us.

I shall only add, that there is ground to believe some men will endeavour to persuade the parliament to take this affair into consideration before all others; because it was the first thing done in the last session of the English parliament; and the bill having past there almost without debate, they will make use of that as an argument why it should do so here. What the considerations were which moved that parliament to do so, I will not presume to determine, neither is it my business; circumstances of affairs may be different in different nations: sure I am, that in this particular they are different, that a greater number of men, in proportion to the people in each nation, will fall under uneasy circumstances by such an act in Scotland, than has been found to have done in England.

The second discourse

The affairs of which I have spoken in the preceding discourse, are such as the present conjuncture makes a proper subject for the approaching session of parliament: but there are many other things which require no less their care, if the urgent and pressing distresses of the nation be considered. I shall therefore with all due respect to the parliament offer my opinion concerning two, which I presume to be of that nature.

The first thing which I humbly and earnestly propose to that honourable court is, that they would take into their consideration the condition of so many thousands of our people who are at this day dying for want of bread.[24] And to persuade them seriously to apply themselves to so indispensable a duty, they have all the inducements which those most powerful emotions of the soul, terror and compassion, can produce. Because from unwholesome food diseases are so multiplied among the poor people, that if some course be not taken, this famine may very probably be followed by a plague; and then what man is there even of those who sit in parliament that can be sure he shall escape? And what man is there in this nation, if he have any compassion, who must not grudge himself every nice bit and every delicate morsel he puts in his mouth,

[24] See fn 11 above.

when he considers that so many are already dead, and so many at that minute struggling with death, not for want of bread but of grains, which I am credibly informed have been eaten by some families, even during the preceding years of scarcity. And must not every unnecessary branch of our expence, or the least finery in our houses, clothes or equipage, reproach us with our barbarity, so long as people born with natural endowments, perhaps not inferior to our own, and fellow citizens, perish for want of things absolutely necessary to life?

But not to insist any more upon the representation of so great a calamity, which if drawn in proper colours, and only according to the precise truth of things, must cast the minds of all honest men into those convulsions which ought necessarily to be composed before they can calmly consider of a remedy; and because the particulars of this great distress are sufficiently known to all, I shall proceed to say, that though perhaps upon the great want of bread, occasioned by the continued bad seasons of this and the three preceding years, the evil be greater and more pressing than at any time in our days, yet there have always been in Scotland such numbers of poor, as by no regulations could ever be orderly provided for; and this country has always swarmed with such numbers of idle vagabonds, as no laws could ever restrain. And indeed when I considered the many excellent laws enacted by former parliaments for setting the poor to work, particularly those in the time of King James the sixth, with the clauses for putting them in execution, which to me seemed such as could not miss of the end, and yet that nothing was obtained by them,[25] I was amazed, and began to think upon the case of other nations in this particular, persuaded that there was some strange hidden root of this evil which could not be well discovered, unless by observing the conduct of other

---

[25] The first Scottish Poor Law was the temporary Act of 1574, made permanent in 1579. It was modelled closely on the English Statutes of 1572 and 1575, with the result that the machinery for administering the Act was hardly adapted to Scottish circumstances. A further Act in 1592 identified Kirk Sessions as appropriate agents, while justices of the peace, named in the 1579 Act, were finally instituted in Scotland in 1609, and instructed to control vagrants and administer apprenticeships in an Act of 1617. If Fletcher exaggerated the efficacy of the clauses for executing the Acts, he was none the less right to suppose that little or nothing was achieved. See Rosalind Mitchison, 'North and South: the development of the gulf in Poor Law practice', in R. A. Houston and I. D. Whyte (eds.), *Scottish Society 1500–1800* (Cambridge, 1989), pp. 200–5.

governments. But upon reflection I found them all subject to the same inconveniencies, and that in all the countries of Europe there were great numbers of poor, except in Holland, which I knew to proceed from their having the greatest share in the trade of the world. But this not being a remedy for every country, since all cannot pretend to so great a part in trade, and that two or three nations are able to manage the whole commerce of Europe; yet there being a necessity that the poor should every where be provided for, unless we will acknowledge the deficiency of all government in that particular, and finding no remedy in the laws or customs of any of the present governments, I began to consider what might be the conduct of the wise antients in that affair. And my curiosity was increased, when upon reflection I could not call to mind that any antient author had so much as mentioned such a thing, as great numbers of poor in any country.

At length I found the original of that multitude of beggars which now oppress the world, to have proceeded from churchmen, who (never failing to confound things spiritual with temporal, and consequently all good order and good government, either through mistake or design) upon the first publick establishment of the christian religion, recommended nothing more to masters, in order to the salvation of their souls, than the setting such of their slaves at liberty as would embrace the christian faith, though our Saviour and his apostles had been so far from making use of any temporal advantages to persuade eternal truths, and so far from invading any man's property, by promising him heaven for it, that the apostle Paul says expressly,

> In whatever condition of life every one is called to the Christian faith, in that let him remain. Art thou called being a slave? Be not concerned for thy condition; but even though thou mightest be free, chuse to continue in it. For he who is called whilst a slave, becomes the freeman of the Lord; and likewise he that is called whilst a free-man, becomes the slave of Christ, who has paid a price for you, that you might not be the slaves of men. Let every one therefore, brethren, in whatever condition he is called, in that remain, in the fear of God.[26]

---

[26] First Epistle to the Corinthians, 7:20–4.

That the interpretation I put upon this passage, different from our translation, is the true meaning of the apostle, not only the authority of the Greek fathers, and genuine signification of the Greek particles, but the whole context, chiefly the first and last words (which seem to be repeated to inforce and determine such a meaning) clearly demonstrate. And the reason why he recommends to them rather to continue slaves (if they have embraced the christian faith in that condition) seems to be that it might appear they did not embrace it for any worldly advantage, as well as to destroy a doctrine which even in his days began to be preached, that slavery was inconsistent with the christian religion; since such a doctrine would have been a great stop to the progress of it. What the apostle means by saying, we ought not to be the slaves of men, I shall shew hereafter.[27]

This disorder of giving liberty to great numbers of slaves upon their profession of Christianity, grew to such a height, even in the time of Constantine the great, that the cities of the empire found themselves burdened with an infinite number of men, who had no other estate but their liberty, of whom the greatest part would not work, and the rest had been bred to no profession. This obliged Constantine to make edicts in favour of beggars; and from that time at the request of the bishops, hospitals and alms-houses, not formerly known in the world, began to be established. But upon the rise of the Mahometan religion, which was chiefly advanced by giving liberty to all their slaves, the Christians were so molested by the continual rebellion of theirs, that they were at length forced to give liberty to them all; which it seems the churchmen then looked upon as a thing necessary to preserve the christian religion, since in

---

[27] Compared with that of the Authorised Version (probably what Fletcher had in mind by 'our translation'), Fletcher's rendering of the passage differed crucially in verse 21. He has: 'Art thou called being a slave? Be not concerned for thy condition; but even though thou mightest be free, chuse to continue in it.' The Authorised Version reads: 'Art thou called being a servant? Care not for it: but if thou mayest be made free, use it rather.' The earlier Coverdale and Geneva translations are very similar to those of the Authorised Version. These renderings have been supported by the New English Bible: 'Were you a slave when called? Do not let that trouble you; but if a chance of liberty shall come, take it.' However, this version also gives a variant reading which is in line with Fletcher's: 'but even if a chance of liberty should come, choose rather to make good use of your servitude'.

many of the writings, by which masters gave freedom to their slaves, 'tis expressly said, they did so, to save their own souls.

This is the rise of that great mischief, under which, to the undoing of the poor, all the nations of Europe have ever since groaned. Because in antient times, so long as a man was the riches and part of the possession of another, every man was provided for in meat, clothes and lodging; and not only he, but (in order to increase that riches) his wife and children also: whereas provisions by hospitals, alms-houses, and the contributions of churches or parishes, have by experience been found to increase the numbers of those that live by them. And the liberty every idle and lazy person has of burdening the society in which he lives, with his maintenance, has increased their numbers to the weakening and impoverishing of it: for he needs only to say, that he cannot get work, and then he must be maintained by charity. And as I have shewn before, no nation except one only (which is in extraordinary circumstances) does provide by publick work-houses for their poor: the reason of which seems to be, that publick work-houses for such vast numbers of people, are impracticable except in those places where (besides a vast trade to vend the manufactured goods) there is an extraordinary police, and that though the Hollanders by reason of the steddiness of their temper, as well as of their government (being a commonwealth) may be constant to their methods of providing for the poor; yet in a nation, and under a government like that of France, though vast publick work-houses may be for a while kept in order, 'twill not be long before they fall into confusion and ruin. And indeed (next to Plato's republick, which chiefly consists in making the whole society live in common)[28] there is nothing more impracticable than to provide for so great a part of every nation by publick work-houses. Whereas when such an œconomy comes under the inspection of every master of a family, and that he himself is to reap the profit of the right management; the thing not only turns to a far better account, but by reason of his power to sell those workmen to others who may have use for them, when he himself has a mind to alter

---

[28] Plato, *The Republic* (*c.* 380 BC), esp. Books III–V, presented arguments for a political society ruled by Guardians and their auxiliaries, who would have neither private property nor families, but would be provided for out of common property and a pool of wives, and would thus be free to devote themselves to the life of the community. Fletcher owned more than one edition of *The Republic*.

his course of life, the profit is permanent to the society; nor can such an œconomy, or any such management ever fall into confusion.

I doubt not, that what I have said will meet, not only with all the misconstruction and obloquy, but all the disdain, fury and out-cries, of which either ignorant magistrates, or proud, lazy and miserable people are capable. Would I bring back slavery into the world? Shall men of immortal souls, and by nature equal to any, be sold as beasts? Shall they and their posterity be for ever subjected to the most miserable of all conditions; the inhuman barbarity of masters, who may beat, mutilate, torture, starve, or kill so great a number of mankind at pleasure? Shall the far greater part of the common-wealth be slaves, not that the rest may be free, but tyrants over them? With what face can we oppose the tyranny of princes, and recommend such opposition as the highest virtue, if we make our-selves tyrants over the greatest part of mankind? Can any man, from whom such a thing has once escaped, ever offer to speak for liberty? But they must pardon me if I tell them, that I regard not names, but things; and that the misapplication of names has confounded every thing. We are told there is not a slave in France; that when a slave sets his foot upon French ground, he becomes immediately free: and I say, that there is not a freeman in France, because the king takes away any part of any man's property at his pleasure; and that, let him do what he will to any man, there is no remedy. The Turks tell us, there are no slaves among them, except Jews, Moors, or Christians; and who is there that knows not, they are all slaves to the grand Seignior, and have no remedy against his will? A slave properly is one, who is absolutely subjected to the will of another man without any remedy: and not one that is only subjected under certain limitations, and upon certain accounts necessary for the good of the commonwealth, though such an one may go under that name. And the confounding these two conditions of men by a name common to both, has in my opinion been none of the least hardships put upon those who ought to be named servants. We are all sub-jected to the laws; and the easier or harder conditions imposed by them upon the several ranks of men in any society, make not the distinction that is between a freeman and a slave.

So that the condition of slaves among the antients, will upon serious consideration appear to be only a better provision in their governments than any we have, that no man might want the necessities of life, nor any person able to work be burdensome to the commonwealth. And they wisely judged of the inconveniences that befal the most part of poor people, when they are all abandoned to their own conduct. I know that these two conditions of men were confounded under the same name, as well by the antients as they are by us; but the reason was, that having often taken in war the subjects of absolute monarchs, they thought they did them no wrong if they did not better their condition: and as in some of their governments the condition of slaves was under a worse regulation than in others, so in some of them it differ'd very little, if at all, from the condition of such a slave as I have defined. But I do not approve, and therefore will not go about to defend any of those bad and cruel regulations about slaves. And because it would be tedious and needless to pursue the various conditions of them in several ages and governments, it shall be enough for me to explain under what conditions they might be both good and useful, as well as I think they are necessary in a well-regulated government.

First then, their masters should not have power over their lives, but the life of the master should go for the life of the servant. The master should have no power to mutilate or torture him; that in such cases the servant should not only have his freedom (which alone would make him burdensome to the publick) but a sufficient yearly pension so long as he should live from his said master. That he, his wife and children, should be provided for in clothes, diet, and lodging. That they should be taught the principles of morality and religion; to read, and be allowed the use of certain books: that they should not work upon sundays, and be allowed to go to church: that in every thing, except their duty as servants, they should not be under the will of their masters, but the protection of the law: that when these servants grow old, and are no more useful to their masters, (lest upon that account they should be ill-used) hospitals should be provided for them by the publick: that if for their good and faithful service, any master give them their freedom, he should be obliged to give them likewise wherewithal to subsist, or put them in a way of living without being troublesome to the commonwealth: that they should wear no habit or mark to distinguish them from hired servants: that any man should be punished who gives them the opprobrious name of slave. So, except it were that they could possess nothing, and might be sold, which really would be but an alienation of their service without their consent, they would live in a much more comfortable condition (wanting nothing necessary for life) than those who having a power to possess all things, are very often in want of every thing, to such a degree, that many thousands of them come to starve for hunger.

It will be said, that notwithstanding all these regulations, they may be most barbarously used by their masters, either by beating them outragiously, making them work beyond measure, suffer cold or hunger, or neglecting them in their sickness. I answer, that as long as the servant is of an age not unfit for work, all these things are against the interest of the master: that the most brutal man will not use his beast ill only out of a humour; and that if such inconveniences do sometimes fall out, it procceds, for the most part, from the perverseness of the servant: that all inconveniences cannot be obviated by any government; that we must chuse the least; and that to prevent them in the best manner possible, a particular magistrate might be instituted for that end.

The condition of such a servant is to be esteemed free; because in the most essential things he is only subject to the laws, and not to the will of his master, who can neither take away his life, mutilate, torture, or restrain him from the comforts of wife and children: but on the other hand, for the service he does, is obliged to ease him of the inconveniences of marriage, by providing for him, his wife, and children, clothes, food, and lodging: and the condition of a bashaw, or great lord, under arbitrary government (who for the sake, and from a necessity of what they call government, has joined to the quality of a slave the office of a tyrant, and imagines himself a man of quality, if not a little prince, by such pre-eminence) is altogether slavish; since he is under the protection of no law, no not so much as to his life, or the honour of his wife and children; and is subjected to stronger temptations than any man, of being a slave to men in St. Paul's sense, which is a worse sort of slavery than any I have yet mentioned. That is of being subservient to, and an instrument of the lusts of his master the tyrant: since if he refuse slavishly to obey, he must lose his office, and perhaps his life. And indeed men of all ranks living under arbitrary government (so much preached and recommended by the far greater part of churchmen) being really under the protection of no law, (whatever may be pretended) are not only slaves, as I have defined before, but by having no other certain remedy in any thing against the lust and passions of their superiors, except suffering or compliance, lie under the most violent temptations of being slaves in the worst sense, and of the only sort that is inconsistent with the christian religion. A condition (whatever men may imagine) so much more miserable than that of servants protected by the laws in all things necessary for the subsistence of them and their posterity, that there is no comparison.[29]

I shall now proceed to the great advantages the antients received from this sort of servants. By thus providing for their poor, and making every man useful to the commonwealth, they were not only able to perform those great and stupendous publick works, high-ways, aqueducts, common-shores, walls of cities, sea-ports, bridges, monuments for the dead, temples, amphitheatres, theatres, places for all manner of exercises and education, baths, courts of justice, market-places, publick walks, and other magnificent works for the use and conveniency of the publick, with which Egypt, Asia, Greece, Italy, and other countries were filled; and to adorn them with stately pillars and obelisks, curious statues, most exquisite sculpture and painting: but every particular man might indulge himself in any kind of finery and magnificence; not only because he

---

[29] Fletcher provides one of the clearest and most systematic accounts in the classical republican canon of the difference between personal and political slavery, and of why only the latter was to be regarded as true slavery. Political slavery was subjection to the arbitrary, unchecked power of a ruler, who was thereby a tyrant or despot. Contemporaries' use of the concept of political slavery was often much more rhetorical than this: many examples are to be found in the anti-standing army writings of the English radical whig John Trenchard, *An Argument shewing that a Standing Army is inconsistent with a Free Government, and absolutely destructive to the Constitution of the British Monarchy* (London, 1697), and *A Short History of Standing Armies* (London, 1698). David Hume may have had Fletcher in mind when he wrote in a footnote to the essay 'Of the Populousness of Ancient Nations' (1752):

> Some passionate admirers of the ancients, and zealous partisans of civil liberty, (for these sentiments, as they are, both of them, in the main, extremely just, are found to be almost inseparable) cannot forbear regretting the loss of this institution; and whilst they brand all submission to the government of a single person with the harsh denomination of slavery, they would gladly reduce the greater part of mankind to real slavery and subjection. (*The Philosophical Works of David Hume*, eds. T. H. Green and T. H. Grose (London 1874–5), III, p. 385; this essay is not included in the Cambridge Texts edition of *David Hume: Political Essays*, ed. K. Haakonssen.)

had slaves to perform it according to his fancy, but because all the poor being provided for, there could be no crime in making unnecessary expences, which are always contrary, not only to christian charity, but common humanity, as long as any poor man wants bread. For though we think that in making those expences, we employ the poor; and that in building costly houses, and furnishing them, making fine gardens, rich stuffs, laces and embroideries for apparel, the poor are set to work; yet so long as all the poor are not provided for, (though a man cannot reproach himself in particular why it is not done) and that there is any poor family in a starving condition, 'tis against common humanity (and no doubt would have been judged to be so by the antients) for any man to indulge himself in things unnecessary, when others want what is absolutely necessary for life, especially since the furnishing of those things to them, does employ workmen as well as our unnecessary expences. So that the antients, without giving the least check to a tender compassion for the necessities of others (a virtue so natural to great minds, so nicely to be preserved and cherished) might not only adorn their publick buildings with all the refinements of art, but likewise beautify their private houses, villas and gardens with the greatest curiosity. But we by persisting in the like, and other unnecessary expences, while all the poor are not provided for (example, vanity, and the love of pleasure, being predominant in us) have not only effaced all the vestiges of christian charity, but banished natural compassion from amongst us, that without remorse we might continue in them.

This explains to us by what means so much virtue and simplicity of manners could subsist in the cities of Greece, and the lesser Asia, in the midst of so great curiosity and refinement in the arts of magnificence and ornament. For in antient times great riches, and consequently bad arts to acquire them, were not necessary for those things; because if a man possessed a moderate number of slaves, he might chuse to employ them in any sort of magnificence, either private or publick, for use or ornament, as he thought fit, whilst he himself lived in the greatest simplicity, having neither coaches nor horses to carry him, as in triumph, through the city; nor a family in most things composed like that of a prince, and a multitude of idle servants to consume his estate. Women were not then intolerably expensive, but wholly imployed in the care of domestick affairs.

Neither did the furniture of their houses amount to such vast sums as with us, but was for the most part wrought by their slaves.

Another advantage which the antients had by this sort of servants, was, that they were not under that uneasiness, and unspeakable vexation which we suffer by our hired servants, who are never bred to be good for any thing, though most of the slaves amongst the antients were. And though we bestow the greatest pains or cost to educate one of them from his youth, upon the least cross word he leaves us. So that 'tis more than probable this sort of servants growing every day worse, the unspeakable trouble arising from them, without any other consideration, will force the world to return to the former.

Among the antients, any master who had the least judgment or discretion, was served with emulation by all his slaves, that those who best performed their duty, might obtain their liberty from him. A slave, though furnished with every thing necessary, yet possessing nothing, had no temptation to cheat his master; whereas a hired servant, whilst he remains unmarried, will cheat his master of what may be a stock to him when married; and if after his marriage he continue to serve his master, he will be sure to cheat him much more. When the antients gave freedom to a slave, they were obliged to give him wherewithal to subsist, or to put him into a way of living. And how well and faithfully they were served by those they had made free, (whom from a long experience of their probity and capacity, they often made stewards of their estates) all antient history does testify. Now, we having no regular way to enable a servant to provide sufficient maintenance for his family, when he becomes independent on his master, his bare wages (out of which he is for the most part to provide himself with many necessaries for daily use) not being enough for that purpose, and no way left but to cheat his master, we ought not to expect any probity or fidelity in our servants, because, for want of order in this point, we subject them to such strong temptation.

I might insist upon many other advantages the antients had in the way they were served, if to persuade the expedient I propose, I were not to make use of stronger arguments than such as can be drawn from any advantages; I mean those of necessity.

There are at this day in Scotland (besides a great many poor families very meanly provided for by the church-boxes, with others, who by living upon bad food fall into various diseases) two hundred thousand people begging from door to door. These are not only no way advantageous, but a very grievous burden to so poor a country. And though the number of them be perhaps double to what it was formerly, by reason of this present great distress, yet in all times there have been about one hundred thousand of those vagabonds, who have lived without any regard or subjection either to the laws of the land, or even those of God and nature; fathers incestuously accompanying with their own daughters, the son with the mother, and the brother with the sister. No magistrate could ever discover, or be informed which way one in a hundred of these wretches died, or that ever they were baptized. Many murders have been discovered among them; and they are not only a most unspeakable oppression to poor tenants, (who if they give not bread, or some kind of provision to perhaps forty such villains in one day, are sure to be insulted by them) but they rob many poor people who live in houses distant from any neighbourhood. In years of plenty many thousands of them meet together in the mountains, where they feast and riot for many days; and at country weddings, markets, burials, and other the like publick occasions, they are to be seen both men and women perpetually drunk, cursing, blaspheming, and fighting together.[30]

These are such outrageous disorders, that it were better for the nation they were sold to the gallies or West Indies, than that they should continue any longer to be a burden and curse upon us. But numbers of people being great riches, every government is to blame that makes not a right use of them. The wholsomeness of our air, and healthfulness of our climate, affords us great numbers of people, which in so poor a country can never be all maintained by manufactures, or publick work-houses, or any other way, but that which I have mentioned.

And to shew that former parliaments struggling with this, otherwise insuperable, difficulty, have by the nature of the thing been as it were forced upon remedies tending towards what I have proposed: by an act of parliament in the year 1579, any subject of sufficient estate is allowed to take the child of any beggar, and

---

[30] No modern historian would venture such estimates of vagabondage – or such a characterisation of lifestyle; the *Scottish Population History*, p. 170, judges Fletcher's estimates 'worthless'.

educate him for his service, which child is obliged to serve such a master for a certain term of years; and that term of years extended by another act made in the year 1597, for life.[31] So that here is a great advance towards my proposition; but either from some mistake about christian or civil liberty, they did not proceed to consider the necessity of continuing that service in the children of such servants, and giving their masters a power of alienating that service to whom they should think fit. The reason for the first of these is, that being married in that sort of service, their masters must of necessity maintain their wife and children, and so ought to have the same right to the service of the children as of the father. And the reason for the power of alienation is, that no man is sure of continuing always in one sort of employment; and having educated a great many such children when he was in an employment that required many servants, if afterwards he should be obliged to quit it for one that required few or none, he could not without great injustice be deprived of the power of alienating their service to any other man, in order to reimburse to himself the money he had bestowed upon them; especially since the setting them at liberty would only bring a great burden on the publick.

Now what I would propose upon the whole matter is, that for some present remedy of so great a mischief, every man of a certain estate in this nation should be obliged to take a proportionable number of those vagabonds, and either employ them in hedging and ditching his grounds, or any other sort of work in town and country; or if they happen to be children and young, that he should educate them in the knowledge of some mechanical art, that so every man of estate might have a little manufacture at home which might maintain those servants, and bring great profit to the master, as they did to the antients, whose revenue by the manufactures of such servants was much more considerable than that of their lands. Hospitals and alms-houses ought to be provided for the sick, lame and decrepit, either by rectifying old foundations or instituting new. And for example and terror three or four hundred of the most

---

[31] 'Act for the punishment of strong and idle beggars and the relief of the poor and impotent' (1579), *The Acts of the Parliaments of Scotland, III: 1567–92* (1814), pp. 139–41; 'Strong beggars, vagabonds and Egyptians should be punished' (1597), *Acts of the Parliaments of Scotland, IV: 1593–1625* (1816), p. 140.

notorious of those villains which we call jockys,[32] might be presented by the government to the state of Venice, to serve in their gallies against the common enemy of Christendom.

But these things, when once resolved, must be executed with great address, diligence, and severity; for that sort of people is so desperately wicked, such enemies of all work and labour, and, which is yet more amazing, so proud, in esteeming their own condition above that which they will be sure to call slavery; that unless prevented by the utmost industry and diligence, upon the first publication of any orders necessary for putting in execution such a design, they will rather die with hunger in caves and dens, and murder their young children, than appear abroad to have them and themselves taken into such a kind of service. And the Highlands are such a vast and unsearchable retreat for them, that if strict and severe order be not taken to prevent it, upon such an occasion these vagabonds will only rob as much food as they can out of the low-country, and retire to live upon it in those mountains, or run into England till they think the storm of our resolutions is over, which in all former times they have seen to be vain.

Nor indeed can there be a thorough reformation in this affair, so long as the one half of our country, in extent of ground, is possessed by a people who are all gentlemen only because they will not work; and who in every thing are more contemptible than the vilest slaves, except that they always carry arms, because for the most part they live upon robbery. This part of the country being an inexhaustible source of beggars, has always broke all our measures relating to them. And it were to be wished that the government would think fit to transplant that handful of people, and their masters (who have always disturbed our peace) into the low-country, and people the Highlands from hence, rather than they should continue to be a perpetual occasion of mischief to us. 'Tis in vain to say, that whatever people are planted in those mountains, they will quickly turn as savage, and as great beggars as the present inhabitants; for the mountains of the Alps are greater, more desert, and more condemned to snows that those of the Highlands of Scotland, which are everywhere cut by friths and lakes, the richest in fishing of any

---

[32] Jockie: a Scots' term for a vagrant or gypsy.

in the world, affording great conveniences for transportation of timber and any other goods; and yet the Alps which have no such advantages are inhabited every where by a civilized, industrious, honest, and peaceable people: but they had no lords to hinder them from being civilized, to discourage industry, incourage thieving, and to keep them beggars that they might be the more dependent; or when they had any that oppressed them, as in that part of the mountains that belongs to the Swiss, they knocked them on the head.

Let us now compare the condition of our present vagabonds with that of servants under the conditions which I have proposed, and we shall see the one living under no law of God, man or nature, polluted with all manner of abominations; and though in so little expectation of the good things of another life, yet in the worst condition of this, and sometimes starved to death in time of extraordinary want. The other, though sometimes they may fall under a severe master (who nevertheless may neither kill, mutilate, nor torture them, and may be likewise restrained from using them very ill by the magistrate I mentioned) are always sure to have food, clothes and lodging; and have this advantage above other men, that without any care or pains taken by them, these necessaries are likewise secured to their wives and children. They are provided for in sickness, their children are educated, and all of them under all the inducements, encouragements and obligations possible to live quiet, innocent and virtuous lives. They may also hope, if they shew an extraordinary affection, care and fidelity, in the service of their master, that not only they and their families shall have their intire freedom, but a competency to live, and perhaps the estate of the master intrusted to their care. Now if we will consider the advantages to the nation by the one, and the disadvantages arising from the other sort of men, we shall evidently see, that as the one is an excessive burden, curse and reproach to us, so the other may inrich the nation, and adorn this country with publick works beyond any in Europe, which shall not take the like methods of providing for their poor.[33]

---

[33] Fletcher's draconian solutions to the problems of poverty and vagrancy were not taken too seriously by contemporaries, and secured nothing like the support he received for his proposals for constitutional change five years later. What he advocated did, as he pointed out, build on the coercive aspects of earlier Scottish

This proposal I hope may be a remedy, not only to that intolerable plague of idle vagabonds who infest the nation; but by providing a more regular maintenance for them, go a great way towards the present relief of other poor people who have been oppressed by them. That which follows is calculated to remove the principal and original cause of the poverty which all the commons of this nation lie under, as well as those straitning difficulties in which men of estates are by our present method of husbandry inevitably involved.

The causes of the present poverty and misery in which the commonalty of Scotland live, are many, yet they are all to be imputed to our own bad conduct and mismanagement of our affairs. 'Tis true, trade being of late years vastly increased in Europe, the poverty of any nation is always imputed to their want of that advantage. And though our soil be barren, yet our seas being the richest of any in the world, it may be thought that the cause of all our poverty has been the neglect of trade, and chiefly of our own fishing: nevertheless were I to assign the principal and original source of our poverty, I should place it in the letting of our lands at so excessive a rate as makes the tenant poorer even than his servant whose wages he cannot pay; and involves in the same misery day-labourers, tradesmen, and the lesser merchants who live in the country villages and towns; and thereby influences no less the great towns and wholesale merchants, makes the master have a troublesome and ill-paid rent, his lands not improved by inclosure or otherwise, but for want of horses and oxen fit for labour, everywhere run out and abused.

The condition of the lesser freeholders or heritors (as we call them) is not much better than that of our tenants; for they have no stocks to improve their lands, and living not as husbandmen but as gentlemen, they are never able to attain any: besides this, the unskilfulness of their wretched and half-starved servants is such, that their lands are no better cultivated than those laboured by

---

legislation for poor relief, but the tendency of subsequent discussion was against anything which smacked of a return to slavery. One of the fullest later eighteenth-century discussions of slavery and its decline since the ancient world was that by John Millar, in *The Origin of the Distinction of Ranks* (1770, 3rd edn 1779), ed. W. C. Lehman, in *John Millar of Glasgow* (Cambridge, 1960). See pp. 318–19 for two paragraphs added to the second edition of the work, which may have been written with Fletcher's scheme in mind.

beggarly tenants.[34] And though a gentleman of estate take a farm into his own hands, yet servants are so unfaithful or lazy, and the country people such enemies of all manner of inclosure, that after having struggled with innumerable difficulties, he at last finds it impossible for him to alter the ordinary bad methods, whilst the rest of the country continues in them.

The places in this country which produce sheep and black cattle, have no provision for them in winter during the snows, having neither hay nor straw, nor any inclosure to shelter them or the grass from the cold easterly winds in the spring; so that the beasts are in a dying condition, and the grass consumed by those destructive winds, till the warm weather, about the middle of June, come to the relief of both. To all this may be added the letting of farms in most part of those grazing countries every year by roop or auction. But our management in the countries cultivated by tillage is much worse, because the tenant pays his rent in grain, wheat, barley or oats: which is attended with many inconveniences, and much greater disadvantages than a rent paid in money.[35]

Money rent has a yearly balance in it; for if the year be scarce, all sorts of grain yield the greater price; and if the year be plentiful, there is the greater quantity of them to make money. Now a rent paid in corn has neither a yearly, nor any balance at all; for if a plentiful year afford a superplus, the tenant can make but little of it; but if the year be scarce, he falls short in the payment of his corn, and by reason of the price it bears, can never clear that debt by the rates of a plentiful year, by which means he breaks, and

---

[34] Freeholders or heritors were landowners whose land was held in direct 'fee' of the Crown; in feudal terms, they were tenants-in-chief of the Crown. Their land passed by inheritance to their heirs. Only freeholders were entitled to vote in the Scottish counties. Given this restricted definition, the number of 'freeholders' was proportionally much smaller in Scotland than in England; and larger estates were the norm in Scotland. Here, however, Fletcher comments on the position of lesser freeholders.

[35] Fletcher's critique of the state of Scottish agriculture starts with the methods of letting lands to tenants. He distinguishes between grazing or upland areas, in which farms are let by an annual auction (roup), and arable areas, in which longer leases (tacks) might be available, but where rent was paid in kind, and in particular in grain. His observation seems to have been broadly accurate. Longer, written leases were being introduced into the arable lowlands at the end of the seventeenth century, while annual, verbal leases by auction persisted (into the nineteenth century) on upland estates in the Borders. See Ian Whyte, *Agriculture and Society in Seventeenth-Century Scotland* (Edinburgh, 1979), pp. 152–62.

contributes to ruin his master. The rent being altogether in corn, the grounds must be altogether in tillage; which has been the ruin of all the best countries in Scotland. The carriage of corn paid for rent, to which many tenants are obliged, being often to remote places, and at unseasonable times, destroys their horses, and hinders their labour. And the hazard of sending the corn by sea to the great towns, endangers the loss of the whole. The master runs a double risque for his rent, from the merchant as well as the tenant; and the merchant making a thousand difficulties at the delivering of the corn if the price be fallen, the bargain sometimes ends in a suit at law. The selling of corn is become a thing so difficult, that besides the cheats used in that sort of commerce, sufficient to disgust any honest man, the brewers, bakers, and sometimes the merchants who send it abroad, do so combine together, that the gentleman is obliged to lay it up, of which the trouble as well as loss is great. This causes him to borrow money for the supply of his present occasions, and is the beginning of most men's debts. We may add to this, that by a rent in corn, a man comes to have one year a thousand pound rent, and the next perhaps but six hundred, so that he never can make any certain account for his expence or way of living; that having one year a thousand pound to spend, he cannot easily restrain himself to six hundred the next; that he spends the same quantity of corn (and in some places where such things are delivered instead of rent), hay, straw, poultry, sheep and oxen, in a dear, as in a plentiful year, which he would not do if he was obliged to buy them. Now the tenant in a plentiful year wastes, and in a scarce year starves: so that no man of any substance will take a farm in Scotland; but every beggar, if he have got half a dozen wretched horses, and as many oxen, and can borrow corn to sow, pretends to be a tenant in places where they pay no other rent than corn.

I know there are many objections made to what has been said concerning the advantages which a rent paid in money has above one paid in corn; but certainly they are all so frivolous, that every man upon a little reflection may answer them to himself. For the chief of them are, either that the tenant will squander away money when he gets it into his hands; or that the master can get a better price for the corn by selling it in gross to merchants in the adjacent towns, or else by sending it to be sold at a great distance. To the first I answer, that no substantial man will squander away money because he has got it into his hands, though such beggars as we now have for tenants might be apt to do so. And to the second, that the hazard of sending corn from one place of the kingdom to another by sea, and the prejudice the tenants suffer from long carriages by land, do in part balance the supposed advantage; besides, if those wholesale bargains were not so frequently made, nor the corn so often carried to be sold at the great towns, the merchants would be obliged to send to the country markets to buy, and the prices in them would rise. In short, the changing of money-rent into corn, has been the chief cause of racking all the rents to that excessive rate they are now advanced. And upon reflection it will soon appear, that the turning of money-rents into rents of corn, has been the invention of some covetous wretches, who have been the occasion that all masters now live under the same uneasiness, and constant care, which they at first out of covetousness created to themselves; and all to get as much as was possible from poor tenants, who by such means are made miserable, and are so far from improving, that they only run out and spoil the ground, ruin their neighbours by borrowing, and at length break for considerable sums, though at first they were no better than beggars.[36]

The method of most other countries is; that all rents are paid in money; that masters receiving a fine, grant long leases of their grounds at easy rents: but this supposes the tenant a man of considerable substance, who cannot only give a fine, but has wherewithal to stock, and also to improve his farm. But in Scotland no such men are willing to take farms; nor in truth are the masters willing to let them, as they do in other countries.[37] And though the

---

[36] The payment of rent in kind (ferme) was traditional throughout Scottish agriculture, Lowland as well as Highland, and was still prevalent at the end of the seventeenth century. (It was not a recent innovation, as Fletcher seems to suggest.) Commutation into money rent had begun by the end of the seventeenth century, but only became widespread in the first half of the eighteenth century: Whyte, *Agriculture and Society*, pp. 192–4; and T. M. Devine, *The Transformation of Rural Scotland. Social Change and the Agrarian Economy 1660–1815* (Edinburgh, 1994), pp. 8–9, 23–5.

[37] A 'fine' was a fee payable on entering or taking up a tenancy: as Fletcher observes, a high entry fine was often accompanied by a moderate annual rental. The advantage to the landowner lay in the receipt of a cash sum on effecting the lease; as long as they were not fixed by custom, both fine and rent could be adjusted upwards when the lease was determined. The system was characteristic of – though by no means universal in – English agriculture. The emergence in Scot-

masters may pretend, that if they could find substantial tenants, they would let their grounds as they do in other places; and men of substance, that if they could have farms upon such conditions, they would turn tenants; yet we see evident marks of the little probability there is that any such thing can be brought about without a general regulation. For in the west and north countries where they let land in feu (or fee) the superiors are so hard, that besides the yearly feu-duty, they make the feuer pay at his first entrance the whole intrinsick value of the land; and the people, though substantial men, are fools and slaves enough to make such bargains.[38] And in the same countries, when they let a small parcel of land to a tradesman, they let it not for what the land is worth, but what both the land and his trade is worth. And indeed 'tis next to an impossibility to alter a general bad custom in any nation, without a general regulation, because of inveterate bad dispositions and discouragements, with which the first beginnings of reformations are always attended. Besides, alterations that are not countenanced by the publick authority, proceed slowly; and if they chance to meet with any check, men soon return to their former bad methods.

The condition then of this nation, chiefly by this abuse of racking the lands, is brought to such extremity, as makes all the commonalty miserable, and the landlords, if possible, the greater slaves, before they can get their rents and reduce them into money. And because this evil is arrived to a greater height with us, than I believe was ever known in any other place; and that, as I have said, we are in no disposition to practise the methods of most other countries, I think we ought to find out some new one which may surmount all difficulties, since in things of this nature divers methods may be proposed very practicable, and much better than any that hitherto have been in use.

I know that if to a law prohibiting all interest for money, another were joined, that no man should possess more land than so much as he should cultivate by servants, the whole money, as well as

land of a class of substantial tenants had to wait until the second half of the eighteenth century.

[38] 'Superior' was a feudal term denoting a freehold landowner who held the 'superiority' over his lands. If these were let in 'feu', the tenant, or 'feuar', would pay a substantial cash sum on entry, and a fixed annual 'feu-duty', set initially at the level of an economic rent. Provided that he and his heirs could pay the entry-fine, the tenant or feuar enjoyed security of possession in perpetuity.

people of this nation, would be presently employed, either in cultivating lands, or in trade and manufactures; that the country would
be quickly improved to the greatest height of which the soil is capable, since it would be cultivated by all the rich men of the nation;
and that there would still be vast stocks remaining to be employed
in trade and manufactures. But to oblige a man of a great estate in
land to sell all, except perhaps two hundred pounds sterling a year
(which he might cultivate by his servants) and to employ the whole
money produced by the sale of the rest, in a thing so uncertain as
he would judge trade to be, and for which 'tis like he might have
no disposition or genius, being a thing impracticable: and also to
employ the small stocks of minors, widows, and other women
unmarried, in trade or husbandry, a thing of too great hazard for
them; I would propose a method for our relief, by joining to the
law prohibiting all interest of money, and to the other, that no man
should possess more land than so much as he cultivates by his
servants, a third law, obliging all men that possess lands under the
value of two hundred pounds sterling clear profits yearly, to cultivate them by servants, and pay yearly the half of the clear profits
to such persons as cultivating land worth two hundred pounds sterling a year, or above, shall buy such rents of them at twenty years
purchase. The project in its full extent may be comprehended in
these following articles.

All interest of money to be forbidden.

No man to possess more land than he cultivates by servants.

Every man cultivating land under the value of two hundred
pounds sterling clear profits a year, to pay yearly the half of the
clear profits to some other man who shall buy that rent at twenty
years purchase; and for his security shall be preferred to all other
creditors.

No man to buy or possess those rents, unless he cultivate land
to the value at least of two hundred pounds sterling clear profits
yearly.

Minors, women unmarried, and persons absent upon a publick
account, may buy or possess such rents, though they cultivate no
lands.[39]

---

[39] This and the preceding paragraph (i.e. the fourth and fifth 'articles' of Fletcher's
proposals) were marked to be deleted in the mss emendations to David Fletcher's
copy of the *Second Discourse*: see the List of Variants. A number of such changes

By the first article, discharging all interest of money, most men who have small sums at interest, will be obliged to employ it in trade, or the improvement of land.

By the second, that no man is to possess more land, than so much as he cultivates by his servants, the whole land of the kingdom will come into the hands of the richest men; at least there will be no land cultivated by any man who is not the possessor of it. And if he have a greater estate than what he cultivates, he may lay out money upon improvements; or if he have bought a small possession, though he may have no more money left, he may, by selling one half of the rent, procure a sum considerable enough, both to stock and improve it. So that in a few years the country will be every where inclosed and improved to the greatest height, the plough being every where in the hand of the possessor. Then servants, day-labourers, tradesmen, and all sorts of merchants, will be well paid, and the whole commons live plentifully, because they will all be employed by men of substance: the ground by inclosure, and other improvements, will produce the double of what it now does; and the race of horses and black cattel will be much mended.

By the other articles; that no man cultivating land under the value of two hundred pounds sterling clear profits yearly, can purchase rents upon land from any other man; but is obliged to pay yearly the half of the clear profits, to such persons as shall buy them at twenty years purchase; and that only those who cultivate land worth at least two hundred pounds sterling a year, can buy such rents; the men of great land estates having sold all their lands, except so much as may yield two hundred pounds sterling yearly, or so much above that value as they shall think fit to cultivate, may secure, if they please, the whole money they receive for their lands, upon those rents which the lesser possessors are obliged to sell. And so those who had formerly their estates in lands ill cultivated, and corn-rents ill paid, as well as the other three sorts of persons excepted from the general rule, and mentioned in the last article, will have a clear

are indicated on this copy: their concern with detail makes it unlikely that anyone other than Andrew Fletcher himself was responsible for them. The changes are all in the direction of simplifying the proposals and the accompanying explanations. Although they probably date from late in Fletcher's life, they almost certainly indicate his concern lest these proposals in particular be misunderstood. For doubts as to the success of the effort, see below, note 41.

rent in money coming in without trouble, for payment of which they are to be secured in the lands of the said lesser possessors before all creditors. The reason of excepting three sorts of persons before-mentioned from the general rule, is evident; because (as has been said) it were unreasonable to oblige minors, or women unmarried, to venture their small stocks in trade or husbandry: and much more that those who are absent upon a publick account, should be obliged to have any stock employed that way, since they cannot inspect either.

The small possessors by this project are not wronged in any thing; for if they are obliged to pay a rent to others, they receive the value of it. And this rent will put them in mind, not to live after the manner of men of great estates, but as husbandmen, which will be no way derogatory to their quality, however antient their family may be.

The method to put this project in execution is, first to enact; that interest for money should fall next year from six per cent. to five, and so on, falling every year one per cent. till it cease: and to make a law, that all those who at present possess lands under the value of two hundred pounds sterling clear profits yearly, should cultivate them by servants, and sell the half of the clear profits at twenty years purchase to the first minor, woman unmarried, or person absent upon a publick account, who should offer money for them; and in default of such persons presenting themselves to buy, they should be obliged to sell such rents to any other persons qualified as above: and likewise to make another law, that whoever possesses lands at present to the value of two hundred pounds sterling clear profits yearly, or more, should at least take so much of them as may amount to that value, into their own hands. This being done, the yearly falling of the interest of money would force some of those who might have money at interest, to take land for it: others calling for their money, would buy estates of the landed men, who are to sell all except so much as they cultivate themselves: and the prohibition of interest producing many small possessors, would afford abundance of rents upon land to be bought by rich men; of which many might probably be paid out of those very lands they themselves formerly possessed. So that all sorts of men would in a little time fall into that easy method for their affairs, which is proposed by the project.

What the half of the yearly clear profits of any small possessors may be, the usual valuation of lands, in order to publick taxes, which because of improvements must be frequently made, will ascertain.

But it will be said, that before any such thing can every where take place in this nation, all teinds (or tithes) and all sorts of superiorities, must be transacted for, and sold; that the tenures of all lands must be made allodial, to the end that every man may be upon an equal foot with another; that this project, in order to its execution, does suppose things, which though perhaps they would be great blessings to the nation upon many accounts, and in particular by taking away the seeds of most law-suits, and the obstructions to all sorts of improvements; yet are in themselves as great and considerable as the project itself.[40]

Indeed I must acknowledge, that any thing calculated for a good end is (since we must express it so) almost always clogged with things of the same nature: for as all bad, so all good things are chained together, and do support one another. But that there is any difficulty, to a legislative power (that is willing to do good) of putting either this project, or the things last named in execution, I believe no man can shew. Sure I am, that it never was nor can be the interest of any prince or commonwealth, that any subject should in any manner depend upon another subject: and that it is the interest of all good governments at least to encourage a good sort of husbandry.[41]

[40] 'Teinds' were tithes, payable to the parish ministers; 'allodial' land was land wholly owned by its proprietor, with no feudal obligations. Fletcher would appear to be conceding that his proposals required the abolition of all feudal tenures.

[41] As the mss emendations to David Fletcher's copy of the *Second Discourse* confirm (see fn 39 above and the List of Variants), Fletcher thought carefully about his proposals for agrarian reform, and was anxious to ensure that they were coherent in detail. In this he had limited success. In his hostility to great landowners, whom Fletcher charged with neglecting to improve their lands, he set the tone for much of the subsequent literature of agrarian improvement; but his specific prescriptions were never followed up. Despite the care Fletcher took in setting them out, their likely outcome was by no means clear, even supposing that a Scottish parliament had possessed the authority and the administrative powers to implement them.

Fletcher evidently wanted to keep estates to a moderate size, by requiring that they be directly farmed, while those with an income lower than the threshold of £200 sterling a year would be obliged to sell the rent of a part of their lands in order to secure capital for their improvement. By these means great landowners would gradually become wealthy owner-farmers, whose income would be directed

I know these proposals, by some men who aim at nothing but private interest, will be looked upon as visionary: it is enough for me, that in themselves, and with regard to the nature of the things, they are practicable; but if on account of the indisposition of such men to receive them, they be thought impracticable, it is not to be accounted strange; since if that indisposition ought only to be considered, every thing directed to a good end is such.

Many other proposals might be made to the parliament for the good of this nation, where every thing is so much amiss, and the publick good so little regarded. Amongst other things, to remove the present seat of the government, might deserve their consideration: for as the happy situation of London has been the principal cause of the glory and riches of England, so the bad situation of Edinburgh has been one great occasion of the poverty and uncleanliness in which the greater part of the people of Scotland live.

A proposal likewise for the better education of our youth would be very necessary: and I must confess I know no part of the world where education is upon any tolerable foot.[42] But perhaps I have presumed too much in offering my opinion upon such considerable matters as those which I have treated.

Since I finished the preceding discourses I am informed, that if the present parliament will not comply with the design of continuing

---

away from interest-bearing funds by an enforced reduction in the rate of interest, and into the purchase of rents from lesser landholders, or into investments in manufactures and trade. Poorer freeholders, by contrast, would become rent-paying tenants on at least part of their lands, but by gaining capital to improve their holdings they could expect to become substantial tenant farmers. Obvious difficulties, however, arise from Fletcher's failure to make provision either for increases in productivity or for inflation. He may have hoped that these would enable the lesser landholders to pass the £200 rental qualification, and to buy out those who owned their rents, creating an ever-larger class of owner-farmers. But the greater resources available to wealthy landowners are likely to have given them a continuing competitive advantage, leading to a renewed concentration of land-ownership.

[42] A later pamphlet containing such a proposal has been attributed to Fletcher: *Proposals for the Reformation of Schools and Universities, in order to the better education of youth, humbly offered to the serious consideration of the High Court of Parliament*, (1704); but the evidence for the attribution is inconclusive. See also fn 7 to the *Account of a Conversation*.

the army, they shall immediately be dissolved, and a new one called. At least those of the presbyterian persuasion, who expect no good from a new parliament, are to be frighted with the dissolution of the present (which has established their church-government) and by that means induced to use their utmost endeavours with the members for keeping up the army, and promoting the designs of ill men:[43] but I hope no presbyterian will ever be for evil things that good may come of them; since thereby they may draw a curse upon themselves instead of a blessing. They will certainly consider that the interest which they ought to embrace, as well upon the account of prudence, as of justice and duty, is that of their country; and will not hearken to the insinuations of ill men who may abuse them, and when they have obtained the continuation of the army, endeavour to persuade his majesty and the parliament, to alter the present government of the church, by telling them, that presbyterian government is in its nature opposite to monarchy, that they maintain a rebellious principle of defensive arms, and that a church government more suitable and subservient to monarchy ought to be established.

Now if at this time the presbyterians be true to the interest of their country, all those who love their country, though they be not of that persuasion, will stand by them in future parliaments, when they shall see that they oppose all things tending to arbitrary power: but if they abandon and betray their country, they will fall unpitied. They must not tell me, that their church can never fall, since it is the true church of God. If it be the true church of God, it needs no crooked arts to support it. But I hope they will not deny that it may fall under persecution; which they will deserve, if they go along with the least ill thing to maintain it.

---

[43] Immediately after the Revolution, the first session of William's parliament abolished episcopacy in July 1689; an Act establishing Presbyterian government followed in the second session, in June 1690: *Source Book of Scottish History*, III, pp. 213–15.

A
DISCOURSE
Concerning the
AFFAIRS
OF
SPAIN

Written in the month of July 1698

Naples 1698

Advertisement

I have written of the causes of the decline [*decadenza*] in the affairs of Spain, of the measures required for its recovery [*per riordinarla*], of the interests of the princes who are pretenders to that crown, and of the ease with which the prince who attains it may move towards making himself lord of the world [*per insignorirsi del mondo*]; not in order to favour a government as damaging to good customs and destructive of the general happiness of men, as one which is universal [*un universale*], and as are all governments, whether republics or monarchies, whose greatness rests on excessive wealth and power: but rather by putting all the other princes and states on their guard against whoever should pursue that ambition, to frustrate such a design, and spare the world from so much ruin. Following this line of reasoning it should be easy to show which are the best governments, which nourish the virtues [*le virtù*] and are of most benefit to mankind; as also to show how great an opportunity the subjects of the Spanish crown will have on the death of their King to gain those advantages, and to enjoy the benefits of peace, of liberty and of good government.[1]

---

[1] This Advertisement ('*AVVISO*') was not printed at the same time as the original pamphlet, but was subsequently added to a number of copies; a slightly revised version is given as a mss correction in David Fletcher's copy (see the List of Variants). It appears to have been written to remove any doubt about the ironic purpose of the *Discourse* itself.

Discourse[2]

The Empire of Spain [*l'Imperio di Spagna*] is so well adapted to be the foundation of that of the world that when the present King dies, an event which his ill-health makes likely within a few years, perhaps a few months, if from among all the pretenders to an empire

---

[2] While the language and place of publication of the *Discorso* present puzzles, answers to which I have offered in the Introduction, the actual subject-matter is relatively clear: the work is an analysis of possible outcomes of the death of the last Habsburg king of Spain, the sickly Charles II. On the throne since 1665 (when he was four), Charles II was never expected to live as long as he did; but by 1698 his end was imminently expected. Since he had no children of his own, and no other male heir, the Spanish Habsburg line would end with him. From the mid-1660s the other ruling houses of Europe had devoted much diplomatic energy to speculating on the succession. The alternatives were that one candidate should inherit the monarchy as a whole, or that the monarchy should be broken up, its various territories being parcelled out between other ruling houses. The composite character of the monarchy, consisting of multiple, formally distinct kingdoms and principalities within Spain itself, in Italy, in the Netherlands and in the New World, made it possible to envisage a great variety of combinations of territories. Castilians naturally favoured the preservation of a single monarchy, as did the other Spanish and Italian kingdoms and territories, which had enjoyed considerable informal autonomy since the failure of attempts to centralise the monarchy in the early seventeenth century. Fearful that one of their number would acquire overwhelming power within Europe, however, other ruling houses preferred to think in terms of a division of the spoils, and favoured partition. Negotiations for a Partition Treaty began in the 1660s, but were interrupted by the wars provoked by the territorial ambitions of Louis XIV in every decade after 1670. The issue came to the fore again during the Nine Years' War which began in 1689, after William had successfully claimed the British thrones; and when that war ended in the Peace of Ryswick in 1697, a new urgency entered negotiations, resulting in the formal Partition Treaties of 1698 and 1700. To prevent partition, Charles II attempted to will the monarchy entire upon a single successor. His first choice, in 1698, was Joseph Ferdinand, son of the elector of Bavaria, who died early in 1699; subsequently he countered the second Partition Treaty of 1700 by nominating Philip of Anjou, Louis XIV's grandson, who became Philip V of Spain.

But at the time of writing this lay in the future: Fletcher was still free to consider the Spanish Succession as an open question. He thus discusses the present condition of Spain, offering a pioneering analysis of the reasons for its decline, the better to suggest how it might yet be enabled to recover; this analysis is accompanied by a discussion of the interests of different candidates for the succession, and of the ways in which they might combine their territories with those of Spain to achieve universal monarchy. Further notes on both the candidates and the territories to be exchanged are included at appropriate points below. Fletcher's purpose in proposing these exchanges was almost certainly ironic; but as will be observed in the notes, the final settlement of the Spanish Succession War at the Peace of Utrecht (1713) was to involve precisely the kind of arbitrary territorial redistribution which Fletcher envisaged.

[*imperio*] which is disordered rather than ruined and undone, there succeeds a wise and vigorous prince, it is most unlikely that he will restrain his ambitions. I have therefore undertaken to discuss the interests of the princes who are pretenders to the crown of Spain; the decline in the affairs of that country, and the means which will be necessary to revive it [*riordinarla*] and to fit it to acquire the empire of the world [*l'imperio del mondo*].

Not that I am unaware of my limited capacity, or that there are many of superior abilities who can better forsee what will happen on the death of the present King of Spain; but in the belief that in a matter as serious as this a variety of opinions will help men to form a better judgement, I too have resolved to offer my thoughts: which if they do not always contain the best conjectures, may often direct a higher and more penetrating mind towards them.

I shall, then, seek to demonstrate that a state which has fallen may be re-established in a manner that will support new superstructures [*che bastasse à superstruttioni nuove*]; and to make myself still clearer, it will be necessary first to show the causes of the decline in the affairs of Spain; and the separation of its states being one of the principal such causes, I shall speak of the exchange or barter [*cambio o permutazione*] of states, as the most effective remedy for this weakness; I shall then discuss the various interests of the princes which aspire to the crown of Spain; the means by which they can attain it; the advantages which they would bring to Spain; the obstacles which they would meet and how these might be overcome; and how easily the exchange of a few states would enable those princes, by taking their time, to prepare themselves without incurring suspicion for universal monarchy [*monarchia universale*]; finally I shall demonstrate that whichever of those princes becomes King of Spain, he would be able, through an expedition to subdue Africa, reformation in the affairs of Spain, and the acquisition of the empire of the sea [*imperio del mare*] (for all of which he will have excellent opportunities), to advance far towards becoming lord of the world [*per insignorirsi del mondo*].

But before I begin to reason on these things, in order to gain close and undivided attention for what I have to say, I want to point out that a King of Spain holds an advantage possessed by no other prince who would command the world; and that is, the situation of Spain. The choice of a situation suited for the acquisition and maintenance of a great empire is of such importance that while any other deficiency may be remedied by laws and good orders [*ordini*], a bad situation is irreparable. The peoples of the north have never been able to acquire a great empire without leaving their own countries; it was for lack of an appropriate situation that Carthage and Egypt were never able to become masters of the world; and the Romans only lost that mastery as a result of Constantine's unhappy choice of Byzantium as the seat of the empire. It is true that in these times, when distant navigations have revealed to us many new countries and powerful governments over almost the entire globe, Egypt has come to seem well-placed to dominate the world, being positioned between the two great continents of Asia and Africa, with the Mediterranean Sea for communications with Europe and America, and the Red Sea for those with the East; but the barren countries and great deserts which surround it on two sides, and which, except for the sea, virtually cut it off from the rest of the world, as well as the great power of several governments at a distance from it and the weakness of nearer countries, have largely counter-balanced these advantages of its situation. To render this situation more convenient would seem to require a canal between the two seas; a project which not even the power of ancient Egypt, or the wealth of the Persians, or the strength of the Moors and the Turks has been able to carry out; and which in any case is said to be impracticable because of Egypt's low situation. But a natural canal having joined the Mediterranean Sea to the Ocean, it seems to me that there cannot be a more suitable or advantageous situation from which to acquire the world, as also for the residence of the prince who would govern it, than one close to these straits; whether it be Lisbon on account of its excellent coast, or Cartagena with its convenient harbour for galleys, or Seville for its fertile, agreeable fields, or the ancient city of Cadiz for its port and strong situation, or Tangiers for its sheltered position towards the sea and its fertile surroundings. To demonstrate the incomparable excellence of these sites, I say therefore that the straits of Gibraltar being in effect the meeting-point for the great seas which border all the countries of the world, and offering such facilities for the easy and speedy carriage of armies and military stores, a city close to them would more than any other possess the greatest advantage in attaining universal empire [*l'imperio dell' universo*]. Which advantage is increased still further by the consideration that from among all the countries of which we have knowledge, it is difficult to identify any on either side of the straits whose coast lines are of greater importance. Being situated at the extremity of the old world, it has all of the new to the west; which, even though it is distant, can be reached in a short time, while the return by a different route is made sure by winds which blow regularly from the same direction. To the north lie Spain, Portugal, the British Isles, France, the Netherlands, Germany and the states which surround the Baltic sea. To the east France, Italy, Dalmatia, Greece, Muscovy, Asia Minor and Greater Asia, Egypt and the Barbary Coast are accessible by navigating the Mediterranean; to the south are Africa, and (by the passage of the Cape of Good Hope) the East Indies, and those vast empires of Persia, the Mogul, China and Japan.[3]

As proof of how tempting it will be for a prince to entertain such ambitions, it is certain that those, princes and others, who have laid the foundations of future greatness, either by founding new kingdoms or republics, or by restoring those which have fallen, have always obtained greater praise than those who have subsequently carried their power to its highest point. Those who have enlarged their dominions have been accorded only the honour which their actions merited; but the glory of the founder has always been equal to that of the empire itself. It is true indeed that examples of restorers of fallen governments are extremely rare, and that the glory of these exceeds even that of the founders of new states: because these, in the words of Machiavelli, 'finding the material at their disposal, faced no greater difficulty that that of giving it a convenient form; whereas the others have to reform disorders which age has rendered great and intractable; further, matter so corrupted needs a long time to be purified, and to recover its initial virtue [*virtù*]; and time itself is subject to many accidents, the least of

---

[3] As David Armitage has pointed out, in 'The Scottish vision of empire: intellectual origins of the Darien venture', in John Robertson (ed.), *A Union for Empire. Political Thought and the Union of 1707* (Cambridge, 1995), pp. 107–9, Fletcher's analysis of the advantages of a position such as the Straits of Gibraltar can be read as a commentary on the possibilities of the Isthmus of Darien, long identified as the narrowest point on the American continent between the Atlantic and Pacific Oceans (and much later to be the site of the Panama Canal). Written, as the title-page stated, in July 1698, the *Discourse* coincided with the sailing of the first Scottish ships to Darien.

which may be enough to renew the disorder.'[4] But true as this is, it will nevertheless be shown in the following discourse that any wise and spirited prince who succeeds to the crown of Spain would be able not only to lay the foundations of a formidable power, but to advance it to considerable strength within his own lifetime. To begin, however, to discuss the subjects proposed above; and first to demonstrate the causes of the decline in the affairs of Spain; I say that the House of Austria, by marriage with the Houses of Burgundy and then of Spain, both of which had already united many rich provinces, partly by the same means of marriage and partly by conquests, and then by the accidental discovery of the Indies and the election of Charles V to the Empire, was without effort or endeavour on its part suddenly elevated to a disproportionate greatness.[5] But following the fate of other things of this world which have grown in the same manner without having put down the roots needed to nourish it, or to support its great bulk, it was not long before its weakness led to the monarchy's precipitous decline, from which it only with difficulty escaped complete ruin. It is true that King Ferdinand had laid some foundations for the future greatness of Spain. His constant intrigues and initiatives formed numerous ministers and statesmen [*huomini di stato*], while the long wars which he undertook with such success in the Kingdom of Granada and in Italy so trained and disciplined his troops, and in particular his infantry, that they had no equal in the world in their capacity for hardship and in battle. These were the arms which at Pavia, and on the river Elbe, brought that great work of fortune to the pinnacle of glory; and after, in the Netherlands, sustained for a while its declining greatness.[6] But even these troops were to suffer from the disorders which were daily undermining the empire, and which

---

[4] I have been unable to identify a passage corresponding to this in Machiavelli's works. The challenge facing the reformer of a corrupt state is a theme of the *Discourses* rather than the *Prince*: it is discussed at some length in the *Discourses*, I.xviii and (especially) III.i.

[5] The 'Indies' (in Italian 'India') denoted Peru.

[6] Charles V defeated Francis I of France at Pavia in 1525, and the German Protestant princes at Muhlberg, near the Elbe, in 1547; but neither victory was definitive. The long war to maintain Spanish rule in the Netherlands lasted from 1566 until 1609, when a truce effectively acknowledged the independence of the seven northern provinces; war resumed on the expiry of the Truce in 1621, but the independence of the United Provinces was confirmed by the Peace of Westphalia in 1648.

soon exhausted the wise counsellors and undermined their advice. Swollen by so much greatness, which the princes and their ministers believed had been acquired by their own efforts and their own virtue, when it was none other than the work of fortune, their heads full of visions, they plotted undertakings from which could result only harm and loss: to the point that they have in recent years abandoned the fabric of the monarchy to the workings of fortune, in the belief that greatness of spirit alone would be enough to ward off its blows, without giving any further thought to the means required to preserve it. First Charles V, who had such an opportunity to make himself master of the world, consumed all his time in running from one province to another without forming one sound project which would be worthy of his rank. Such was his predicament (his states being disunited, and his power so greatly envied), it seemed that there could be no other remedy but to aspire to a still higher level of greatness. So swollen was the power of Philip that it was enough to nourish once again hopes of a world monarchy [*monarchia del mondo*]; but even he, with all the appearance of a wise, grave, constant, astute and politic prince, could not impose order on affairs already completely disordered; nor had he any successes apart from the acquisition of Portugal, a truly great gain, but one which like all the others was the work of fortune. Nor did he introduce among the people of Spain, who should be the strength and, so to speak, the seat [*domicilio*] of his empire, any sort of industry, whether in agriculture, in manufactures, in commerce or in navigation; for all of which they had considerable opportunities; and for the last, so great a need. Instead the little ships of the English traversed his seas with impunity; attacked his greatest carracks, which his subjects did not know how to sail; and exploited the impossibility of defending the immense shore-lines of his dominions with forts and garrisons, by raiding and plundering wherever they pleased, just as the pirates of the same nation do today. That King and his Spaniards lived entirely on the mines of the Indies; the gold and silver of which, passing out of their hands, served only to enrich their enemies, the English, the French and the Dutch, who provided the Spanish with their manufactures, and other necessities of life. Because he did not put in order the affairs of the Indies, where in the time of Ferdinand and Charles more than twenty million men [*huomini*] were killed (an eternal reproach, and a loss irreparable for centuries), while his subjects continued to destroy those peoples and steal their gold, as had happened under Charles and Ferdinand because they never thought of encouraging any industry, Philip, as a Spanish author says, derived not one *maravedí* of permanent revenue from that whole, vast and populous world; which became instead a desert.[7] Because of this, and because of the waste and disorder in his expenditure, that prince fell into great financial difficulties, and his successors, through the usury of the Genoese and other foreigners, into extreme poverty. He also diminished the population of Spain itself (which Ferdinand had already rid of the Jews [*Marani*]), by the expulsion of the Moors [*Mori*] from Granada as enemies of the faith (the rock on which the House of Austria perpetually founders), by the repopulation of the Indies, and by the need to sustain armies and garrisons in so many places.[8] For, not wishing to govern his distant states by relying on the affections of his peoples, maintaining their traditional privileges and ancient customs; nor to establish colonies, which is one of the best means of securing them; but everywhere introducing by force of arms new constitutions and an absolute government [*ordini nuovi e un governo assoluto*], it was essential that the garrisons were composed entirely or mostly of Spaniards: with the result that Spain, which should have been drawing people from the provinces to itself in order maintain them in subjection, was instead exhausted of men and money in favour of the provinces, and hence became incapable of new conquests, clinging with difficulty to its old possessions.[9] This

[7] The *maravedí* was the Castilian money of account. One gold ducat was officially worth 375 *maravedís*, and a silver real was worth 34 *maravedís*.

[8] Philip II ordered the expulsion of the Moors or Moriscos from Granada following their unsuccessful rebellion (the second Rebellion of the Alpujarras) in 1568–70. (They were subsequently expelled from all the Spanish kingdoms by Philip III between 1608 and 1614; the Jews had suffered this fate in 1492.) On this and other episodes in Spanish history to which Fletcher refers, the authoritative modern account is J. H. Elliott, *Imperial Spain 1469–1716* (Harmondsworth, 1970).

[9] The analysis of the failure of the Spanish monarchy to establish its authority in its distant possessions is particularly rich in echoes of Machiavelli: the options once open to the Spanish as new princes were all discussed in *The Prince* and the *Discourses*. Winning the affections of the people by confirmation of existing privileges is discussed at a number of points in *The Prince*, particularly chs. iii and v; that the sending of colonies of one's own subjects offers a better solution is argued in *The Prince*, ch. iii, while the Romans' use of colonies as a means of rewarding their soldiers and securing new territories is considered in the *Discourses*, Book II,

will be clear if we consider the wars of the Low Countries, the most obvious reason for the decline of Spain, as they continue to be today: like a running sore, the seventeen provinces have continually drained away the aliment which should have nourished the empire of Spain.

I repeat, then, that the violation of the ancient privileges of these countries, from a wish to introduce absolute government and the Inquisition, was very bad policy, which combined with the cruelty of the Duke of Alva made these peoples obstinately hostile.[10] But the Spanish troops were so excellent, that they would easily have overcome this difficulty, despite the extremely strong situation of several of the provinces, and even in the absence of measures to restore order [*mettervi ordine*] by the king, were it not that the distance of Flanders from Spain made it difficult and expensive to convey troops to the former, so that not only they, but often the orders for them did not arrive in time to meet the emergencies which are always a feature of war, and which the English and the French, being closer, were in a position to foment easily and speedily. So blind was that prince, that he behaved as if Flanders had become the seat of his empire (even though, as has been said, its affairs were conducted with so much difficulty and expense, and he himself was absent), and sought, before the Flemings had been defeated, to make war from there on France and England, as his successors were later to do on the Palatinate.[11] This great mistake not only caused him to lose his dominion over seven of those provinces, and ruined his grand designs in France and England, but reduced all his affairs to severe straits: which the French in more

chs. vi–vii. Conversely, the Romans' absorption of the defeated and consequent enrichment of Rome itself is the subject of *Discourses* II. iii. The use of arms to support new orders is a theme central to both works: *Prince*, ch. vi, and *Discourses*, I.v–vi, II.i–iv. Where Fletcher has broken with Machiavelli is in questioning both the efficacy and the justice of a reliance on arms to subjugate other peoples: *pace* Machiavelli, the cost of arms could not be discounted, and an 'absolute government' was a political evil.

[10] Sent by Philip II to the Netherlands as Governor in 1567, the duke of Alva (or Alba) won a reputation for severity against heretics and rebels; by the time of his departure in 1573 virtually the whole of the Netherlands was involved in the rebellion.

[11] Fletcher refers to Philip II's use of Flanders as a base for the war against England begun with the Armada of 1588, and for intervention in the French Wars of Religion in the 1590s; under Philip IV, Spanish armies from Flanders invaded the Lower Palatinate in 1622, in the early stages of the Thirty Years' War.

recent times having become aware of, they now seek to concentrate their fighting and the greater part of their forces in these areas close to Paris, to their own great advantage, and the lasting damage of the Spaniards. Even today their leaving to the Crown of Spain a remnant of these provinces has no other end than to weaken Spanish arms, and to prevent them from being employed elsewhere, while enhancing the glory of the French. When the German armies defeated the French at the encounters of Trèves and Altenheim, the following Spring we saw the French King march into Flanders to restore his reputation.[12] To ensure that these provinces are even more burdensome and damaging to Spain, the French have now seized the best part of the country, while leaving the Spaniards with many large towns requiring sizeable garrisons to defend them. Even if the French were to acquire the rest of Flanders, moreover, they would enjoy similar advantages in the state of Milan; for there too the French can make war more easily than Spain, re-inforcements being closer by land and sea from Provence and the Dauphiné than they are from Spain. Thus France, because it can make war from a position of strength [*con più vantaggio*] will always be provoking it in the separated states of the monarchy; until as a result of their ruin Spain itself becomes exhausted and, incapable of further defence, is the last to fall.

From all that has been said above it can be seen that the causes of the decline of the empire of Spain have been the lack of good orders [*ordini*] within its government, and the disunity and isolation of its states, between which lies the vigorous kingdom of France, its perpetual enemy. We shall first discuss the latter cause, because it seems reasonable that it should be remedied without delay, given the necessity which will face whichever prince succeeds to the crown of Spain of alienating or exchanging some of his provinces for others; and also because the establishment of good orders within the government will require more time.

It was wisely said by a happy and quick-witted observer that Spain and the Indies weighed less when Flanders and the Spanish states in Italy were added to them. In our age those states have reduced them almost to nothing: it would have been to the advan-

---

[12] Imperial forces defeated the French at Crequi in 1675, and thus briefly enabled the Elector of Trier (Trèves) to assert his independence of French influence. But within a year the elector had died and French influence was restored.

tage of Spain if Charles V had alienated the provinces of Flanders, adding them to the Empire, or giving them to whoever had the strength to defend them from the French; or if Philip, instead of retaining dominion over some of the provinces at the cost of a ruinous war, had granted all of that people their liberty; or if the present King had ceded the remnant to the French, rather than holding onto them to the great advantage of the latter. So little do men understand their own affairs; such great and infinite miseries do peoples suffer simply for lack of sound reflection. But because this is the way things are, and it seems almost ridiculous to seek to persuade princes to abandon states to their enemies, or to leave government to the people, as if they would have been capable of it; because the remedy of colonies (although the most effective in such cases) cannot be adopted owing to the depopulation of Spain, nor any other which will be slow, since the affairs of that kingdom are reduced to such a state that they require a remedy whose effect is immediate, in order to allow time for good orders to be established in its government; after much thought I have found no alternative but the alienation or exchange of some of the above-mentioned provinces for others whose situation is more convenient for the empire of Spain.

But before I show which these countries are, and how such exchanges may be carried out, I shall observe that permutations of countries which are effected by exchange are much easier and happier than those which result from war; the latter, for the most part achieved only with infinite pains and difficulties, generally result in nothing that a treaty or a marriage could not have realised without any such inconvenience: and I shall further observe, that the object of the exchange being always the utility of princes and peoples, it is to be wondered that so few have occurred, and that these have been of so little note; were it not very well known that ambition, the mother of wars, is always stronger in the breasts of men than more modest and useful inclinations. If any should say that exchanges, especially those of great importance, present so many difficulties that they are impracticable; I answer that in exchanges made by agreement there should be no difficulty where all the contracting parties find it to their advantage; and that where any difficulty does arise, it is the result of weakness and a lack of greatness in minds hesitant and unwilling to choose the wise and useful course in affairs of great moment. Of this we have a notable example in the same Philip who has been so often mentioned above; persuaded that dominion over the Netherlands was damaging to him, he alienated it by the marriage of Isabella to the Archduke Albert.[13] But in the absence of heirs of their own, the remedy failed, and he had not the strength to alienate it in any other way; which would have been a better policy than to retain it at all. And should it be argued that when a prince or a republic wishes to alienate a province by exchange or otherwise, the province may reclaim its liberty, and should not be obliged to submit to the authority of another when its own prince no longer wishes to rule it; it may be answered, that such a province finding it (as may be supposed) more in its interest [*più suo utile*] to submit to the new lord, than it was to be under the old, will always consent; and that it is not necessary for its lord to declare his wish to alienate it completely (even if this is his intention) before the province has given its consent to the exchange. There is no such difficulty, however, in provinces which are subject to absolute authority, where the prince can make the exchange without the participation of the people with the same justice as he exercises his absolute government over them.

From what has been said above, it follows that in exchanging its disconnected states (which are not only useless but damaging to it), Spain should be contented with little in return. But this being a doctrine difficult to persuade either peoples or princes to accept, I intend to propose the exchange of states of a value equal or not much inferior to the value of the Spanish ones; an exchange which would be as much in the interests of Spain as a great good is to a very great loss. Coming therefore to the various interests of the princes who aspire to the crown of Spain; to the means by which they can obtain it, and the advantages which they would bring to Spain; to the obstacles which they would encounter, and the ways of overcoming them; and to the ease with which the exchange of a number of states would enable them to prepare, over a period of

---

[13] At the very end of his reign Philip was persuaded to grant the government of the Netherlands to his younger daughter, Isabella and her husband, Albert of Austria, youngest brother of the emperor and Philip's nephew. In principle they were rulers of all seventeen provinces; in practice of those remaining after the revolt. They ruled together until Albert's death in 1621, and Isabella ruled alone until her own death in 1633.

time and without being suspected, for universal monarchy [*monarchia universale*], I say, that the King of Portugal should offer to conjoin his dominions with those of Spain, obtaining that crown for himself:[14] and that for the Spaniards as much as for the Portuguese this would be a good, secure and easily achieved solution: because there is no country in the world more convenient to Spain, for its situation and many other reasons, than Portugal, a state which on many occasions has been powerful enough to wage a vigorous war in the bowels of Spain itself. By this union the dominions of Spain in America, which ought to count for more than they have hitherto, will be enlarged by Brazil; and through the Portuguese crown Spain will also acquire places in Africa and Asia which offer outstanding opportunities for commerce and navigation, so necessary to its empire. And if the Spaniards are as wise as they are reputed to be, they would transfer their court to Lisbon, a move by which they will derive many benefits. For besides the advantage of its excellent situation, convenient for commerce and the largest fleets, and thus well-adapted for the conquest of the world, and the residence of the prince who should rule it, the Portuguese will then be content to give up the use of their own language and customs, and with them every memory of being an independent people or government. The whole enormous country between the sea and the Pyrenees would become one united body. But if the Spaniards remain obstinate in their prejudices, and wish to remain in Madrid, it should still be possible for them to accommodate their empire to the situation of this city (adapted as it is to rule all Spain, though only Spain), instead of choosing the situation to fit the empire. If it is said, that the Spanish grandees and courtiers will not care to see their court enlarged by that of Portugal, and that the succession of that king's eldest son would be more welcome to them, since it would give them the opportunity to enrich themselves during his minority; it

---

[14] The reigning king of Portugal in 1698 was Pedro II. His candidacy for the Spanish succession was based on his distant descent from the younger daughter of Ferdinand and Isabella; it was considered possible by the main powers, but never gained serious support. Portugal had been annexed to the Spanish monarchy in 1580, but had broken out in revolt in 1640, in the name of the duke of Braganza, who became John IV. Strengthened by the recapture of Brazil from the Dutch in 1654, Portugal was alone among the provincial kingdoms of the Spanish monarchy in winning its independence, which was formally recognised by Spain in 1668. Pedro II was recognised as king in the same year, taking power from his brother Alfonso.

may equally be said that had the Kings of Spain, who were persuaded by the frauds of those same courtiers that to conquer the
Indies it was necessary to exterminate its peoples, realised the
deception and put a stop to the spilling of the blood of so many
millions of men, they would have denied their Spanish subjects the
means of enriching themselves; and that if the present King had
taken as his wife the late Infanta of Portugal, Don John and the
other malcontents at court would not have had such a near and
convenient retreat to escape to: excellent reasons, worthy even of
them![15] Truly I believe that the unjust interests of these men have
been, at all critical moments, the immediate cause of the ruin of
Spain. But besides that the design of this discourse is not to continue its disorders, I say that if a German or French prince should
ascend the throne, offices and ministerial positions will be taken in
greater numbers by the nobility of those nations than they would
be by the Portuguese; and that a King of Spain being always
engaged in enormous undertakings, as will become clear in what
follows, there will be no lack of opportunities for any who would
advance themselves by their virtue [*la virtù*]. But if the King of
Portugal, having acquired the crown of Spain, wishes to remain
undisturbed, and to prepare himself for the empire of the world
without incurring suspicion, it will be necessary for him, with the
consent of the people of Spain, to alienate Luxemburg to the
Empire, in return for certain fiefs in Italy; likewise Ostend and the
remnant of the province of Flanders to the English in return for
certain islands which they possess in America, and in particular for
Jamaica, a haven for pirates damagingly close to the fleets and colonies of the Indies; and the rest of the Netherlands to the Dutch, in
return for various strongholds which they possess in America,
Africa and Asia, which with those ceded by the English will do
much to secure the peace of the Indies. The Netherlands, being so
close to Paris, and in the hands of three such great powers, will
form the strongest of barriers against the ambition of France; and
this in turn would give these nations a motive to remain closely

---

[15] Fletcher appears to have mis-remembered the circumstances of the coups by
which Don John (Don Juan José, illegitimate son of Philip IV) attempted to gain
power: in 1668 he had fled to Aragon and Catalonia, before marching on Madrid
in 1669; on the failure of this effort, he retired to Aragon as viceroy, returning at
the head of another army in 1677, when he finally achieved his objective.

allied to Spain. The people of the Netherlands, after such great, prolonged misfortunes, having patrons who would protect them, would enjoy some repose. If to the above exchanges could be added that of Tuscany for the Duchy of Milan and the Kingdom of Sardinia, Spain would be secured on every side; because the port of Leghorn would offer the most convenient channel for reinforcements, whether from Spain or from Naples and Sicily, which otherwise can be conveyed to Milan only with the utmost difficulty.[16] Situated behind the barriers of the Lombard Alps and the Appenines, Tuscany would be difficult for the French to attack other than by sea: the condition of the Florentines, currently oppressed by excessive taxes (their prince knowing no other way of keeping them in subjection), would be made more tolerable by their being employed in the defence of Italy against the French; and the Milanese, no longer subject to government by foreigners, a condition they abhor, would have an Italian prince of their own, residing constantly in Milan. It will perhaps be said that the Grand Duke will never consent to such an exchange; and that he will never leave a dominion, in which his family is anciently established, to go to live in others exposed to war.[17] To which I reply that Milan and Sardinia are countries of the same province [*della medesima provincia*], language, customs and religion as that prince, and that the wealth of the Duchy, and the dignity of the Kingdom, with such an enlargement of dominion, are worthy of his consent.[18] But on

---

[16] Leghorn was the English name for Livorno (which is used in the Italian original); it was the port most visited by English merchant shipping, serving as an entrepot for trade with other parts of Italy, not least the South.

[17] The Grand Duke of Tuscany at this time was Cosimo III (1670–1723); the Medici family had ruled the duchy since 1530, and for a hundred years before that they had been the principal family in Florentine politics.

[18] The duchy of Milan had reverted to Charles V as an imperial fief on the death of the last Sforza duke in 1535; Charles conferred it on his son Philip in 1540, and thereafter it had remained part of the Spanish monarchy. In the latter part of the sixteenth century it became the vital staging-post for Spanish armies en route for the Netherlands.

Sardinia had been subject to the crown of Aragon since the early fifteenth century, and remained part of the Spanish monarchy for the next two centuries; during the Spanish Succession War it was to be captured by the emperor, along with the kingdoms of Naples and Sicily. At the Peace of Utrecht the emperor kept Sardinia and Naples but was obliged to cede Sicily to Savoy; in 1720, however, he successfully swapped Sardinia for Sicily, and the duke of Savoy became king of Sardinia.

accepting this exchange, it would be useful for him to propose another to the Duke of Mantua; I mean that of the Cremonese and Lodesano for Montferrat, a country so much more advantageous to the state of Milan, possession of which would deprive the French of a convenient point of entry into Italy, and the Duke of Savoy of a pretext for quarrelling.[19] For its part the Duchy of Mantua would be sufficiently compensated by the wealth and even more by the situation of the territories it received, both of which adjoin its own land and are remote from the theatres of war. In this way the republics of Venice and Genoa and the princes of Lombardy will have less to fear from the situation of the Spanish dominions in Italy; the Papacy and the republic of Lucca perhaps more than they do now. But the forces which will be under an obligation to join in the defence of Italy against the French will be increased by those of Tuscany, as I have said. If it should be said that it is vain to imagine that a King of Portugal who has no pretension to the crown of Spain by right should succeed to it, above all when the Houses of Austria and France, the two greatest in the world, along with other princes claim the right to the succession; I reply, that I do not speak of the right of succession, leaving that to the Doctors of laws; nor am I concerned with what princes ought to do, which is for Divines to teach; I am speaking of what princes have and will always do, which is, by any means, wherever they can, to enlarge their kingdoms by occupying neighbouring provinces. And if ever a prince deserved to be excused for such ambition, it would be the King of Portugal in this case; bringing such enormous advantages to the Spanish crown, which once relieved of the cancer of Flanders, unburdened of the state of Milan, and reinforced by the kingdom of Portugal, would be able at its leisure [*otiosa*] to use the armies which it presently maintains at great expense in its disconnected states, along with the forces of Portugal, to make a major diversion in Guienne and Languedoc whenever the French should think fit to attack the Empire, Italy, the Netherlands or the British Isles;[20] instead of which today its continual losses do nothing but increase

---

[19] The territories of Cremona and Lodi lay between Milan and Mantua; Montferrat, by contrast, lay to the west of Milan, between the Duchy and Turin, the capital of Savoy.

[20] Guienne and Languedoc were provinces in the south-west and south of France respectively, therefore easily reached from Spain.

the lands and the glory of the French, as has been said above. This King deserves the still further excuse, that if a German or a French prince were to become King of Spain, it is almost inevitable that he would lose his own states: but by adopting the above course, and thus avoiding that danger, the King of Portugal becomes the first King of the world; he makes Portugal and its Indies (freed for ever from war) happy; its nobles and courtiers (repenting of the folly of the late revolution) [*pentitisi della coglioneria dell'ultima rivoluzione*] still happier.[21] As for the great power of the two above-named Houses which dispute the succession, this is a circumstance favourable to the king of Portugal, because being implacable enemies, they will never unite against him. The members of the Empire, Italy, the Swiss, Sweden, Denmark, Poland and Turkey will welcome the humiliation of the House of Austria; and the whole world will be glad to see France lose its hope of possessing the Spanish crown.

Even if the union of Portugal with Spain will not be so welcome to the English, the Dutch, the Hamburgers and others for whom commerce is their chief end; these will still not risk obstructing it, in case they lose their richest trade, which is with Spain, and supply a pretext for the seizure of the immense wealth held by their merchants in that country.

In the second place we shall consider the interests of the Elector of Bavaria; who if he would dissuade the Emperor from pursuing the claims of his sons to the Spanish crown, and advance instead those of the Prince of Bavaria, the Emperor's grandson, must offer to leave the inheritance of the Electorate and its dominions to the Archduke; because unless he has the support of the Emperor, he must despair of the crown of Spain for his son.[22] To induce the

---

[21] Which revolution Fletcher had in mind, and why the nobles and courtiers of Portugal should repent its folly ('*coglioneria*' is a strong term for foolishness), are not immediately obvious. The most recent 'revolution' in Portuguese history was the coup by which the high nobility had brought Pedro II to the throne in 1667–8; but the removal of his incapable brother Alfonso, while personally cruel, was hardly foolish. Perhaps Fletcher had in mind the rebellion of 1640 which had led to the restoration of an independent Portuguese monarchy, reasoning that had the kingdom remained within the Spanish monarchy, the house of Braganza would have been better placed to press its claim for the entire Spanish Succession.

[22] The elector of Bavaria at the time was Max Emmanuel (1679–1726); he had married Emperor Leopold's daughter, making his son, Joseph Ferdinand, the grandson of the emperor and his Spanish first wife, the youngest daughter of Philip IV. Fletcher's proposal is that in order to obtain the Spanish monarchy for his

Emperor to accept this course, in addition to consideration for his grandson, there is the probability that France would not be so opposed to a prince who is not of the House of Austria; and it is safer for the Emperor that the Spanish Monarchy should be with another prince, than that by forcing it to remain in the House of Austria, there should be a risk of its falling to a French prince.[23] The Emperor should see no little gain in enlarging his estate with the dominions of Bavaria, and with its Electorate. As to the other powers of Europe, they would be better pleased with the succession of any prince whatever as King of Spain, than of one from either the House of Austria or that of France; and they would prefer the Prince of Bavaria to any of the pretenders who would add to the dominions of Spain.

The Prince of Bavaria once in possession of the Spanish crown, and wishing likewise to set out, unsuspected, on the road to the empire of the world [*al Imperio del mondo*], in order to make time for re-ordering the affairs of Spain, should, with the agreement of his people, alienate the Netherlands in the manner indicated above; and also make the exchange of Milan and Sardinia for Tuscany; or, should the Grand Duke refuse the exchange, give the state of Milan to the Venetians and the Genoese in return for the Morea and the island of Corsica, which will be easily defended, and convenient for the empire of the Mediterranean sea [*l'Imperio del mare Mediterraneo*]. The Venetians and the Genoese being thus greatly strengthened in Lombardy, they will be an enormous obstacle to France whenever it should wish to invade Italy. This last exchange might similarly be made by the King of Portugal. But rather than that the state of Milan should remain the responsibility of Spain, and give occasion to the French, the Germans, the Swiss and the Duke of Savoy to disturb the peace of Italy, and put themselves in a position

own son, the elector Max Emmanuel should divert the inheritance of the electorate itself to Leopold's second son, the Archduke Charles of Austria. In reality, Joseph Ferdinand was the favoured candidate for the Spanish Succession in 1698, being designated the heir to Spain, the Netherlands and the Spanish overseas territories in the Partition Treaty of 1698, and to the whole monarchy in Charles II's will in the same year; his untimely death early in 1699 brought a sudden end to these prospects.

[23] Fletcher's point is that for the purposes of the Spanish Succession the elector's son would not be seen as belonging to the house of Austria, even though he was also the emperor's grandson.

to attack the other Spanish dominions in that country, it should be alienated by any means possible; either by dividing it between its neighbours, or by conceding to the people their liberty, and joining it to the Swiss Cantons, to form an invincible obstacle to the French every time they should wish to invade Italy.

If the Spaniards were to accept the Duke of Savoy as King, it would bring them enormous advantages;[24] because by uniting his dominions with the state of Milan, and possessing the Alpine passes, the Duke would be master of Lombardy and (with the islands of Sicily and Sardinia) King of two thirds of Italy: from where no less than from Spain itself the monarchy would be able to defy whoever would attack it. It will be said that the Pope, the Venetians, the Genoese, the Grand Duke and the other powers of Italy, jealous of so great an ambition, will unite to oppose such a design. But were they to unite, they would not want immediately to call foreign arms into Italy (a policy always fatal to that country) in order to destroy a greatness which would have arisen without the movement of arms; rather they would seek to set limits to its growth: because there was more to fear from Charles V and his son Philip than there would be from a Duke of Savoy who became King of Spain, and such a greatness will rather enhance the security of Italy against the arms of the French; there being time to call for their assistance, should this prince, not content with the ancient dominions of his dynasty, or those of the Spaniards in Italy, wish to make an attempt on some other state in the country. His security, meanwhile, would lie in the implacable hatred of the two dynasties of France and Austria for each other, which would prevent them from allying against him. But should he wish to gain himself time to plan the monarchy of the world, he would need to alienate the Netherlands in the manner previously described, and to exchange the Cremonese and Lodesano for Montferrat.

---

[24] The current duke of Savoy was Victor Amadeus II, who reigned from 1675 to 1730. The one Italian prince to be an active participant in European diplomacy, the duke's priority was to secure his authority in Savoy-Piedmont, especially against French aggression. Though descended from the daughter of Philip II's first marriage, he was not an immediate candidate for the Spanish Succession in 1698; but he became a reversionary candidate during the subsequent war, and was confirmed in this status at the Peace of Utrecht in 1713. (That is, Savoy would succeed to Spain if the Bourbon line failed.) The Peace also brought Savoy territorial concessions on its border with France, and the kingdom of Sicily.

The whole world would oppose the claims of the Dauphin to the Spanish crown; nevertheless, his father must at first give the appearance of wishing to support them, so that the Spaniards may the more readily accept the Duke of Berry as their King; once accepted, he will easily achieve the joining of the two empires of France and Spain.[25] The French will say that since it is necessary to provide a successor to the Spanish crown, the right of succession lies in the Dauphin; nevertheless, their King, as befits his title of Most Christian King, being opposed to the shedding of Christian blood, and in order not to give an occasion for endless wars, and to fill the world with the fear that such a succession would excite, will be content if his grandson the Duke of Berry is accepted as King.[26] They will also say that the King will send him to Spain not only without armies, or any military escort, but accompanied by his domestics alone; who (on being met by the Spaniards at the border) will all turn back to France, leaving not a single page inside Spain: that all the advantage which will accrue to France will be the honour of giving a King to Spain, who having the same interests as the Spanish themselves, will always follow them. Golden words! And if by this gilding of the sleeping-pill the Spaniards should fall asleep; before they awaken the French would have them all in chains; either by occupying their dominions with French armies, on the pretext of assisting them against attacks by the House of Austria, or by a thousand other means which it is needless to detail.

[25] The dauphin was the French king's eldest son, Louis (1661–1711). Charles, duke of Berry was the third son of the dauphin. As it happened, Fletcher guessed wrong: although Louis XIV at one point suggested that either of the dauphin's younger sons would do, it was the second son, Philip, duke of Anjou, who emerged as the Bourbon candidate for the Spanish Succession, and was designated heir to the entire monarchy by Charles II in his will of 1700. The mistake is acknowledged by the substitution of Anjou for Berry in the manuscript alterations to David Fletcher's copy of the *Discorso* (see List of Variants). Neither Anjou nor Berry was in line to succeed to the French crown; although both the dauphin and his own first son, Louis, duke of Burgundy, predeceased Louis XIV, Burgundy himself had a son, who became Louis XV when his great-grandfather finally died in 1715.

[26] The French claim to the Spanish Succession lay through Louis XIV's marriage to the infanta Maria Theresa, who was Charles II's older half sister by Philip IV's first marriage: failing Charles and any heirs of his, the succession should pass to Philip IV's senior daughter and her line, hence to the dauphin. But the marriage settlement, at the Peace of the Pyrenees of 1659, had required that Maria Theresa renounce all future claims to the Spanish throne on payment of her dowry. The title 'Most Christian King' was traditionally associated with the holder of the Crown of France.

But to lull not only the Spaniards, but all the other peoples of Europe, the French will also propose, that the British King [*il Rè Britannico*] and the Republic of Holland (who alone are qualified) may stand surety for France, giving their word that that kingdom will not take advantage in any way of the succession of the Duke of Berry to the Spanish throne; who possessing that empire independently, will become as much the enemy of France as any Prince of Austria. They will say further, that in giving this guarantee, they will liberate not only the other states of Europe, but also themselves from a most damaging war: that, being exhausted of funds, which they can only regain by commerce, they ought by every means to preserve the peace. And truly the bad conduct of the past war, chiefly in affairs at sea and in the management of public finances, may with reason undermine the will of the English to re-start the war in Flanders (which would be as pernicious to that nation, as neglecting to oppose the designs of France with all the naval force at their disposal). But, besides that the French with their intrigues may succeed in rendering the guarantee useless by embroiling the English against the Dutch, or setting the English against themselves, it appears that there is a hidden poison within those nations themselves, which is anyway at work to precipitate their ruin. This is why in this most corrupt age (in which every aspect of men's condition has worsened, having made themselves vulnerable not by defect of knowledge [*scienza*] but by lack of virtue [*virtù*]) the gross deception by France may perhaps succeed: above all when the peoples of Europe are impoverished and exhausted by war, while France is not sparing of its money on courtiers, or of its promises to princes to assist them in depriving their subjects and neighbours of liberty, and in banishing it from the world.

But if these schemes of the French do not have the success they desire, and which the laxity of this enervated age gives them reason to hope for, so that they find themselves obliged to proceed more openly (the Spanish not wishing to have the Duke as their King), they can still deploy enormous armies and navies to attack the state of Milan, the Kingdom [of Naples], Sicily and Sardinia, pinning all their hopes on the speed of their conquest so that they may pre-empt the Germans: and at the same time by undertaking a defensive war in the Netherlands, and allowing a number of strongholds to be lost to the English and the Dutch, the better to lull them into acquiescence, they might send a small army (to prevent it going short of food) consisting of their most select forces into Spain: luring [*uccellando*] even the Spaniards with the sight of the Duke of Berry at the head of this army, they will attain the summit of their designs: and the Spaniards by the loss of their dominions in Italy will become themselves a province; because once the Duke of Berry has been accepted with an army, the French will dipose of everything in Spain at will.

In order to retain a large part of Italy and exclude the Germans from it, without being suspected by the Italians, they can come to an agreement with the Duke of Savoy; in return for being made King of Naples, he would cede his ancestral dominions to France; and if he were to refuse the exchange, they could easily drive him from his state. But it is unlikely that he would refuse; because once Milan, Naples, Sicily and Sardinia fall into French hands, his position as prince in his old state would be much more precarious than if he were established in Naples. In possessing Naples he would have not only the title of King, but a very rich and delightful country. It is true that his family is long-established in his old dominions, and much loved by his people; but if he governs wisely, he has nothing to fear from his new subjects, who are of the same province, language, customs and religion: and once restored to the true dignity of a kingdom, with an Italian prince of its own instead of being preyed upon by governors, after two hundred years of servitude under Barbarians (as they call the Ultramontanes), that country will be faithful to him.[27]

In this way the Most Christian King, uniting Milan with France, and by possessing the dominions of the Duke of Savoy on both sides of the Alps, would gain such a strong foothold in Italy, that it would be very difficult to chase him from it. Sicily and Sardinia,

---

[27] The kingdom of Naples had been part of the Spanish monarchy since 1504, when it was recaptured from the French by Ferdinand of Aragon; like the kingdoms of Aragon and Sicily, it was thereafter ruled by a viceroy. The kingdom had experienced a major rebellion in 1647, in which the French had intervened; but it was put down, and the kingdom, whose nobility enjoyed extensive privileges, had thereafter remained loyal to the monarchy. In 1707, during the subsequent Spanish Succession War, it was to be seized by the Austrians, who ruled it as their vice-royalty until 1734. Only then, quite unexpectedly, was its independence restored, as a result of its capture by one of the Farnese branch of the Bourbon family, who became Charles III, king of the Two Sicilies (and subsequently, in 1759, Charles III of Spain).

as islands, will be easily defended, and will not arouse the jealousy that would occur were he to keep Naples, and transfer those islands to the Duke.[28] Nor need the King fear that that prince would confederate with the other powers of Italy to attack him; for the King being master [*padrone*] of the sea, and being able to take him in the rear from Sicily, it would be dangerous for a newly-established prince to renounce the King's friendship, seek other friends, and give a people as fickle and changeable as the Neapolitans even the slightest pretext for fresh disorders.[29]

Yet with all this it is beyond doubt that the Pope, the Venetians, and the smaller Republics of Italy will ally with the Empire and the Swiss in order to prevent this establishment of the French in Italy. It is a difficult thing to deceive the Italians: Italian wars have always been fatal to French arms, and it is a country much obstructed by mountains and rivers. The Germans, and in particular the Emperor and the Bavarians, who are the closest, and who both have claims to the Spanish crown, can ally with the Swiss, and by descending from the Alps, can inundate Lombardy with such armies that the French will repent of having made war in that country.

It would perhaps not only be good policy, but positively necessary for France to offer the Elector of Bavaria the state of Milan, with an agreement to be put by him in possession of the Spanish Netherlands. And it is likely that the Elector would accept this measure, should the Emperor refuse his consent to the Elector's obtaining the Spanish crown on the conditions set out above. The states belonging to the Elector in Germany will be sufficiently close to the Duchy of Milan for them to give each other assistance against the Emperor, or whatever Italian power should attack him. The French possessing only Piedmont, and having set up a powerful prince in Italy, would expose their own arms to less suspicion: and in this way keeping the Germans disunited, and gaining an ally against the House of Austria as considerable as the Elector of Bavaria (who has almost always doubled the strength of Austria in

---

[28] Sicily, like Sardinia, had been subject to the Aragonese monarchy since the early fifteenth century, and then became part of the Spanish monarchy, ruled, as Sardinia and Naples, by a viceroy. For its various destinations after the Spanish Succession War, see fn 18.

[29] An allusion to the Neapolitan revolution of 1647, which became notorious throughout Europe as having been instigated by a mere fishseller, one Tommaso Masaniello.

Germany), the French would be able to turn their arms against Spain knowing that they faced no further obstacles in Italy, and with the added convenience of having strengthened their flank against Great Britain and Holland with the Spanish Netherlands.

However, if France can find no means of drawing Bavaria away from its ancient friendship with Austria, it will be obliged to keep Naples and to present the state of Milan to the Duke of Savoy, who having by a combination of old and new dominions become extremely powerful in Lombardy, will be a very faithful confederate against the Germans. French possession of the Kingdom of Naples would also arouse less jealousy among the Italians than if the French held Savoy, the Alps, Piedmont and Milan, countries adjoining and contiguous with France, whose possession would thereby assure them of control of the affairs of Italy. Without naval forces the Germans cannot oppose French arms in Spain, the presence of which will always have the greatest influence in drawing its other dominions along with it.

If, however, the French were to become lords of Spain and of the Spanish Indies after renouncing the Spanish dominions in Italy to the Germans and Italians, they would do great damage to the commerce of the English and the Dutch: with this daily diminishing, those nations within a few years will have been completely driven from the sea by the all-powerful arms of France, to which nothing is now lacking except the seamen with whom they will be supplied by the commerce of the Indies and the Mediterranean, and the wealth which will accrue from it and from the mines of Peru. Indeed so formidable has the power of the Most Christian King become in our time, that should he have the desire to make himself master of any part of the Spanish Monarchy, he must expect to have the whole world allied against him, save perhaps for a few princes to whom he would allow a share of the spoils.

Moreover the fleets of England and Holland give the British King such power at sea, enabling him not only to prevent the French King from conquering America, but to disrupt his conquest of Spain itself, breaking the blockade by the French fleets, that it is very probable he would never allow the French King to succeed to Spain unless he gained a settlement highly advantageous to his people and those of Holland. This will not be less than leaving North America (where they already have many colonies) to the

English, depriving the French of theirs, and transferring to the Dutch the Spanish dominions in the East Indies, along with those that remain to it in the Netherlands. If it is said that these suppositions and demands are intolerable; I reply, that the Most Christian King, by grasping at all the Spanish dominions, would lose them all; that I have demonstrated that wars in Italy are very difficult, and almost impracticable, for the French; and that these concessions to the British King (who cannot accept less, if he would not have the English and the Dutch abandon the sea, as said above) will make everything easy for the King of France, who will retain enough; for by possessing Spain and South America together with France, he can in time easily make himself master of the world, as will be made clear below: and this even without the advantage of moving the seat of the empire to Spain; it being unlikely that France, which is still full of inhabitants, would wish to submit itself to depopulated Spain. But if the French were to consent to this solution, it would seem to be an easy thing for the two empires to be united. And truly the French have become so base under their present servitude, that their King would not have great difficulty in carrying out such a design, on the sole condition that France would have French governors. But such a resolution would seem to the Spaniards to be so incredible, that even if made with complete sincerity, they would never persuade themselves that it was other than a trick; and not only the Spaniards, but all other peoples would be opposed. Besides which, so great a design is beyond the spirit [*animo*] of men, and most of all of princes; being equally incapable of making their memory eternal by works of extraordinary greatness as by those of true virtue [*virtù*].[30]

Let us proceed to discuss the other pretenders. The Archduke seems a very fit successor, being of the same house as the present King, and it being requisite for the crown of Spain to continue in the same house in order to balance the excessive power of France; besides which he adds no other state to Spain; nor any alliances

---

[30] Fletcher's meaning in this paragraph is not altogether clear: in particular, it is unclear which 'design' the French are too base to question, the Spanish unable to believe, and men and their princes now lack the spirit to carry out. It may be the attempt to secure the entire Spanish monarchy, or the willingness to make large concessions to the English and Dutch in order to be able to take the remainder.

beyond those it now enjoys.[31] It is likely that being of the same house, he will be, like his predecessors, a pacific prince; he will not innovate in anything; the world will not realise that Spain has changed its King; and if the Emperor, having made peace with the Ottomans, should give Bavaria some strongholds on the Rhine, to make him always an enemy of France, the French will be the only enemies the Archduke has.[32] Succeeding in this way to the Empire of Spain by the interests of those princes who do not wish to see changes in Europe after the death of the King of Spain, and with every thing quietened, in order to lay the basis for universal empire [*Imperio universale*] he has only to exchange the Spanish Netherlands in the manner stated above, it being necessary to retain the state of Milan as a channel by which assistance can come from his father.

The capital point in all the claims to the crown of Spain being to have the good-will of the Spanish, and to have been called by them, it is likely that the House of Austria, being anciently established in that country, will always have many partisans; while the House of France, because of past hostilities and incompatibility of tempers [*umori*], will have few, and the influence of certain Grandees of Spain corrupted by French money will disappear on the death of the King. However were a French Prince to succeed, even if he should cut himself off in spirit from his own country, and become wholly Spanish, he would not bring such strength to the affairs of Spain as a prince with allies and family connections in Germany; nor would this last advantage be as important as a prince who has powerful dominions there. So that it is likely that the Spaniards, finding their interests [*l'utile*] and their inclinations to be

---

[31] The archduke was Charles, archduke of Austria, second son of Emperor Leopold. Born in 1685, he became the principal Habsburg candidate for the Spanish succession after the death of Prince Joseph Ferdinand of Bavaria. During the subsequent War of the Spanish Succession he assumed the title King of Spain following the allied capture of Barcelona in 1705. But once he had become Emperor (as Charles VI) on the death of his brother in 1711, the anti-French coalition began to disintegrate, and he gave up the claim to the Spanish throne at the Peace of Utrecht.

[32] The Emperor was by 1698 actively negotiating with the Ottomans, negotiations which culminated in 1699 in the Treaty of Carlowitz: this confirmed the Habsburg recapture of Hungary and Croatia, and fixed the frontier on the Danube and between Croatia and Serbia.

joined, will make an offer to the Emperor to accept the King of the Romans as their King, provided that his hereditary dominions are united to the crown of Spain, with no possibility of their future alienation.[33] It is true that such a power will be much envied and feared; it would cause great jealousy among the Germans; and it is probable that the House of Austria would lose the Imperial dignity, which has become virtually its own. But that House would have consolation for its loss by the accession of so many kingdoms. And the Germans will never make a member of the House of France Emperor; but will rather turn to one of their own nation, in order to hold the balance between these two most powerful Houses, together with that of Europe; which will be easier for such an Emperor than for the feeble Venetians, or the fickle English.[34] Nor will the Germans have anything to fear from such a power, France having already become so very powerful in our time. It will perhaps be said that Spain requires a prince who will make his residence there, and Austria another to oppose the Ottomans above the Danube: to which I reply that speedy and potent assistance can be sent from Sicily and the Kingdom of Naples to the nearby countries of Croatia, Bosnia, Rascia, Slavonia and Hungary; and the coasts of Greece can so easily be harried by a naval force kept at Otranto, that the union of states described above would be a sufficient means to bring down the empire of the Turks;[35] and also that so great a

---

[33] The King of the Romans was the title of the Emperor's designated heir, who at this point was his eldest son, Joseph; the title marked a form of pre-election to the imperial title itself, and was thus used to ensure dynastic continuity in what was formally an elective monarchy. But the Habsburgs also possessed hereditary family lands within the Empire, the so-called '*Erblande*', the most important of which were in Austria and south-western Germany. It is these which were to be permanently united with the Spanish Crown; as Fletcher immediately acknowledges, a union of the Empire and the Spanish monarchy was most unlikely.

[34] In the sixteenth century the Venetian Republic had successfully defied both the Spanish monarchy and the Emperor, maintaining its independence by orchestrating anti-Habsburg alliances throughout Europe. By the late seventeenth century, however, the republic had long since abandoned any such European role, becoming a largely passive participant in Italian regional politics.

[35] Rascia was an area west of the river Morava and south of the Danube, straddling Serbia and Bulgaria; Slavonia lay between the Sava and the Drava, west of Belgrade. By the Treaty of Carlowitz, Croatia and Slavonia were confirmed as Habsburg possessions, while Bosnia and Rascia remained under Ottoman rule. Otranto is a port on the Adriatic, almost at the tip of the heel of Italy, thus well situated to command the coasts of Greece which lay opposite. It was then within the kingdom of Naples.

king, even if he were not constantly to be engaged on expeditions, like Charles V, should not bury himself in Spain in imitation of Philip II. But despite being so powerful, this prince too should rid himself of the cancer of Flanders, in the manner indicated earlier, and should place the seat of his empire at Cartagena, to be close to Italy, and to those states that lie opposite to the Turkish empire.[36]

The Popes of Rome have claims over the Kingdom of Naples; but they do not have the military forces to make themselves master of it. Nor is their authority today such that they could offer an equivalent to so valuable a present, were any of the claimants to the Spanish crown willing to cede it to them.[37]

Of private pretenders [*privati pretendenti*] to the Spanish throne there is none who has come to my attention other than the Duke of Medina Celi, descendant of the disinherited Alfonso: but it is unlikely that he or any other Spanish Viceroy can make himself master of the Spanish monarchy, or any part of it; for there are so many powerful princes, who command fleets and armies, to prevent them; and none of the private candidates [*privati*] wishes to cede so high a place to another.[38]

---

[36] Cartagena is a port on the south-east coast of Spain, on the Mediterranean.

[37] The Papacy claimed that the Norman rulers of Naples had done homage in return for their investiture as kings in the eleventh and twelfth centuries, making the kingdom a papal fief. The claim had repeatedly been contested since, and the Spanish had refused to acknowledge papal overlordship. The form of homage included the *chinea*, the ceremonial presentation of a white horse to the pope.

[38] Luis de La Cerda, ninth duke of Medina Celi from the death of his father in 1691, was the viceroy of Naples from 1695 to 1700, having previously been the Spanish ambassador in Rome. His father, the eighth duke, had been Charles II's principal minister after Don Juan, between 1680 and 1685. As 'descendant of the disinherited Alfonso', the duke could claim to be of the Castilian royal line, albeit very distantly: the Alfonso alluded to was the grandson of Alfonso X of Castile (1252–84) by that king's eldest son, Ferdinand de La Cerda, who had predeceased his father in 1275. Although the succession should have gone through Ferdinand de La Cerda as the king's eldest son, the young Alfonso was dispossessed by his uncle, Sancho, the king's second son, who succeeded as Sancho IV of Castile (1284–95). As the so-called 'Infantes of La Cerda' Alfonso and his younger brother Ferdinand gave the La Cerda family a potential claim to the succession.

Fletcher's reference to Medina Celi may also be significant as one of the few indications of a particularly close acquaintance with the affairs of Naples, sufficient to explain his giving the city as the pamphlet's place of publication. The ninth duke's reputation as viceroy of Naples stood highest as a patron of the arts and of Neapolitan men of letters, many of whom were members of an academy which bore his name.

The use of the term '*privato*' as a noun and an adjective reproduces Machiavelli's, as in *The Prince*, chs. vii (Francesco Sforza) and viii (Agathocles).

But there is nothing which could make the position of the prince who succeeds to that crown easier, or would be more likely to spare the people of Spain the alarm and the horrible disorders which will otherwise happen on the death of the present King, than if he were to designate his successor while he still lives, especially if he makes a wise choice. Because his people will be determined by his authority; and many measures can be taken to forestall contrary designs; above all the exchanges which are so necessary to the affairs of Spain, which a prince new to the government [*un prencipe nuovo nel governo*] will find very difficult to carry out against the differing views of the people, who considering names more than things, will murmur against so many changes made by a foreigner: whereas if the changes are effected by the present ruler of Spain, the new King will face only the difficulty of transferring himself to his new realm.

I have spoken of how the above-mentioned princes must behave to obtain the crown of Spain; of the advantages which they would bring to it; of the opposition they will face and the means of overcoming it, and of the benefit which they would acquire from the exchange of certain states, giving them time to reorder the affairs of Spain, and so to prepare themselves without being suspected for universal monarchy [*monarchia universale*]. It remains for me to discuss the means to be adopted by the prince who succeeds to the crown of Spain in order to increase his dominions, and set his successors on the road to the empire of the world. Before doing so, it does not seem to me necessary to prolong this discourse, by demonstrating that should France prevail by the stratagem of offering the Duke of Berry, even if it were to add to its own states only Spain and South America, it could easily by these additions, as I have said above, make itself master of the world; nevertheless, to fulfill my promise, I shall say that we have seen the Most Christian King defy so many princes during the last war, as to make it sufficiently clear that with those additions, which include the mines of Peru, he will be much too powerful for all the other princes of Europe. Leaving aside further discussion of this issue as superfluous, therefore, I shall speak of the measures which should be taken by whichever other pretender obtains the crown of Spain, to set his successors on course for universal empire [*imperio universale*].

To establish good orders [*Lo stabilire buoni ordini*] in a disordered kingdom is a difficult matter, for the reasons given above, and requires the greatest dexterity; above all when the prince is a foreigner, and new to the state which he must reform. In considering which, I cannot do better than offer as an example the Catholic King, Ferdinand, of whom the previously-cited author in his book on the prince says this:

> One can almost call him a new prince; because from a weak king he has become for fame and glory the first King of Christendom. At the beginning of his reign he invaded Granada, and that undertaking was the foundation of his state: for, first, he did it at his leisure, free of any apprehensions of being interrupted; he used it to occupy the spirits of the Castilian barons, who thinking only of the war, had no thought of innovations; by this means he acquired reputation and empire [*riputazione e imperio*] over them, without their realising it. He maintained his armies with money from the Church and the people; and over that long war he laid the foundation of his own militia [*militia sua*], which has since won him such honour.[39]

An incomparable example, highly appropriate to the condition of a new prince of Spain, who if he wishes to imitate that wise king should make his first expedition against the Moors of Barbary. It is true that wars in Africa are difficult; and that the undertakings of Christians in those lands have had little success; but this is because they have taken them lightly, with insufficient, poorly-ordered forces.

In this war against the infidel no-one will impede him, it will give no Christian prince cause for jealousy: the Church and the whole of Italy will supply funds; his people will contribute willingly to such an undertaking, and he cannot do anything more useful and convenient for Spain; since by the conquest of the Kingdoms of Fez and Morocco, countries as fertile as they are near, he will see the centre [*il Domicilio*] of the empire doubled in size by the addition of the other side of the straits.[40] But the advantages he

---

[39] Machiavelli, *The Prince*, ch. xxi. This translation is mine: cf. that in the Cambridge Texts Series edition by Quentin Skinner and Russell Price (Cambridge, 1988), pp. 76–7. Fletcher has omitted a sentence in the original (between the first two sentences in the quoted passage).

[40] The conquest of the Barbary states along the North African coast could expect to command wider support, especially in Italy, because of the constant disruption of Mediterranean trade by their privateering activities, and because of their continued raiding of southern Italy in order to obtain slaves. But in fact both

will gain during the war will be much more considerable than the acquisitions themselves; because, as our author says, the spirits of his subjects being kept occupied, they will think of the war, and not of innovation; he will gain reputation, and empire over them, without their realising it; the war will be the foundation of his militia; and what is most important of all, the reputation of so great an undertaking will give him authority and credit sufficient to introduce new orders [*nuovi ordini*] into the affairs of Spain and the Indies.

Proceeding then to these, it is first necessary to adopt the appropriate means to repopulate Spain and the Indies, accustoming those peoples to agriculture, the mechanical arts and commerce. Many measures might be adopted to repopulate Spain and the Indies; but the want of people is so great that they will all take ages to have an effect unless toleration for all religions is introduced. I do not ignore the oppposition that will be raised by the clergy, who out of their own particular interests (alien to the spirit of peace, and of the Gospels) are mortal enemies to all those who do not submit to their will; but to this can be opposed reason of state, and extreme necessity [*la ragion di stato, e la somma necessità*]. And truly it is high time that the Spaniards were disabused in this matter (as many of them today are), and left to the French this fatal error of government, of tormenting and persecuting peoples on account of their religion, and not wishing to have subjects who differ in their opinions on the highest and most difficult mysteries: and the French have been the more fools, not to have been able to learn from the experience of the Spaniards.[41] But if these were to choose the policy of toleration, the Indies would once again fill with people, and Spain would become very populous; which is the only sufficient basis for a great empire; and the clergy themselves will have the opportunity to con-

Machiavelli and Fletcher were mistaken in holding up Ferdinand as an example of a king who saw the advantage of making war in North Africa: it had been Isabella's policy, not Ferdinand's, and he pursued it reluctantly and half-heartedly after her death. Subsequent expeditions against Tunis (1534–5) and Algiers (1541) by Charles V had had only temporary success, as had Don John of Austria's capture of Tunis in 1573.

[41] A reference to the intolerance which had led to the successive expulsions of the Jews and the Moors from Spain in the late fifteenth and sixteenth centuries; and to the withdrawal of toleration from the Huguenots by seventeenth-century French kings, culminating in Louis XIV's Revocation of the Edict of Nantes in 1685.

vert many to the faith, in the same way as did our Redeemer. The increase of population will in turn lead to an increase in agriculture, the mechanical arts, commerce and navigation: and from the example of foreigners, the Spaniards will begin gradually to apply themselves to work and industry; the great inclination which that nation has always had to leisure [*ozio*], and idleness, being one of the principal causes of its weakness.[42] But this remedy not being enough on its own, it would have to be combined with laws and the most rigorous regulations, as for the cure of an obstinate evil: and to attract and induce foreigners to stay, as well as to protect the inhabitants [*nativi*] themselves, it will be necessary to provide all subjects, even in the remotest provinces, with exact, speedy and inexpensive justice; to punish with the most horrible torments the cruelties that are committed secretely in the Indies: and by the example of the prince, which for this purpose is the most powerful of all, to correct that fantastic pride [*orgoglio fantastico*], which is so inconsistent with any good government.

The increase of commerce and navigation will add to the number of seamen, and will render them more expert and practiced for the navy [*militia del mare*], which the prince, by imitating the orders [*ordini*] of the English, the Dutch and the French, should promote in every way, and make his principal object; because with it (as I have already said, when discussing the situation of Spain) he would be able to acquire and hold the empire of the world more easily than any other prince. As for the reformation of the land forces [*la militia di terra*], to which the Spanish nation is so well suited that in the past age it has seemed as if military glory had become theirs alone, it will be necessary to restore their discipline, imitating the ancient orders [*ordini antichi*] of the Romans in matters of arms and field warfare, and those of the French in seiges. There is an infinity of other things to say on this subject, but it is enough for me to have said the most necessary; above all in discussing princes, who have so many advantages in reforming a government [*per riformare*

---

[42] The damage done to Spain by population loss was by now a cliché of the literature on the decline of the monarchy; it had been made much of by the reason of state theorist Giovanni Botero, in *The Reason of State* (1589), trans. P. J. and D. P. Waley (London, 1956), Book VII, p. 143. Unlike Botero and other Catholic commentators, however, Fletcher takes reason of state to point to toleration as the remedy.

un governo], being able to act alone, and to do so much by their example.

If once these foundations have been laid, I had to make a prognosis of what was to happen, I would not hesitate to affirm that for that prince to win the world nothing remains except to acquire the empire of the sea [*del imperio del mare*]: indeed it would be a great blunder to think of increasing his empire yet further [*l'imperio suo più oltre*],[43] without acquiring it: because he would then face great difficulties in making war in countries distant from Spain, and still greater ones in retaining his conquests. On the other hand, if he were to attack his neighbours in Europe, he would inadvertently disclose the design of universal monarchy, and provoke the fiercest hostility. The French, English and Dutch, who are the maritime powers, would interrupt communications between Spain and its other dominions; they would destroy its fleets, harry its commerce, and ruin everything which provided a foundation for its greatness. In acquiring the empire of the sea our prince will have great advantages, being master of extensive coasts, and of convenient and capacious ports on every side save the north, where there are the maritime forces of the above three nations. To supply this deficiency, while proceeding with discretion, he needs to ally with one of those nations against the other two, obtaining from the ally passage into all its ports, and even, if possible, one for garrisoning by Spanish soldiers, to serve as a magazine for naval stores. And this course will give fewer grounds for suspicion if from the beginning he were to retain the port of Ostend. It will also be appropriate, in order to avoid suspicion, to employ only a part of his forces on that side, and with the other during the same period to wipe out the fleets and colonies of his enemies in the Indies, Africa and the Mediterranean, where he is at his strongest; always paying the utmost respect to the interests of his ally until he has driven the two other nations from the sea, and there remains only the one to contend with. To this acquisition of the empire of the sea the prince must commit the greatest strength he can, and put virtually all his glory into the success of the enterprise, for it is here that all the difficulty lies; once won, he leaves the world in chains for his suc-

---

[43] An echo, perhaps, of the famous motto of Emperor Charles V, *Plus Ultra*, which accompanied the emblem of a ship sailing beyond the Pillars of Hercules.

cessors, needing nothing to cap his labour but time and the continuation of the above good orders. For once the dominion of the sea has been acquired, the remaining European colonies in America, Africa and the East Indies will fall unopposed into his hands. France, which after this should be the next to be attacked, being weakened by the expulsion of the Calvinists; missing the present King, and the good order into which he has put his affairs; and having neither men, other than nobles, nor horses who are fit for war, as a result of the great misery of the people, will be unable to resist; the English and the Dutch, having lost the sea, will become poor and of small importance. Italy is sunk in effeminacy [*effeminata*], and drained by the clergy and its own luxury. Germany, which alone remains of any account, may put up some resistance, but it will not be long or vigorous against such forces. The empire of the Turks, having become utterly corrupt, and now attacked by sea and land, will be easily destroyed; those of Persia, Muscovy, the Mogul, of the Tartars, of China and Japan, like so many empty names, will vanish before such a power: they will serve only to provide trophies, displaying the strange diversity and richness of the arms and dress of those enfeebled nations; among whom will shine above all other names that of the restorer of the empire [*del ristoratore del Imperio*].

The End

A SPEECH

upon the

STATE OF THE NATION

In April 1701

Gentlemen,

It seems at first view hard to determine, whether you would be
more obliged to one who should persuade you of the miserable and
irretrievable condition, into which you are precipitating yourselves,
and the rest of Europe; or to him, who after you are convinced,
should shew you how to escape.[1] But as it is a much more difficult

---

[1] Of all Fletcher's writings this is the hardest to ascribe a context and an intended
readership. The manuscript emendations to the title in David Fletcher's copy
tacitly admit this: the title becomes 'A Speech supposed to be spoke in ye House
of Com. upon the Partition Treaty', and it begins 'Mr Speaker' instead of 'Gentlemen'. While a speech by Fletcher to the English House of Commons was an
obvious impossibility, the fiction was a common pamphleteers' device, and indicates that Fletcher wished to address an English as well as a Scottish readership.
Following the deliberately esoteric *Discorso delle cose di Spagna*, the *Speech* of 1701
would seem to be a further attempt to explain the implications and dangers of the
Spanish Succession crisis, now that the last Habsburg king, Charles II, had finally
died. Since the writing of the *Discorso* successive Partition Treaties had been
negotiated in 1698 and 1699 (see note 5 below); but these had been superseded
in 1700 by Charles II's decision to make a will in which the whole monarchy was
left to Philip, duke of Anjou, on condition that the Spanish thrones must be kept
separate from that of France. The will was promptly accepted by Louis XIV
instead of the Partition Treaty, and Philip of Anjou became Philip V of Castile
and the other kingdoms and territories of the monarchy. Although a French succession to the Spanish monarchy was precisely what the other powers in Europe
had long sought to prevent, the Dutch were initially inclined to accept the new
reality, and Fletcher evidently feared that William would persuade the English to
do the same. The purpose of the work appears to have been to warn that this was
William's intention, and that he would attempt to strengthen his own position at
the expense of the English parliament's by negotiating territorial acquisitions in
the Netherlands as the price of his acceptance of the Bourbon succession in Spain.

work to convince you of the true state of affairs; so it seems to have this advantage, that when you know your danger, the frightful and terrible circumstances of your present condition will certainly make you improve every opportunity, and lay hold upon every thing that may in the least contribute to save you: and this will be the more easy for you to do, since such means are now in your power, as could hardly be expected on the like occasion; and which, if you neglect, you have resolved your own ruin. You were formerly convinced, that the French King was a dangerous neighbour, powerful and vigilant; that there was no end of his designs, no relying on his treaties; that he could corrupt not only those who under your princes had the management of publick affairs, but even your princes themselves. The least increase of his power at sea, every inconsiderable fort taken by him in Flanders, alarmed you in the highest degree. You were jealous of his secret treaties with your princes, and so industrious, that you discovered one in which the abolition of parliaments, and suppression of your liberties were expressly stipulated; provided England would remain his ally, and not oppose the designs he had formed against the house of Austria, and the rest of Europe.[2] You were then alarmed that no care was taken of the protestant religion abroad, and began from thence, and the debaucheries of your princes, to suspect them of inclining to a religion that allows men to live ill, and consecrates the arbitrary power of kings. But now, as if there were not the least ground to suspect any of these things, you are very easy: you concur with the designs of France and the court in every thing. France is too powerful to be opposed; you are too poor, and too much in debt to make war. Yet France has seized the whole Spanish monarchy; and, if suffered to enjoy it quietly, he who formerly was able to oppose, may thereafter trample on the rest of mankind. 'Tis no longer Condé, Linck, and the sluices of Newport he pretends: his troops fill Brussels, Antwerp, and the Spanish Gelderland. Ostend and Newport are by our good conduct added to Dunkirk, in order to receive his royal fleets, and harbour his pirates, who are to enrich themselves with the ruin of our trade. In this state of things you

---

[2] Probably a reference to the Secret Treaty of Dover, made by Charles II with Louis XIV in 1670: see below, note 4.

are for preserving the peace of Europe; which would be yet much better secured by your slavery.[3] When King Charles the second went to Dover, and the French King came to Calais, gallantry and diversion seemed to be the only business of the two courts. 'Twas not then and in those places publickly known that there was a secret treaty, yet you not only suspected one, but the design and intention of it also; and your suspicions were found to be well grounded.[4] Now though two great armies have been witnesses that the Mareschal de Bouflers and Earl of Portland were for several days imployed in making a treaty (and sure 'twas a secret one, since none of you yet know what it was) you have not to this day taken the least notice of it.[5] But can any man suspect the minister of a prince, who is said to have rejected a crown, and that of no contemptible country, by refusing to join in that very treaty of Dover? Can he, that in a private condition resisted the arts of France, be supposed, now he is master of three kingdoms, and of a powerful state, to risk them all at once, and yield to those arts he before despised? To this, whatever other answer I could give, I shall only say at present that we have always but too just ground to suspect all secret and close negotiations with France. But it seems you thought it not worth your inquiry, whether these negotiations were for your advantage or ruin. You will say, what ground was there of suspicion? For

[3] Fletcher's point is that, by the succession of his grandson to the Spanish crown, Louis XIV had acquired at a stroke the major strongpoints of the Spanish Netherlands, including Antwerp and Brussels, when in the preceding war he had struggled to obtain lesser prizes, such as Condé, much nearer to France. In particular, Louis had now added Ostend and Newport to Dunkirk (which had been sold back to Louis by Charles II in 1662) as Channel ports from which French privateers could harass British shipping and trade.

[4] The Treaty of Dover, agreed on 1 June 1670, was secretly negotiated between Charles II and Louis XIV; its full terms were known only to a small circle of ministers. Ostensibly it provided for a fresh Dutch War, in which England would be the ally of France. Further, undisclosed terms committed Charles II to declare himself a Catholic when the condition of his kingdom permitted, in return for French subsidies and even the loan of French troops. These additional terms were soon leaked, and the so-called 'Secret Treaty' was published in 1682.

[5] The Partition Treaties of 1698 and 1699, by which Emperor Leopold, Louis XIV and William III had sought to agree on a division of the Spanish monarchy, were both negotiated in secret. William Bentinck, earl of Portland, a Dutchman who was one of William's closest advisers, was one of the chief negotiators. Parliament's anger when it learnt of these negotiations made it readier to accept the will of the late Spanish king and the succession of Philip of Anjou. Fletcher's argument was intended to demonstrate the folly of such acquiescence.

nothing appeared. I say, that of all others was the greatest. But who was it, that first as commissionated, and after as embassador, was employed to treat? Was he an Englishman? And how were the plenipotentiaries of this nation used at the formal treaty? Were they not as pageants brought in to attend the show? Or as so many cyphers, that without the Dutchmen, who made the figure, could signify nothing? Yet this advantage we had, that the King having not been owned till the conclusion of the treaty, the abandoning of the protestant religion at Reswick cannot with any colour of justice be imputed to English ministers, but only to the plenipotentiaries of Holland: and you could not by any means conceive or entertain the least suspicion of indirect dealing in the private treaty, when you saw yourselves and your religion so fairly dealt with in that which was publick. Yet methinks, the abandoning of our antient allies, and entring into the closest and most intire correspondence with France that has ever been seen between the two courts, ought to have moved you a little, and made you doubtful that a bargain was struck, unless you can think France uncapable of entring into any that may be to your disadvantage. Here indeed I know not what to say for you: and the best account I can give of your careless indifference, must be to set before you your present condition; which yet I fear will both offend and terrify you; I wish it may not throw you into despair. But such distempers are only to be cured by violent remedies: and I had rather venture your displeasure in doing my duty, than obtain the friendship of your enemies by omitting it. 'Tis then thus. The English nation have now nothing remaining but the outward appearance and carcase, as I may call it, of their antient constitution. The spirit and soul is fled. Jealousy for publick liberty is vanished. The court has so often renewed the same arts, methods and counsels, and so often made trial of the several parties in the kingdom, as well as of the alliance of France, in order to compass their ends, that the nation begins to grow weary of opposing the same things, and very wisely thinks that there can be no danger of such attempts as have so often failed. Besides, you are grown weary of that old and antiquated care and concernment for the publick: or at least have given it a new and better turn. Some of you improving your morals, which are so necessary for the preservation of liberty, in constant gaming, as others do their politicks and skill in military matters by laying wagers. And even stock-jobbing makes you deeply concerned for the publick affairs. Long sessions of parliament furnish great opportunities of knowing the interests of the several parties; by which you must needs know that of the nation, since the nation is made up of parties. And the court by frequent shifting from one party to another, has forced you to double your attendance upon them. So that as well those who are at this time to go off the guard, as those who are coming on, being equally willing, the one to continue, and the other to enter upon duty, the court craftily keeps both parties under arms, whilst the country has nothing to trust to, but a weak, unpaid and disorderly militia party.[6] And now I think I have sufficiently shewn the causes of your present indifference; since having so much business at home, you can hardly attend to what is doing abroad. Yet one would think that a certain affair transacted abroad, in which your ministers are said to have had no small part, and which has made so great a noise in the world, might deserve a little consideration, and oblige you to make some reflection upon the motives of that undertaking. Especially since it is of so extraordinary a nature, as to be the first of the kind, and like to prove of such consequence, as may involve the world in troubles and calamities, which perhaps may be of equal duration with its frame. And though, as a prodigious comet, it has alarm'd the rest of the world, you did not see it 'till of late, and 'tis already vanished by the shutting of your eyes. As to what it may portend, you think it as foolish to enquire, as wise men do to attend the dreams of astrologers. In this I wish I could defend you; but that being utterly impossible, there remains nothing to be done, except only charitably to undeceive you, and shew, if you had time to spare from your great application to maintain the interests of your several parties, what consequences you must necessarily draw from things you all know and acknowledge. By this time you see 'tis the partition-treaty I mean.[7] I say then that from the first appearance of that treaty, it

---

[6] Fletcher identifies the only principled opponents of the court as those who had campaigned in 1697–8 for a reduction in the size of the army, arguing instead for a defence based on the navy and a national militia. The leader of this group within the Commons was Robert Harley, later earl of Oxford; outwith parliament, the campaign against a standing army had been led by the radical Whigs John Trenchard, Walter Moyle and John Toland. Fletcher had written his *Discourse concerning Militias and Standing Armies* (1697) in support of their cause. But his sharp words on the weakness of the militia party may indicate that he now wished to distance himself from them.

[7] See above, note 5.

was not only evident, but foretold by thousands even of the most ordinary capacity, that it would unavoidably throw the whole Spanish monarchy into the house of Bourbon. If some men of more penetration did happen so far to refine, as to put any other construction upon the treaty, it only proceeded from a charitable opinion they had taken up, that the design could not be so black, as it has since appeared by the conduct of most of the partitioners, ever since the death of the King of Spain: which has demonstrated to the world with what intention it was made. The letter of this treaty tells us of preserving the peace of Europe by dismembring the Spanish monarchy; but the spirit throws it intire into the family of Bourbon, intails an endless war upon Christendom, breaks the balance, which has preserved its liberty for two hundred years, and will consequently banish all remains of freedom both civil and religious from among men.[8] This treaty like an alarum-bell rung over all Europe: Pray God it may not prove to you a passing-bell. Poor helpless Spain, rather than divide the child, chose to give it intire to the harlot, to whom it did not belong. And she has got it; for the Solomon who commanded to divide the child, did it not in order to do justice. Instead of the preservation of the peace of Europe (for no great mischief was ever designed, but piety was still pretended) Europe must from this time be either in a posture of war, and so consumed by taxes; or in actual war, wasted by bloodshed and rapine, 'till she be forced to hold out her hands to the shackles, and submit to a worse condition. These are the glorious works of such governours as the world thinks they cannot be without; perhaps too truly: I mean those who are to execute God's judgements upon them. 'Tis evident a treaty was made, which if it had taken effect even in the plain meaning of the words, had broken the balance of Europe, and destroyed your trade in the Mediterranean, under the plausible pretence of avoiding a greater evil, into which it was contrived to throw you. Yet after all, you are positively resolved to rely upon the faith of those who contrived and concerted this, and

[8] The 'balance of Europe' was the term used to describe the result of the rivalry between the Habsburg and Bourbon monarchies in the seventeenth century: by balancing each other's ambition, neither had been able to establish a universal monarchy. The maintenance of this 'balance' became a declared principle of British policy in 1702, when it was invoked as a formal justification for declaring war on France.

obstinately bent to continue in peace, when the rest of Europe are to make the last push for their liberty. As those who are marked out for ruin are first bereft of understanding; so you who see nothing but sham upon sham played upon you, seem to be altogether uncapable of making the least reflection to what end they are designed.

You plainly see that those who have the direction of your affairs, have broken the balance of Europe, and delivered a great part of the world into the hands of France. Yet to this hour it cannot enter into your heads that this was done for any end, nor can you allow it the least reflection. 'Tis true, wise men love not to determine suddenly: you take yet a surer way not to mistake in your determination, which is, not to think. 'Tis commonly said, that in this world nothing is to be had for nothing: but you make no doubt, that almost one half of the world may be given for nothing. The proverb I own is meant of money, and of private persons: but you are of opinion, that princes may be more disinterested, and less wise; or at least, that 'tis not much your business to enquire whether it be so or not. Besides, there is nothing to direct you in an enquiry touching this whole affair, there being no manner of resemblance between this treaty and that of Dover. For though the French King was a party concerned in both; yet he is now grown old, and would willingly, if you permit, pass the rest of his days in peace, and only apply himself to redress the disorders, and restore the vigour of the Spanish monarchy. The condition of the Dutch is much altered since the Dover treaty; for then they were partitioned, but now they are risen to the quality of partitioners. And we are in absolute security that nothing can be stipulated to our prejudice, since he who then gloriously refusing a crown, broke the measures of King Charles and of France, now treats for us, and remains still as generously disinterested as ever, no advantage appearing to accrue by the treaty either to him or his. So that the Dover treaty affording no light at all in this affair, it still remains an impenetrable mystery, why France is allowed so many rich provinces in possession, and so many in reversion. For if the duke of Anjou be any more than a viceroy, 'tis in the power of his grandfather to make him less, and dispose of him and his dominions at his pleasure. But I have found the secret. You will say, pray what is it? What you might have found out as well as I, if you had any goodness in you. 'Twas the pious design of preserving the peace of Europe, on which you see the whole treaty is founded. You will answer; all the world knows this as well as you. Ay; but you don't sufficiently reflect upon the eminent degree of that piety, so clearly demonstrated in a perfect resignation of all that the world calls honour and security, in order to continue the peace and quiet of the poor people of Europe. This was the thing that made us first sacrifice the balance of Christendom, together with a considerable part of our trade. After which, when, by the perfidiousness of our new allies, this treaty, that had cost us such a sacrifice to obtain, was impudently broken to the ruin of the balance, and putting ourselves and antient allies into the most imminent dangers, we took so high an affront, so irreparable an injury with such an absolute resignation, and exemplary patience, as neither by word or deed to shew the least mark of resentment. But like true Christians, that we might do good to those who used us despitefully, and by ways of meekness and condescension, bring them back to a sense of what they owe to us, we delayed the calling of the great council of the nation, till they had sent the new King to his kingdom, and put themselves into a posture of seizing Milan and Flanders, which they have since effected. And now we are so moderate, to ask only a most inconsiderable or rather ridiculous security; perhaps because the French King is now become more solvent. Truly, if we design not to enter into a war, we need not be nice upon any security; for all securities are alike, if France be permitted to increase in power. As to the security of a fleet, I say, that a people, who are resolved to have peace with their neighbours, at a time when 'tis highly the interest of their neighbours to keep peace with them, stand not in need of a fleet, unless it be to make a war of taxes upon themselves. And if the enemy contrary to his present interest, should unite his whole sea-force to attack us, such a fleet as we are now setting out, is exactly calculated to receive damage and affront. But peace, cautionary towns, and moderate fleets will secure our trade, till we have freed ourselves from debt, and are grown so rich, that we can make war when we please. That is, after our enemies shall have disabled all those that we may now have for our allies, and be at leisure to deal with us alone. The honour indeed will be great to be single in the attack, against a power that has baffled the rest of the world: but I fear the danger will be no less; for they always go hand in hand. You'll ask perhaps, what one would have the nation do? Both houses have damned the treaty; and some considerable men may possibly be punished for it. I know there is yet more done; for by excusing the late chancellor, the blame is thrown upon the King; since in all free governments, somebody must be answerable for whatever is done with relation to the publick. But hitherto nothing has been so much as thought of to retrieve us from that ruin, into which the treaty throws us. This is that, which one might justly expect from the nation; and not that they should content themselves with railing at the treaty, whilst they are allowing and concurring in the execution of the real and pernicious design of it. Some will say: let the Emperor and the Dutch be principals in this war; we who formerly were at the greatest expence in opposing France, will now be accessaries, and come in when we think fit. It would seem by this reasoning, that the power of France is diminished, and that you can overtake the growth of it when you please. Who told you that the Dutch, if they find themselves abandoned by you now, will not for the sake of their trade resolve to have peace at any rate? If the Emperor be abandoned by both, is not the business at an end? What business? All opposition, by which the French may be hindered from bringing the affairs of Spain into order, and uniting those vast dominions to their empire. And this naturally leads me again to consider what return may be expected for the contrivance and execution of a treaty so infinitely advantageous to France. For whatever I have said before of a certain pious design; I fear I shall hardly persuade this wicked age of it. And though the Heathens thought virtue a sufficient reward for itself; yet the christian religion with more truth and solidity has accompanied it with other advantages. If then the dominions accruing to France by this treaty, may justly be accounted the greatest that ever were procured for any nation, the returns ought certainly to be the greatest that can be made; or such as the benefactor puts the highest value upon. You'll say, 'tis hard to judge of them; and that if I would insinuate any thing by the mention I made of the Dover treaty, the insinuation is ridiculous in a weakly man, without any probability of issue. I answer, if there should be such a tendency, I hope you do not take it for a virtuous inclination, and consequently ought to judge of it by the temper of the person, and the unreasonableness of every vicious disorder of the mind. No well-natured, generous, unthinking people, can ever penetrate the thoughts of a designing man. Does not an old miser, even though he want issue, increase in covetousness to the last hour of his life? Is ambition a less passion than avarice? Is not the conquest of free men more noble than that of slaves? Did ever any hero refuse to die in a great battle in which kingdoms and powerful states were to fall with him, and serve for trophies to his hearse? But I will shew you the thing in another view, which perhaps will suit better with your temper and disposition. You all say, every prince would be absolute; and this inclination you think so agreeable to the nature of man, that no one can be without it. And indeed it would be strange you should trust them with so much power, under the greatest temptations of employing it that way, if you thought it a great crime to do so. Besides, 'tis not their interest to use arbitrary power cruelly. And you do not know what condition a prince, who in order to good designs should obtain it, might at his death leave you: perhaps in greater liberty than you ever enjoyed. If then pursuant to these or the like thoughts his M[ajesty] should have judged that the monarchy of Spain will prove a burden to the French, and rather weaken than strengthen them; by exhausting their treasures and men in defending and repeopling those countries: If he should have considered, that nothing can so effectually oppose the great and growing power of France, as the united and neighbouring force of England and Holland; countries abounding in people, riches, and store of shipping; provided that force were upon a right foot, as well in respect to secrecy, as the unanimity of counsel and command, flowing from an unjarring direction, not subject to the storms of a H[ouse] of C[ommons] or the capricio's of a free people, little conversant in foreign affairs; (which you will allow to be a very natural thought in a prince.) I say, if upon these considerations, the K[ing] seeing the confederacy falling to pieces, and open force ineffectual, proposed to himself, in order to obtain an advantageous peace, and lay a sure foundation for the destruction of France, to blind them with the ruinous fantom of Spain, and promise to enter into any measures they should propose, in order to deliver it to them, in case they would assist him to establish himself both here and in Holland. Was this design so criminal? Or could France do less for such a benefactor? I am afraid, I have put such a mask of innocence on this affair, that you will begin to like it. And in an age, when divisions and exchanges of countries are so frequently mentioned, who knows, whether the agreement may not be, to unite the whole seventeen provinces to the crown of England, and in lieu of them to give the kingdom of Portugal to Spain, which is a country as much more convenient for Spain than Flanders, as accession of strength is more advantageous than ruin. What a glorious government would the three kingdoms and the seventeen provinces be? Might they not, when united under one wise and absolute prince (for people of such different tempers, and so emulous of each other in trade, seem necessarily to require it) bid defiance not only to France, but to the world? Might they not for ever establish in themselves the empire of the sea, with an entire monopoly of trade;[9] especially if it should please him to crown all his other actions, by leaving them possessed of such immunities as might secure the continuation of their trade for ever? Is there, after all, such a probable way of resisting the power of France? Or is it not the only way of saving both us and our religion, which is our main concern? You being men of understanding, I resolve to leave it thus with you, though you should think me a courtier. For according to the judgement you shall make of what I have said, it will appear, whether it be possible to save you or not, and consequently whether it be to any purpose to give you or myself any farther trouble.[10]

Τυραννος ἐων, τυραννῳ συγκατεργαζεται
Herodot. Urania.[11]

---

[9] English commentators had previously accused the Dutch of harbouring this ambition, and thus of seeking to establish a universal monarchy by sea: John Evelyn, *Navigation and Commerce, Their Original and Progress* (London, 1674).

[10] Fletcher was in effect accusing William III of the ambition to create for himself an absolute monarchy, which by combining the three kingdoms of England, Scotland and Ireland with all seventeen provinces of the Netherlands, would be more than a match for the new Bourbon monarchy of France and Spain. The implication is not that this would contribute to a better balance of power in Europe; by capturing the 'empire of the sea', William would be in a position to rival Louis XIV in the pursuit of universal monarchy.

[11] Herodotus, *Histories*, Book VIII ('Urania'), para. 142: 'a tyrant himself, he would be a tyrant's assistant'.

SPEECHES
by a
MEMBER OF THE PARLIAMENT

Which
Began at Edinburgh the 6th of May, 1703.

Edinburgh;
Printed in the Year MDCCIII.

Advertisement

Some of the following Speeches are not placed in the order they were spoken; but in such an order as the matters they contain seem to require.[1]

[1] A new parliament was called for May 1703, in order to confirm the accession of Anne as Queen of Scotland, to settle the succession to the throne thereafter, and to raise supply. The previous parliament, which had held its last session in June 1702, was the one elected in 1689, to which Fletcher had addressed the *Two Discourses concerning the Affairs of Scotland* in 1698. Its final session had met later than the stipulated number of days after Anne's accession, with the result that its legality, and the legality of its Acts, had been questioned. Since then Commissioners for Union had been appointed and had begun negotiations for a formal treaty of union between Scotland and England; but the negotiations had stalled by February 1703. The court therefore had no option but to call a new parliament, with fresh elections, if it was to settle the succession and raise money. The question of the succession was critical, for Queen Anne was no longer expected to have surviving heirs, and the exiled Catholic Stewarts were waiting for an opportunity to return, while their Jacobite supporters at home were sufficiently numerous to pose a substantial political threat to the Protestant interest. The English parliament had already settled the succession on the House of Hanover by the Act of Settlement of 1701; this made no mention of the Crown of Scotland, but the Scots understood it to be an implicit demand to adopt the same succession.

Fletcher, who had not been a member of the previous parliament, was now elected as one of the members for the county of East Lothian. In the following notes his speeches will whenever possible be dated from four sources: *The Acts of the Parliament of Scotland; XI: 1702–1707* (1824), pp. 29–112 [hereafter: *APS XI*]; *The Proceedings of the Parliament of Scotland: begun at Edinburgh, 6th May 1703. With an Account of all the material Debates which occur'd during that Session*, an anonymous account, unofficially compiled (1704) [hereafter: *Proceedings*]; [George Ridpath], *An Account of the Proceedings of the parliament of Scotland, which met at Edinburgh, May 6, 1703* (1704) [hereafter: Ridpath, *Account*]; Sir David Hume of Crossrig, *A Diary of the Proceedings in the Parliament and Privy Council of Scotland 21 May 1700–7 May 1707* (Edinburgh: Bannatyne Club, 1828) [hereafter: Hume, *Diary*]. On the evidence of these, it would seem that the speeches were delivered on dates in the following order:

26 May 1703	Speech I
28 May	II
17 June	XVII
22 June	III
22 June or 1 July	IV
7 July	V
7 July	VI
2 or 7 August	XII
10 August	VII
10 August	VIII
16 August	IX
20 (or 17) August	X
20 August	XI
9 September	XIII
13 or 14 September	XV
14 September	XVI
15 September	XIV.

I

My Lord Chancellor,[2]

I am not surprized to find an act for a supply brought into this house at the beginning of a session. I know custom has for a long time made it common. But I think experience might teach us, that such acts should be the last of every session; or lie upon the table, 'till all other great affairs of the nation be finished, and then only granted. 'Tis a strange proposition which is usually made in this house; that if we will give money to the crown, then the crown will give us good laws: as if we were to buy good laws of the crown, and pay money to our princes, that they may do their duty, and comply with their coronation oath. And yet this is not the worst; for we have often had promises of good laws, and when we have given the sums demanded, those promises have been broken, and the nation left to seek a remedy; which is not to be found, unless we obtain the laws we want, before we give a supply. And if this be a sufficient reason at all times to postpone a money-act, can we be blamed for doing so at this time, when the duty we owe to our country, indispensably obliges us to provide for the common safety in case of an event, altogether out of our power, and which must necessarily dissolve the government, unless we continue and secure it by new laws; I mean the death of her Majesty, which God in his mercy long avert? I move therefore, that the house would take into consideration what acts are necessary to secure our religion, liberty, and trade, in case of the said event, before any act of supply, or other business whatever be brought into deliberation.

Act concerning offices, &c.
brought in by the same member.

The estates of Parliament taking into their consideration, that to the great loss and detriment of this nation, great sums of money are yearly

---

[2] An Act for Supply was introduced on 19 May, and its First Reading moved on 26 May, but it was countered by an Overture given by the marquis of Tweeddale that parliament should first consider an Act for Securing the Religion, Liberty and Trade of the Kingdom, settling the conditions of government after the decease of Her Majesty and the heirs of her body. A lengthy debate ensued, and continued on 28 May, until the Overture was accepted. Fletcher's speech was probably given on 26 May (Hume, *Diary*, p. 100), and the accompanying draft of an Act concern-

carried out of it, by those who wait and depend at court, for places and preferments in this kingdom: and that by Scotsmen, employing English interest at court, in order to obtain their several pretensions, this nation is in hazard of being brought to depend upon English ministers: and likewise considering, that by reason our princes do no more reside amongst us, they cannot be rightly informed of the merit of persons pretending to places, offices, and pensions; therefore our Sovereign Lady, with advice and consent of the estates of parliament, statutes and ordains, that after the decease of her Majesty (whom God long preserve) and heirs of her body failing, all places and offices, both civil and military, and all pensions, formerly conferred by our Kings, shall ever after be given by parliament, by way of ballot.

II

My Lord Chancellor,[3]

When our Kings succeeded to the crown of England, the ministers of that nation took a short way to ruin us, by concurring with their inclinations to extend the prerogative in Scotland; and the great places and pensions conferred upon Scots-men by that court, made them to be willing instruments in the work. From that time this nation began to give away their privileges one after the other, though they then stood more in need of having them enlarged. And as the collections of our laws, before the union of the crowns, are full of acts to secure our liberty, those laws that have been made since that time are directed chiefly to extend the prerogative. And that we might not know what rights and liberties were still ours, nor be excited by the memory of what our ancestors enjoyed, to recover those we had lost, in the two last editions of our acts of parliament the most considerable laws for the liberty of the subject are industriously and designedly left out.[4] All our affairs since the

---

ing Offices was read on 28 May. The Lord Chancellor to whom the speech was formally addressed was the earl of Seafield.

[3] Not referred to by any of the four sources, it seems likely to have been given on 28 May, to reinforce the case for the preceding draft of an Act.

[4] The most recent general collections of Scottish Acts were those of Sir T. Murray, *The Laws and Acts of Parliament made by James I–Charles II* (Edinburgh, 1681); and Sir James Steuart, *An Index and Abridgement of the Acts of Parliament made by James I . . . Charles II* (Edinburgh, 1685); another edition, *continued to the Ninth Session of the current Parliament* (Edinburgh, 1702).

union of the crowns have been managed by the advice of English ministers, and the principal offices of the kingdom filled with such men, as the court of England knew would be subservient to their designs: by which means they have had so visible an influence upon our whole administration, that we have from that time appeared to the rest of the world more like a conquered province, than a free independent people. The account is very short: whilst our princes are not absolute in England, they must be influenced by that nation; our ministers must follow the directions of the prince, or lose their places, and our places and pensions will be distributed according to the inclinations of a king of England, so long as a king of England has the disposal of them: neither shall any man obtain the least advancement, who refuses to vote in council and parliament under that influence. So that there is no way to free this country from a ruinous dependence upon the English court, unless by placing the power of conferring offices and pensions in the parliament, so long as we shall have the same king with England. The antient Kings of Scotland, and even those of France, had not the power of conferring the chief offices of state, though each of them had only one kingdom to govern, and that the difficulty we labour under, of two kingdoms which have different interests governed by the same king, did not occur. Besides, we all know that the disposal of our places and pensions is so considerable a thing to a king of England, that several of our princes, since the union of the crowns, have wished to be free from the trouble of deciding between the many pretenders. That which would have given them ease, will give us liberty, and make us significant to the common interest of both nations. Without this, 'tis impossible to free us from a dependence on the English court: all other remedies and conditions of government will prove ineffectual, as plainly appears from the nature of the thing; for who is not sensible of the influence of places and pensions upon all men and all affairs? If our ministers continue to be appointed by the English court, and this nation may not be permitted to dispose of the offices and places of this kingdom to balance the English bribery, they will corrupt every thing to that degree, that if any of our laws stand in their way, they will get them repealed. Let no man say, that it cannot be proved that the English court has ever bestowed any bribe in this country. For they bestow all offices and pensions; they bribe us, and are masters of us at our own cost. 'Tis nothing but an English interest in this house, that those who wish well to our country, have to struggle with at this time. We may, if we please, dream of other remedies; but so long as Scots-men must go to the English court to obtain offices of trust or profit in this kingdom, those offices will always be managed with regard to the court and interest of England, though to the betraying of the interest of this nation, whenever it comes in competition with that of England. And what less can be expected, unless we resolve to expect miracles, and that greedy, ambitious, and for the most part necessitous men, involved in great debts, burdened with great families, and having great titles to support, will lay down their places, rather than comply with an English interest in obedience to the prince's commands? Now to find Scotsmen opposing this, and willing that English ministers (for this is the case) should have the disposal of places and pensions in Scotland, rather than their own parliament, is matter of great astonishment; but that it should be so much as a question in the parliament, is altogether incomprehensible: and if an indifferent person were to judge, he would certainly say we were an English parliament. Every man knows that princes give places and pensions by the influence of those who advise them. So that the question comes to no more than, whether this nation would be in a better condition, if in conferring our places and pensions the prince should be determined by the parliament of Scotland, or by the ministers of a court, that make it their interest to keep us low and miserable. We all know that this is the cause of our poverty, misery and dependence. But we have been for a long time so poor, so miserable and depending, that we have neither heart nor courage, though we want not the means, to free ourselves.

III

My Lord Chancellor,[5]

Prejudice and opinion govern the world to the great distress and ruin of mankind; and though we daily find men so rational as to charm by the disinterested rectitude of their sentiments in all other

---

[5] Ridpath, *Account*, p. 132, dates this speech to 22 June. A draft Act of Security had been introduced on 28 May, and was considered on 1, 3 and 9 June; there was an interval before consideration resumed on 22 June.

things, yet when we touch upon any wrong opinion with which they have been early prepossessed, we find them more irrational than any thing in nature; and not only not to be convinced, but obstinately resolved not to hear any reason against it. These prejudices are yet stronger when they are taken up by great numbers of men, who confirm each other through the course of several generations, and seem to have their blood tainted, or, to speak more properly, their animal spirits influenced by them. Of these delusions, one of the strongest and most pernicious, has been a violent inclination in many men to extend the prerogative of the prince to an absolute and unlimited power. And though in limited monarchies all good men profess and declare themselves enemies to all tyrannical practices, yet many, even of these, are found ready to oppose such necessary limitations as might secure them from the tyrannical exercise of power in a prince, not only subject to all the infirmities of other men, but by the temptations arising from his power, to far greater. This humour has greatly increas'd in our nation, since the union of the crowns; and the slavish submissions, which have been made necessary to procure the favours of the court, have cherished and fomented a slavish principle. But I must take leave to put the representatives of this nation in mind, that no such principles were in this kingdom before the union of the crowns; and that no monarchy in Europe was more limited, nor any people more jealous of liberty than the Scots. These principles were first introduced among us after the union of the crowns, and the prerogative extended to the overthrow of our antient constitution, chiefly by the prelatical party; though the peevish, imprudent, and detestable conduct of the presbyterians, who opposed these principles only in others, drove many into them, gave them greater force, and rooted them more deeply in this nation.[6] Should we not be ashamed to embrace opinions contrary to reason, and contrary to the sentiments of our ancestors, merely upon account of the uncharitable and insupportable humour and ridiculous conduct of bigots of any sort? If then no such principles were in this nation, and the constitution

---

[6] The 'Prelatical Party' refers to those who supported the attempts of the Stewarts to impose episcopacy on the Scottish Church: after the Revolution these became avowed Episcopalians. The 'Presbyterians' are here broadly identified with those who adhered to the National Covenant of 1638, and who thereafter fought to get the Crown to accept a presbyterian form of church government.

of our government had greatly limited the prince's power before the union of the crowns; dare any man say he is a Scots-man, and refuse his consent to reduce the government of this nation, after the expiration of the intail, within the same limits as before that union?[7] And if since the union of the crowns, every one sees that we stand in need of more limitations; will any man act in so direct an opposition to his own reason, and the undoubted interest of his country, as not to concur in limiting the government yet more than before the union, particularly by the addition of this so necessary limitation for which I am now speaking? My Lord, these are such clear demonstrations of what we ought to do in such conjunctures, that all men of common ingenuity must be ashamed of entring into any other measures. Let us not then tread in the steps of mean and fawning priests of any sort, who are always disposed to place an absolute power in the prince, if he on his part will gratify their ambition, and by all means support their form of church-government, to the persecution of all other men, who will not comply with their impositions. Let us begin where our ancestors left before the union of the crowns, and be for the future more jealous of our liberties, because there is more need. But I must take upon me to say, that he who is not for setting great limitations upon the power of the prince, particularly that for which I am speaking, in case we have the same king with England, can act by no principle, whether he be a presbyterian, prelatical, or prerogative-man, for the court of St. Germains, or that of Hanover;[8] I say, he can act by no principle unless that of being a slave to the court of England for his own advantage. And therefore let not those who go under the name of prerogative-men, cover themselves with the pretext of principles in this case; for such men are plainly for the prerogative of the English court over this nation, because this limitation is demanded only in case we come to have the same king with England.

[7] An 'intail' or entail was the device by which an inheritance (usually of land) was passed down through the generations, on terms which prevented the current possessor from alienating, dividing or redirecting the inheritance. Fletcher uses the term here to refer to the Stewart succession to the Scottish Crown, which was by now expected to determine on Anne's death, none of her children having survived.

[8] St Germains was short-hand for the exiled House of Stewart, which Louis XIV had allowed to establish its court in the palace of St Germains in Paris. Hanover referred to the family holding the electorate of Hanover, which had already been designated to succeed to the English Crown.

Act for the security of the kingdom,
brought in by the same member.[9]

The estates of parliament considering, that when it shall please God to afflict this nation with the death of our Sovereign Lady the Queen (whom God of his infinite mercy long preserve) if the same shall happen to be without heirs of her body, this kingdom may fall into great confusion and disorder before a successor can be declared. For preventing thereof, our Sovereign Lady, with advice and consent of the estates of parliament, statutes and ordains, that if at the foresaid time, any parliament or convention of estates shall be assembled, then the members of that parliament or convention of estates shall take the administration of the government upon them: excepting those barons and burroughs, who at the foresaid time shall have any place or pension, mediately or immediately of the crown: whose commissions are hereby declared to be void; and that new members shall be chosen in their place: but if there be no parliament or convention of estates actually assembled, then the members of the current parliament shall assemble with all possible diligence: and if there be no current parliament, then the members of the last dissolved parliament, or convention of estates, shall assemble in like manner: and in those two last cases, so soon as there shall be one hundred members met, in which number the barons and burroughs beforementioned are not to be reckoned, they shall take the administration of the government upon them: but neither they, nor the members of parliament, or convention of estates, if at the time foresaid assembled, shall proceed to the weighty affair of naming and declaring a successor, 'till twenty days after they have assumed the administration of the government: both that there may be time for all the other members to come to Edinburgh, which is hereby declared the place of their meeting, and for the elections of new barons and burroughs in place above-mentioned. But so soon as the twenty days are elapsed, then they shall proceed to the publishing by proclamation the conditions of government, on which they will receive the successor to the imperial crown of this realm;[10] which in

---

[9] Fletcher's draft Act of Security was introduced on 22 June, and was ordered to be printed: *APS XI*, p. 63; Ridpath, *Account*, p. 132.

[10] The Scottish Crown had been regarded as an 'imperial' crown since the mid-fifteenth century: technically this indicated that the crown itself was 'closed' over the head of the king; in principle it asserted that the kingdom was completely independent, acknowledging neither pope nor emperor, let alone any other king

the case only of our being under the same king with England, are as follows.

1   *That elections shall be made at every Michaelmas head-court for a new parliament every year; to sit the first of November next following, and adjourn themselves from time to time, till next Michaelmas: that they chuse their own president, and that every thing shall be determined by ballotting, in place of voting.*[11]

2   *That so many lesser barons shall be added to the parliament, as there have been noblemen created since the last augmentation of the number of the barons; and that in all time coming, for every nobleman that shall be created, there shall be a baron added to the parliament.*[12]

3   *That no man have vote in parliament, but a nobleman or elected member.*

4   *That the king shall give the sanction to all laws offered by the estates; and that the president of the parliament be impowered by his majesty to give the sanction in his absence, and have ten pounds sterling a day salary.*

5   *That a committee of one and thirty members, of which nine to be a quorum, chosen out of their own number, by every parliament, shall, during the intervals of parliament, under the king, have the administration of the government, be his council, and accountable to the next parliament; with power in extraordinary occasions, to call the parliament together: and that in the said council, all things be determined by ballotting in place of voting.*[13]

or prince, as superior over it. The status was still being challenged by English historical propagandists, and on 30 June the Scottish parliament condemned 'a book publisht by the title of *Historia Anglo-Scotica* by D. Drake M.D. and dedicated to Sir Edward Seymour, containing many false and injurious reflections upon the soveraignty and independency of this crown, and nation, to be burnt by the hand of the hangman': *Proceedings*, p. 22. See William Ferguson, 'Imperial Crowns: a neglected facet of the background to the Treaty of Union', *Scottish Historical Review*, 53 (1974).

[11] The Michaelmas Head Court was the annual meeting of the freeholders of the county, these alone being entitled to vote. Fletcher is demanding annual elections to parliament; by 'ballotting' he meant secret voting, but probably did not also mean that representatives should be chosen by lot.

[12] Lesser barons were members of the Second Estate, while the titled nobility were the First Estate. Commissioners of the Shires (such as Fletcher was for East Lothian) were lesser barons.

[13] This would replace the Committee of the Articles, the standing committee of the Scottish parliament, whose membership, by skilful manipulation, had come to depend on the choice of the crown, and which as a result had enabled the Crown to control parliamentary proceedings and legislation.

6   *That the king without consent of parliament shall not have the power
     of making peace and war; or that of concluding any treaty with any
     other state or potentate.*

7   *That all places and offices, both civil and military, and all pensions
     formerly conferred by our kings, shall ever after be given by
     parliament.*

8   *That no regiment or company of horse, foot, or dragoons be kept on
     foot in peace or war, but by consent of parliament.*

9   *That all the fencible men of the nation, betwixt sixty and sixteen, be
     with all diligence possible armed with bayonets, and firelocks all of a
     calibre, and continue always provided in such arms with ammunition
     suitable.*[14]

10   *That no general indemnity, nor pardon for any transgression against
     the publick, shall be valid without consent of parliament.*

11   *That the fifteen senators of the college of justice shall be incapable of
     being members of parliament, or of any other office, or any pension:
     but the salary that belongs to their place to be increased as the parlia-
     ment shall think fit: that the office of president shall be in three of
     their number to be named by parliament, and that there be no extra-
     ordinary lords. And also, that the lords of the justice court shall be
     distinct from those of the session, and under the same restrictions.*[15]

12   *That if any king break in upon any of these conditions of government,
     he shall by the estates be declared to have forfeited the crown.*

*Which proclamation made, they are to go on to the naming and
declaring a successor: and when he is declared, if present, are to read to
him the claim of right and conditions of government abovementioned,
and to desire of him, that he may accept the crown accordingly; and he
accepting, they are to administer to him the oath of coronation: but if
the successor be not present, they are to delegate such of their own number
as they shall think fit, to see the same performed, as said is: and are to
continue in the administration of the government, until the successor his
accepting of the crown, upon the foresaid terms be known to them:
whereupon having then a king at their head, they shall by his authority*

---

[14] 'Fencible men' were those capable of bearing arms.

[15] The highest courts in Scotland were the Court of Session, for civil cases, and the
High Court of Justiciary, for criminal cases. The Court of Session consisted of 14
lords of session and a lord president; the Justiciary Court of a lord justice clerk
and other judges drawn from the lords of session. Fletcher proposed to alter these
arrangements by dividing the two courts, and by sharing the lord presidency
among three judges.

declare themselves a parliament, and proceed to the doing of whatever shall be thought expedient for the welfare of the realm. And it is likewise by the authority aforesaid declared, that if her present majesty shall think fit, during her own time, with advice and consent of the estates of parliament, failing heirs of her body, to declare a successor, yet nevertheless, after her Majesty's decease, the members of parliament or convention shall in the several cases, and after the manner above-specified, meet and admit the successor to the government, in the terms and after the manner as said is. And it is hereby further declared, that after the decease of her Majesty, and failing heirs of her body, the forementioned manner and method shall in the several cases be that of declaring and admitting to the government all those who shall hereafter succeed to the imperial crown of this realm; and that it shall be high treason for any man to own or acknowledge any person as king or queen of this realm, till they are declared and admitted in the abovementioned manner. And lastly, it is hereby declared, that by the death of her Majesty, or any of her successors, all commissions, both civil and military, fall and are void. And that this act shall come in place of the seventeenth act of the sixth session of King William's parliament.[16] *And all acts and laws, that any way derogate from this present act, are hereby in so far declared void and abrogated.*

IV

My Lord Chancellor,[17]

'Tis the utmost height of human prudence to see and embrace every favourable opportunity: and if a word spoken in season does for the most part produce wonderful effects; of what consequence and advantage must it be to a nation in deliberations of the highest moment; in occasions, when past, for ever irretrievable, to enter into the right path, and take hold of the golden opportunity, which

---

[16] The 17th Act of the sixth session of William's parliament was the Act of Security of 1696, which provided that all commissions, civil or military, should remain in force on the death of the sovereign: *APS X*, pp. 59–60.

[17] Ridpath, *Account*, pp. 140ff., presents this speech as following directly on from the Limitations, and as being given in their defence, which would date it also to 22 June. Alternatively, it might have been given on 1 July, when Fletcher moved that before approving the Act of Security parliament should first consider the Limitations to be put on the next successor to the throne: *Proceedings*, p. 22; Hume, *Diary*, p. 112.

makes the most arduous things easy, and without which the most inconsiderable may put a stop to all our affairs? We have this day an opportunity in our hands which if we manage to the advantage of the nation we have the honour to represent, we may, so far as the vicissitude and uncertainty of human affairs will permit, be for many ages easy and happy. But if we despise or neglect this occasion, we have voted our perpetual dependence on another nation. If men could always retain those just impressions of things they at some times have upon their minds, they would be much more steddy in their actions. And as I may boldly say, that no man is to be found in this house, who at some time or other has not had that just sense of the miserable condition to which this nation is reduced by a dependence upon the English court, I should demand no more but the like impressions at this time to pass all the limitations mentioned in the draught of an act I have already brought into this house; since they are not limitations upon any prince, who shall only be king of Scotland, nor do any way tend to separate us from England; but calculated merely to this end, that so long as we continue to be under the same prince with our neighbour nation, we may be free from the influence of English councils and ministers; that the nation may not be impoverished by an expensive attendance at court, and that the force and exercise of our government may be, as far as is possible, within ourselves. By which means trade, manufactures, and husbandry will flourish, and the affairs of the nation be no longer neglected, as they have been hitherto. These are the ends to which all the limitations are directed, that English councils may not hinder the acts of our parliaments from receiving the royal assent; that we may not be ingaged without our consent in the quarrels they may have with other nations; that they may not obstruct the meeting of our parliaments, nor interrupt their sitting; that we may not stand in need of posting to London for places and pensions, by which, whatever particular men may get, the nation must always be a loser, nor apply for the remedies of our grievances to a court, where for the most part none are to be had. On the contrary, if these conditions of government be enacted, our constitution will be amended, and our grievances be easily redressed by a due execution of our own laws, which to this day we have never been able to obtain. The best and wisest men in England will be glad to hear that these limitations are settled by us. For though the ambition of courtiers lead them to desire an uncontroulable power at any rate; yet wiser men will consider that when two nations live under the same prince, the condition of the one cannot be made intolerable, but a separation must inevitably follow, which will be dangerous if not destructive to both. The senate of Rome wisely determined in the business of the Privernates, that all people would take hold of the first opportunity to free themselves from an uneasy condition; that no peace could be lasting, in which both parties did not find their account; and that no alliance was strong enough to keep two nations in amity, if the condition of either were made worse by it.[18] For my own part, my lord Chancellor, before I will consent to continue in our present miserable and languishing condition after the decease of her Majesty, and heirs of her body failing, I shall rather give my vote for a separation from England at any rate. I hope no man who is now possessed of an office, will take umbrage at these conditions of government, though some of them seem to diminish, and others do intirely suppress the place he possesses: for besides the scandal of preferring a private interest before that of our country, these limitations are not to take place immediately. The Queen is yet young, and by the grace of God may live many years, I hope longer than all those she has placed in any trust; and should we not be happy, if those who for the future may design to recommend themselves for any office, could not do it by any other way than the favour of this house, which they who appear for these conditions will deserve in a more eminent degree? Would we rather court an English minister for a place than a parliament of Scotland? Are we afraid of being taken out of the hands of English courtiers, and left to govern ourselves? And do we doubt whether an English ministry, or a Scots parliament will be most for the interest of Scotland? But that which seems most difficult in this question, and in which, if satisfaction be given, I hope no man will pretend to be dissatisfied with these limitations, is the interest of a

[18] The Privernates were the inhabitants of Privernum, a city of the Volscians, south of Rome. After intermittent conflict with the Romans between 358 and 329 BC, when the city finally submitted, the Privernates were admitted to citizenship of Rome. This was granted following a debate in the senate in which one of the deputation from Privernum challenged the Romans to offer a good peace, for otherwise it could not be expected to last. Fletcher follows Livy, Book VIII, ch. xxi, and Machiavelli, *Discorsi*, II.xxiii, who quotes extensively from Livy's account of the debate.

king of Great Britain. And here I shall take liberty to say, that as the limitations do no way affect any prince that may be king of Scotland only, so they will be found highly advantageous to a king of Great Britain.[19] Some of our late kings, when they have been perplexed about the affairs of Scotland, did let fall such expressions, as intimated they thought them not worth their application. And indeed we ought not to wonder if princes, like other men, should grow weary of toiling where they find no advantage. But to set this affair in a true light: I desire to know, whether it can be more advantageous to a king of Great Britain to have an unlimited prerogative over this country in our present ill condition, which turns to no account, than that this nation grown rich and powerful under these conditions of government, should be able upon any emergency to furnish a good body of land forces, with a squadron of ships for war, all paid by ourselves, to assist his Majesty in the wars he may undertake for the defence of the protestant religion and liberties of Europe. Now since I hope I have shewn, that those who are for the prerogative of the kings of Scotland, and all those who are possessed of places at this time, together with the whole English nation, as well as a king of Great Britain, have cause to be satisfied with these regulations of government, I would know what difficulty can remain; unless that being accustomed to live in a dependency and unacquainted with liberty, we know not so much as the meaning of the word; nor if that should be explained to us, can ever persuade ourselves we shall obtain the thing, though we have it in our power by a few votes to set ourselves and our posterity free. To say that this will stop at the royal assent, is a suggestion disrespectful to her Majesty, and which ought neither to be mentioned in parliament, nor be considered by any member of this house. And were this a proper time, I am confident I could say such things as being represented to the Queen, would convince her, that no person can have greater interest, nor obtain more lasting honour by the enacting of these conditions of government, than her Majesty. And if the nation be assisted in this exigency by the good offices of his grace the high

---

[19] Fletcher's reference to a 'king of Great Britain' did not reflect current usage. Although James VI and I had himself proclaimed 'King of Great Britain', the title was not acknowledged in statute by either the Scottish or English parliaments, and was not used by any of his Stewart successors, until it was formally created for Queen Anne in the Acts of Union in 1707.

Commissioner, I shall not doubt to affirm, that in procuring this
blessing to our country from her Majesty, he will do more for us,
than all the great men of that noble family, of which he is
descended, ever did; though it seems to have been their peculiar
province for divers ages, to defend the liberties of this nation against
the power of the English and the deceit of courtiers.[20] What further
arguments can I use to persuade this house to enact these limitations, and embrace this occasion, which we have so little deserved?
I might bring many; but the most proper and effectual to persuade
all, I take to be this: that our ancestors did enjoy the most essential
liberties contained in the act I have proposed: and though some few
of less moment are among them which they had not, yet they were
in possession of divers others not contained in these articles: that
they enjoyed these privileges when they were separated from England, had their prince living among them, and consequently stood
not in so great need of these limitations.[21] Now since we have been
under the same prince with England, and therefore stand in the
greatest need of them, we have not only neglected to make a due
provision of that kind, but in divers parliaments have given away
our liberties, and upon the matter subjected this crown to the court
of England: and are become so accustomed to depend on them, that
we seem to doubt whether we shall lay hold of this happy opportunity to resume our freedom. If nothing else will move us, at least
let us not act in opposition to the light of our own reason and
conscience, which daily represents to us the ill constitution of our
government; the low condition into which we are sunk, and the
extreme poverty, distress, and misery of our people. Let us consider

[20] The high commissioner was appointed by the Queen to act in her stead in the
Parliament. On this occasion the high commissioner was James Douglas, second
duke of Queensberry. The Douglas family had led the struggle against the English
(and, often, against the Scottish) crown since the fourteenth century. But this was
the same Queensberry that Fletcher had so sharply criticised for deserting his
command in the *Two Discourses concerning the Affairs of Scotland*: see above,
p. 47.

[21] Fletcher's sweeping, perhaps deliberately inexact claim that the Scots had enjoyed
these liberties prior to the Union of the Crowns in 1603 is hard to verify: given
the power exercised in the Scottish parliament by the Committee of the Articles,
the claim is improbable. Although he did not say so, Fletcher's programme of
Limitations did, however, bear a significant resemblance to the legislation enacted
by the Covenanter Parliament in 1641, and to the demands of 'the Club' of radical
members of the Estates in 1689. (While not a member of that parliament, Fletcher
had been associated with the Club.)

whether we will have the nation continue in these deplorable circumstances, and lose this opportunity of bringing freedom and
plenty among us. Sure the heart of every honest man must bleed
daily, to see the misery in which our commons, and even many of
our gentry live; which has no other cause but the ill constitution of
our government, and our bad government no other root, but our
dependence upon the court of England. If our kings lived among
us, 'twould not be strange to find these limitations rejected. 'Tis
not the prerogative of a king of Scotland I would diminish, but the
prerogative of English ministers over this nation. To conclude,
these conditions of government being either such as our ancestors
enjoyed, or principally directed to cut off our dependence on an
English court, and not to take place during the life of the Queen;
he who refuses his consent to them, whatever he may be by birth,
cannot sure be a Scots-man by affection. This will be a true test to
distinguish, not whig from tory, presbyterian from episcopal, Hanover from St. Germains, nor yet a courtier from a man out of place;
but a proper test to distinguish a friend from an enemy to his
country. And indeed we are split into so many parties, and cover
ourselves with so many false pretexts, that such a test seems necessary to bring us into the light, and shew every man in his own
colours. In a word, my lord Chancellor, we are to consider, that
though we suffer under many grievances, yet our dependence upon
the court of England is the cause of all, comprehends them all, and
is the band that ties up the bundle. If we break this, they will all
drop and fall to the ground: if not, this band will straiten us more
and more, till we shall be no longer a people.

I therefore humbly propose, that for the security of our religion,
liberty, and trade, these limitations be declared by a resolution of
this house to be the conditions, upon which the nation will receive a
successor to the crown of this realm after the decease of her present
Majesty, and failing heirs of her body, in case the said successor
shall be also King or Queen of England.

V

My Lord Chancellor,[22]

I am sorry to hear what has been just now spoken from the throne. I know the duty I owe to her Majesty, and the respect that is due to her Commissioner; and therefore shall speak with a just regard to both. But the duty I owe to my country obliges me to say, that what we have now heard from the throne, must of necessity proceed from English councils. If we had demanded that these limitations should take place during the life of her Majesty, or of the heirs of her body, perhaps we might have no great reason to complain, though they should be refused. But that her Majesty should prefer the prerogative of she knows not who, to the happiness of the whole people of Scotland; that she should deny her assent to such conditions of government as are not limitations upon the crown of Scotland, but only such as are absolutely necessary to relieve us from a subjection to the court of England, must proceed from English councils; as well because there is no Scots minister now at London, as because I have had an account, which I believe to be too well grounded, that a letter to this effect has been sent down hither by the lord Treasurer of England, not many days ago.[23] Besides, all men who have lately been at London, well know, that nothing has been more common, than to see Scots-men of the several parties addressing themselves to English ministers about Scots affairs; and even to some ladies of that court, whom for the respect I bear to their relations I shall not name. Now, whether we shall continue under the influence and subjection of the English court; or whether it be not high time to lay before her Majesty, by a vote of this house, the conditions of government upon which we will receive a successor, I leave to the wisdom of the parliament. This I

---

[22] Although printed by Ridpath, *Account*, pp. 290–3, this speech is not dated by him. Consideration of the Acts of Security was resumed on 1 July, and a speech very similar to this is reported in the *Proceedings*, pp. 25–6, to have been given on 7 July; Hume, *Diary*, p. 115, also records that on 7 July Saltoun provoked 'a great hubbub' by claiming that Scotland's kings since the union of the crowns 'were under the influence of English counsels, and it appeared to be so from what the Commissioner had spoke'.

[23] The Lord Treasurer of England at this point was the 1st earl of Godolphin. He advised the queen to reject the Act of Security, and did not relent until 1704, when supply was 'tacked' onto it (making taxes dependent on the Crown's acceptance of the Act of Security).

must say, that to tell us any thing of her Majesty's intentions in this affair, before we have presented any act to that purpose for the royal assent, is to prejudge the cause, and altogether unparliamentary. I will add, that nothing has ever shewn the power and force of English councils upon our affairs in a more eminent manner at any time, since the union of the crowns. No man in this house is more convinced of the great advantage of that peace which both nations enjoy by living under one prince. But as on the one hand, some men for private ends, and in order to get into offices, have either neglected or betrayed the interest of this nation, by a mean compliance with the English court; so on the other side it cannot be denied, that we have been but indifferently used by the English nation. I shall not insist upon the affair of Darien, in which by their means and influence chiefly, we suffered so great a loss both in men and money, as to put us almost beyond hope of ever having any considerable trade; and this contrary to their own true interest, which now appears but too visibly.[24] I shall not go about to enumerate instances of a provoking nature in other matters, but keep myself precisely to the thing we are upon. The English nation did, some time past, take into consideration the nomination of a successor to that crown; an affair of the highest importance, and one would think of common concernment to both kingdoms. Did they ever require our concurrence? Did they ever desire the late King to cause the parliament of Scotland to meet, in order to take our advice and consent? Was not this to tell us plainly, that we ought to be concluded by their determinations, and were not worthy to be consulted in the matter?[25] Indeed, my lord Chancellor, considering their whole carriage in this affair, and the broad insinuations we have now heard, that we are not to expect her Majesty's assent to any limitations on a successor (which must proceed from English council) and considering we cannot propose to ourselves any other relief from that servitude we lie under by the influence of that court; 'tis my opinion, that the house come to a resolution, *That after the decease of her Majesty, heirs of her body failing, we will separate our crown from that of England.*

[24] The second expedition to Darien, sent to relieve the first, had failed in 1700, provoking fierce recrimination at the expense of the English.

[25] A reference to the English Act of Settlement of 1701, on which see note 1.

VI

My Lord Chancellor,[26]

That there should be limitations on a successor, in order to take away our dependence on the court of England, if both nations should have the same king, no man here seems to oppose. And I think very few will be of opinion that such limitations should be deferred till the meeting of the nation's representatives upon the decease of her Majesty. For if the successor be not named before that time, every one will be so earnest to promote the pretensions of the person he most affects, that new conditions will be altogether forgotten. So that those who are only in appearance for these limitations, and in reality against them, endeavour for their last refuge to mislead well-meaning men, by telling them, that 'tis not advisable to put them into the act of security, as well for fear of losing all, as because they will be more conveniently placed in a separate act. My lord Chancellor, I would fain know if any thing can be more proper in an act which appoints the naming and manner of admitting a successor, than the conditions on which we agree to receive him. I would know, if the deferring of anything, at a time when naturally it should take place, be not to put a slur upon it, and an endeavour to defeat it. And if the limitations in question are pretended to be such a burden in the act, as to hazard the loss of the whole, can we expect to obtain them when separated from the act? Is there any common sense in this? Let us not deceive ourselves, and imagine that the act of 1696 does not expire immediately after the Queen and heirs of her body; for in all that act, the heirs and successors of his late Majesty King William are always restrained and specified by these express words, 'according to the declaration of the estates, dated the 11th of April 1689.'[27] So that unless we make a due provision by some new law, a dissolution of the government will ensue immediately upon the death of her

---

[26] Like the previous speech, this was printed out of sequence, and without a date, by Ridpath, *Account*, pp. 293–5. It seems most likely that it was given as a supplement to the previous speech on the same day (7 July) since it resembles the speech abstracted in *Proceedings*, pp. 26–7, for that date; and its content is in line with Hume's observations on the day: Hume, *Diary*, p. 115.

[27] See above, note 16.

Majesty, failing heirs of her body.[28] Such an act therefore being of absolute and indispensable necessity, I am of opinion, that the limitations ought to be inserted therein as the only proper place for them, and surest way to obtain them: and that whoever would separate them, does not so much desire we should obtain the act, as that we should lose the limitations.

VII

My Lord Chancellor,[29]

I hope I need not inform this honourable house, that all acts which can be proposed for the security of this kingdom, are vain and empty propositions, unless they are supported by arms; and that to rely upon any law without such a security, is to lean upon a shadow. We had better never pass this act: for then we shall not imagine we have done any thing for our security; and if we think we can do any thing effectual without that provision, we deceive ourselves, and are in a most dangerous condition. Such an act cannot be said to be an act for the security of any thing, in which the most necessary clause is wanting, and without which all the rest is of no force: neither can any kingdom be really secured but by arming the people. Let no man pretend that we have standing forces to support this law; and that if their numbers be not sufficient, we may raise more. 'Tis very well known this nation cannot maintain so many standing forces as would be necessary for our defence, though we could intirely rely upon their fidelity. The possession of arms is the distinction of a freeman from a slave. He who has nothing, and belongs to another, must be defended by him, and needs no arms: but he who thinks he is his own master, and has any thing he may call his own, ought to have arms to defend himself

---

[28] By speaking of a 'dissolution of the government' Fletcher may have meant to invoke the full force of Locke's concept of dissolution: *Two Treatises of Government* (1689/90), *The Second Treatise*, sections 212–22. If so, this would be one of the few allusions to Locke (other than in the contributions of Daniel Defoe) in the Scottish Union debates. But the use of the term here is too fleeting for much to be built on it.

[29] Printed but not dated by Ridpath, *Account*, pp. 258–60; probably delivered on 10 August, when a clause of the Act of Security for arming all fencible men was debated.

and what he possesses, or else he lives precariously and at discretion. And though for a while those who have the sword in their
power abstain from doing him injuries; yet by degrees he will be
awed into a submission to every arbitrary command. Our ancestors
by being always armed, and frequently in action, defended themselves against the Romans, Danes, and English; and maintained
their liberty against the incroachments of their own princes. If we
are not rich enough to pay a sufficient number of standing forces,
we have at least this advantage, that arms in our own hands serve
no less to maintain our liberty at home, than to defend us from
enemies abroad. Other nations, if they think they can trust standing
forces, may by their means defend themselves against foreign enemies. But we, who have not wealth sufficient to pay such forces,
should not, of all nations under heaven, be unarmed. For us then
to continue without arms, is to be directly in the condition of slaves:
to be found unarmed in the event of her Majesty's death, would
be to have no manner of security for our liberty, property, or the
independence of this kingdom. By being unarmed, we every day
run the risk of our all, since we know not how soon that event may
overtake us: to continue still unarmed, when by this very act now
under deliberation, we have put a case, which happening may separate us from England, would be the grossest of all follies. And if we
do not provide for arming the kingdom in such an exigency, we
shall become a jest and a proverb to the world.

VIII

My Lord Chancellor,[30]
If in the sad event of her Majesty's decease without heirs of her
body, any considerable military force should be in the hands of one
or more men, who might have an understanding together, we are
not very sure what use they would make of them in so nice and
critical a conjuncture. We know that as the most just and honourable enterprizes, when they fail, are accounted in the number of
rebellions; so all attempts, however unjust, if they succeed, always

---

[30] Again, printed but not dated by Ridpath, *Account*, pp. 260–2; probably also delivered on 10 August, when the clause moved by Fletcher at the end of this speech
was proposed, debated and accepted: *Proceedings*, p. 42; *APS XI*, p. 74.

purge themselves of all guilt and imputation. If a man presume he shall have success, and obtain the utmost of his hopes, he will not too nicely examine the point of right, nor balance too scrupulously the injury he does to his country. I would not have any man take this for a reflection upon those honourable persons, who have at present the command of our troops. For besides that we are not certain, who shall be in those commands at the time of such an event, we are to know that all men are frail, and the wicked and mean-spirited world has paid too much honour to many, who have subverted the liberties of their country. We see a great disposition at this time in some men, not to consent to any limitations on a successor, though we should name the same with England. And therefore since this is probably the last opportunity we shall ever have, of freeing ourselves from our dependence on the English court, we ought to manage it with the utmost jealousy and diffidence of such men. For though we have ordered the nation to be armed and exercised, which will be a sufficient defence when done: yet we know not but the event, which God avert, may happen before this can be effected. And we may easily imagine, what a few bold men, at the head of a small number of regular troops, might do, when all things are in confusion and suspence. So that we ought to make effectual provision with the utmost circumspection, that all such forces may be subservient to the government and interest of this nation, and not to the private ambition of their commanders. I therefore move, that immediately upon the decease of her Majesty, all military commissions above that of a captain be null and void.

IX

My Lord Chancellor,[31]

I know 'tis the undoubted prerogative of her Majesty, that no act of this house shall have the force of a law without her royal assent. And as I am confident his grace the high Commissioner is sufficiently instructed, to give that assent to every act which shall be laid before him; so more particularly to the act for the security of the

---

[31] The Act of Security was approved by the House by a majority of 59 on 13 August. This speech was given on 16 August, when a number of speakers pressed for the royal asset to be given to the Act: *Proceedings*, pp. 42–3.

kingdom, which has already past this house: an act that preserves us from anarchy: an act that arms a defenceless people: an act that has cost the representatives of this kingdom much time and labour to frame, and the nation a very great expence: an act that has passed by a great majority: and above all an act, that contains a caution of the highest importance for the amendment of our constitution. I did not presume the other day, immediately after this act was voted, to desire the royal assent; I thought it a just deference to the high Commissioner, not to mention it at that time. Neither would I now, but only that I may have an opportunity to represent to his grace, that as he who gives readily doubles the gift; so his grace has now in his hands the most glorious and honourable occasion, that any person of this nation ever had, of making himself acceptable, and his memory for ever grateful to the people of this kingdom: since the honour of giving the royal assent to a law, which lays a lasting foundation for their liberties, has been reserved to him.

X

My Lord Chancellor,[32]

On the day that the act for the security of the kingdom passed in this house, I did not presume to move for the royal assent. The next day of our meeting I mentioned it with all imaginable respect and deference for his grace the high Commissioner, and divers honourable persons seconded me. If now, after the noble lord who spoke last, I insist upon it, I think I am no way to be blamed. I shall not endeavour to shew the necessity of this act, in which the whole security of the nation now lies, having spoken to that point the other day: but shall take occasion to say something concerning the delay of giving the royal assent to acts passed in this house; for which I could never hear a good reason, except that a Commissioner was not sufficiently instructed. But that cannot be the true reason at this time, because several acts have lain long for the royal assent: in particular, that to ratify a former act, for turning the convention into a parliament, and fencing the claim of right, which no man

---

[32] Fletcher's account of the timing of his speeches on the royal assent in the opening sentences of this speech suggests the date of 20 August; 17 August is also a possibility, in which case 'the other day' would refer to yesterday (16 August); see also *Proceedings*, p. 44.

doubts his grace is sufficiently instructed to pass. We must therefore look elsewhere for the reason of this delay, and ought to be excused in doing this; since so little regard is had, and so little satisfaction given to the representatives of this nation, who have for more than three months employed themselves with the greatest assiduity in the service of their country, and yet have not seen the least fruit of their labours crowned with the royal assent. Only one act has been touched, for recognizing her Majesty's just right, which is a thing of course. This gives but too good reason to those who speak freely, to say that the royal assent is industriously suspended, in order to oblige some men to vote, as shall be most expedient to a certain interest; and that this session of parliament is continued so long, chiefly to make men uneasy, who have neither places nor pensions to bear their charges; that by this means acts for money, importation of French wine, and the like, may pass in a thin house, which will not fail immediately to receive the royal assent, whilst the acts that concern the welfare, and perhaps the very being of the nation, remain untouched.

XI

My Lord Chancellor,[33]

Being under some apprehensions that her Majesty may receive ill advice in this affair, from ministers who frequently mistake former bad practices for good precedents, I desire that the third act of the first session of the first parliament of King Charles the second may be read.

Act the third of the first session, parl. I. Car. II.[34]
Act asserting his Majesty's royal prerogative,
in calling and dissolving of parliaments,
and making of laws.

The estates of parliament now convened by his Majesty's special auth-
ority, considering that the quietness, stability and happiness of the people,

---

[33] Probably also given on 20 August: see *Proceedings*, p. 44.
[34] *APS VII: 1661–69*, pp. 10–11; 11 January 1661: given as the 7th, not the 3rd, Act of the session.

do depend upon the safety of the King's Majesty's sacred person, and the maintenance of his sovereign authority, princely power, and prerogative royal; and conceiving themselves obliged in conscience, and in discharge of their duties to almighty God, to the King's Majesty, and to their native country, to make a due acknowledgment thereof at this time, do therefore unanimously declare, that they will with their lives and fortunes maintain and defend the same. And they do hereby acknowledge, that the power of calling, holding, proroguing, and dissolving of parliaments, and all conventions and meetings of the estates, does solely reside in the King's Majesty, his heirs and successors. And that as no parliament can be lawfully kept, without the special warrant and presence of the King's Majesty, or his Commissioner; so no acts, sentences or statutes, to be passed in parliament, can be binding upon the people, or have the authority and force of laws, without the special authority and approbation of the King's Majesty, or his Commissioner interponed thereto, at the making thereof. And therefore the King's Majesty, with advice and consent of his estates of parliament, doth hereby rescind and annul all laws, acts, statutes or practices that have been, or upon any pretext whatsoever may be, or seem contrary to, or inconsistent with, his Majesty's just power and prerogative above-mentioned; and declares the same to have been unlawful, and to be void and null in all time coming. And to the end that this act and acknowledgment, which the estates of parliament, from the sense of their humble duty and certain knowledge, have hereby made, may receive the more exact obedience in time coming; it is by his Majesty, with advice foresaid, statute and ordained, that the punctual observance thereof be specially regarded by all his Majesty's subjects, and that none of them, upon any pretext whatsoever, offer to call in question, impugn, or do any deed to the contrary hereof, under pain of treason.

My Lord Chancellor,

The questions concerning the King's prerogative and the people's privileges are nice and difficult. Mr. William Colvin, who was one of the wisest men this nation ever had, used to say concerning defensive arms, that he wished all princes thought them lawful, and the people unlawful.[35] And indeed I heartily wish, that something

---

[35] William Colvin was probably William Colvill (d. 1675), minister and principal of Edinburgh University 1652–3 and again from 1662, and author of *Philosophia Moralis Christiana* (Edinburgh, 1670), and of a collection of sermons, *Refreshing*

like these moderate sentiments might always determine all matters in question between both. By the constitution of this kingdom, no act of the estates had the force of a law, unless touched by the King's scepter, which was his undoubted prerogative. The touch of his scepter gave authority to our laws, as his stamp did a currency to our coin: but he had no right to refuse or withhold either. 'Tis pretended by some men, that in vertue of this act, the King may refuse the royal assent to acts passed by the estates of the kingdom. But it ought to be considered, that this law is only an acknowledgment and declaration of the King's prerogative, and consequently gives nothing new to the prince. The act acknowledges this to be the prerogative of the King, that whatever is passed in this house, cannot have the force of a law without the royal assent, and makes it high treason to question this prerogative; because the parliament, during the civil war, had usurped a power of imposing their own votes upon the people for law, though neither the King, nor any person commissionated by him were present: and this new law was wholly and simply directed to abolish and rescind that usurpation, as appears by the tenour and express words of the act; which does neither acknowledge nor declare, that the prince has a power to refuse the royal assent to any act presented by the parliament. If any one should say, that the lawgivers designed no less, and that the principal contrivers and promoters of the act frequently boasted they had obtained the negative, as they call it, for the crown; I desire to know how they will make that appear, since no words are to be found in the act, that shew any such design: especially if we consider, that this law was made by a parliament that spoke the most plainly, least equivocally, and most fully of all others concerning the prerogative. And if those who promoted the passing of this act were under so strong a delusion, to think they had obtained a new and great prerogative to the crown by a declaratory law, in which there is not one word to that purpose, 'twas the hand of heaven that defeated their design of destroying the liberty of their country. I

Streams flowing from the Fulnesse of Jesus Christ (London, 1655). The endings 'in' and 'ill' or 'ille' were used interchangeably in the seventeenth century: the plaintiff in 'Calvin's Case' in 1608 (which naturalised Scots born after James I's accession in England under English Common Law) was one of the grandsons of Lord Colville of Culross. When Fletcher may have heard the sentiments he attributes to Colvin (they are not in Colvill's published works) is not known.

know our princes have refused their assent to some acts since the making of this law: but a practice introduced in arbitrary times can deserve no consideration. For my own part, I am far from pushing things to extremity on either hand: I heartily enter into the sentiments of the wise man I mentioned before, and think the people of this nation might have been happy in mistaking the meaning of this law, if such men as have had the greatest credit with our princes, would have let them into the true sense of it. And therefore those who have the honour to advise her Majesty, should beware of inducing her to a refusal of the royal assent to the act for the security of the kingdom, because the unwarrantable custom of rejecting acts, was introduced in arbitrary times.

XII

My Lord Chancellor,[36]

'Tis often said in this house, that parliaments, and especially long sessions of parliament, are a heavy tax and burden to this nation: I suppose they mean as things are usually managed: otherwise I should think it a great reflection on the wisdom of the nation, and a maxim very pernicious to our government. But indeed in the present state of things, they are a very great burden to us. Our parliament seldom meets in winter, when the season of the year, and our own private affairs bring us to town. We are called together for the most part in summer, when our country business and the goodness of the season make us live in town with regret. Our parliaments are sitting both in seed-time and harvest, and we are made to toil the whole year. We meet one day in three; though no reason can be given why we should not meet every day, unless such a one, as I am unwilling to name, lest thereby occasion should be taken to mention it elsewhere to the reproach of the nation. The expenses of our commissioners are now become greater than those of our kings formerly were: and a great part of this money is laid out upon equipage and other things of foreign manufacture, to the great damage of the kingdom. We meet in this place in the afternoon,

---

[36] According to Ridpath, *Account*, pp. 220–3, this was given on 2 August, in response to an adjournment by the high commissioner of five days, to enable the Convention of the Burghs to meet in Glasgow. Alternatively, Hume, *Diary*, p. 124, suggests 7 August.

after a great dinner, which I think is not the time of doing business; and are in such confusion after the candles are lighted, that very often the debate of one single point cannot be finished, but must be put off to another day. Parliaments are forced to submit to the conveniences of the lords of the session, and meetings of the burroughs; though no good reason can be given, why either a lord of the session or any one deputed to the meetings of the burroughs, should be a member of this house; but on the contrary, experience has taught us the inconvenience of both. When members of parliament, to perform the duty they owe to their country, have left the most important affairs, and quitted their friends many times in the utmost extremity, to be present at this place, they are told they may return again; as we were the other day called together only in order to be dismissed. We have been for several days adjourned in this time of harvest, when we had the most important affairs under deliberation; that as well those who have neither place nor pension might grow weary of their attendance, as those, whose ill state of health makes the service of their country as dangerous, though no less honourable than if they served in the field. Do not these things shew us the necessity of those limitations, I had the honour to offer to this house? and particularly of that for lodging the power of adjournments in the parliament; that for meetings of parliament to be in winter; that for impowering the President to give the royal assent, and ascertaining his salary; with that for excluding all lords of the session from being members of parliament. Could one imagine that in this parliament, in which we have had the first opportunity of amending our constitution by new conditions of government, occasion should be given by reiterating former abuses, to convince all men of the necessity of farther limitations upon a successor? Or is not this rather to be attributed to a peculiar providence, that those who are the great opposers of limitations, should by their conduct give the best reason for them? But I hope no member of this house will be discouraged either by delay or opposition; because the liberties of a people are not to be maintained without passing through great difficulties, and that no toil and labours ought to be declined to preserve a nation from slavery.

XIII

My Lord Chancellor,[37]

I have waited long and with great patience for the result of this session, to see if I could discover a real and sincere intention in the members of this house to restore the freedom of our country in this great and perhaps only opportunity. I know there are many different views among us, and all men pretend the good of the nation. But every man here is obliged carefully to examine the things before us, and to act according to his knowledge and conscience, without regard to the views of other men, whatever charity he may have for them: I say, every man in this place is obliged by the oath he has taken to give such advice as he thinks most expedient for the good of his country. The principal business of this session has been the forming of an act for the security of the kingdom, upon the expiration of the present intail of the crown. And though one would have thought, that the most essential thing which could have entered into such an act, had been to ascertain the conditions on which the nation would receive a successor, yet this has been entirely waived and over-ruled by the house. Only there is a caution inserted in the act, that the successor shall not be the same person who is to succeed in England, unless such conditions of government be first enacted, as may secure the freedom of this nation.[38] But this is a general and indefinite clause, and liable to the dangerous inconveniency of being declared to be fulfilled by giving us two or three inconsiderable laws. So that this session of parliament, in which we have had so great an opportunity of making ourselves for ever a free people, is like to terminate without any real security for our liberties, or any essential amendment of our constitution. And now, when we ought to come to particulars, and enact such limitations as may fully satisfy the general clause, we must amuse ourselves with things of little significancy, and hardly mention any limitation of moment or consequence. But instead of this, acts are brought in for regu-

[37] Given on 9 September, along with the drafts of Acts following: Ridpath, *Account*, pp. 271–8; *Proceedings*, pp. 57–8.

[38] Fletcher's complaint is that the parliament had voted (in August) for an Act of Security, but without the specific Limitations which he had proposed. See Ridpath, *Account*, pp. 242–9 for 'A Copy of the Act of Security'; this differs only slightly from the Act of Security approved by the Crown a year later: *APS XI*, pp. 136–7; *Source Book of Scottish History*, III, pp. 474–7.

lations to take place during the life of the Queen, which we are not to expect, and quite draw us off from the business we should attend. By these methods divers well-meaning men have been deluded, whilst others have proposed a present nomination of a successor under limitations. But I fear the far greater part have designed to make their court either to her Majesty, the house of Hanover, or those of St. Germains, by maintaining the prerogative in Scotland as high as ever, to the perpetual enslaving of this nation to the ministers of England. Therefore I, who have never made court to any prince, and I hope never shall, at the rate of the least prejudice to my country, think myself obliged in discharge of my conscience, and the duty of my oath in parliament, to offer such limitations as may answer the general clause in the act for the security of the kingdom. And this I do in two draughts, the one containing the limitations by themselves; the other with the same limitations, and a blank for inserting the name of a successor. If the house shall think fit to take into consideration that draught which has no blank, and enact the limitations, I shall rest satisfied, being as little fond of naming a successor as any man. Otherwise, I offer the draught with a blank; to the end that every man may make his court to the person he most affects; and hope by this means to please all parties: the court in offering them an opportunity to name the successor of England, a thing so acceptable to her Majesty and that nation: those who may favour the court of St. Germains, by giving them a chance for their pretensions; and every true Scots-man, in vindicating the liberty of this nation, whoever be the successor.

First Draught

Our sovereign Lady, with advice and consent of the estates of parliament, statutes and ordains, that after the decease of her Majesty (whom God long preserve) and failing heirs of her body, no one shall succeed to the crown of this realm that is likewise successor to the crown of England, but under the limitations following, which, together with the oath of coronation and claim of right, they shall swear to observe. That all places and offices, both civil and military, and all pensions formerly conferred by our kings, shall ever after be given by parliament. That a new parliament shall be chosen every Michaelmas head-court, to sit the first of November thereafter, and adjourn themselves from time to time till next Michaelmas; and that they chuse their own president. That a committee of thirty-six members, chosen by and out of the whole parliament, without distinction of estates, shall, during the intervals of parliament, under the king, have the administration of the government, be his council, and accountable to parliament; with power, in extraordinary occasions, to call the parliament together.

Second Draught

Our sovereign Lady, with advice and consent of the estates of parliament, statutes and ordains, that after the decease of her Majesty (whom God long preserve) and heirs of her body failing,   shall succeed to the crown of this realm. But that in case the said successor be likewise the successor to the crown of England, the said successor shall be under the limitations following, &c.

No man can be an enemy to these limitations, in case we have the same king with England, except he who is so shameless a partizan either of the court at St. Germains, or the house of Hanover, that he would rather see Scotland continue to depend upon an English ministry, than that their prerogative should be any way lessened in this kingdom. As for those who have St. Germains in their view, and are accounted the highest of all the prerogative-men, I would ask them, if we should assist them in advancing their Prince to the throne of Great Britain, are we, for our reward, to continue still in our former dependence on the English court? These limitations are the only test to discover a lover of his country from a courtier either to her Majesty, Hanover, or St. Germains. For prerogative-men who are for enslaving this nation to the directions of another court, are courtiers to any successor; and let them pretend what they will, if their principles lead necessarily to subject this nation to another, are enemies to the nation. These men are so absurd as to provoke England, and yet resolve to continue slaves of that court. This country must be made a field of blood, in order to advance a papist to the throne of Britain. If we fail, we shall be slaves by right of conquest; if we prevail, have the happiness to continue in our former slavish dependence. And though to break this yoke all good men would venture their all, yet I believe few will be willing to lie at the mercy of France and popery, and at the same time draw upon themselves the indignation and power of

England, for the sake only of measuring our strength with a much more powerful nation; and to be sure to continue still under our former dependence, though we should happen to prevail. Now of those who are for the same successor with England, I would ask, if in that case we are not also to continue in our former dependence; which will not fail always to grow from bad to worse, and at length become more intolerable to all honest men, than death itself. For my own part I think, that even the most zealous protestant in the nation, if he have a true regard for his country, ought rather to wish (were it consistent with our claim of right) that a papist should succeed to the throne of Great Britain under such limitations as would render this nation free and independent, than the most protestant and best prince, without any. If we may live free, I little value who is king: 'tis indifferent to me, provided the limitations be enacted, to name or not name; Hanover, St. Germains, or whom you will.[39]

XIV

My Lord Chancellor,[40]

His grace the high Commissioner having acquainted this house that he has instructions from her Majesty to give the royal assent to all acts passed in this session, except that for the security of the kingdom, 'twill be highly necessary to provide some new laws for securing our liberty upon the expiration of the present intail of the crown. And therefore I shall speak to the first article of the limitations contained in the short act I offered the other day; not only because 'tis the first in order, but because I persuade myself you all know that parliaments were formerly chosen annually; that they had

---

[39] Despite Fletcher's eloquence, the House ignored his drafts and voted to finish consideration of an Act against the export of wool.

[40] Delivered on 15 September, following the admission by the high commissioner on 10 September that her majesty would give assent to all acts voted in the session except the Act of Security. On 13 September Fletcher's drafts had been considered again, only to be lost on a motion to consider instead the proposals for trade; but on 15 September he successfully led the opposition in blocking the court's attempt to pass an Act of Supply. *APS XI*, pp. 101–4; Ridpath, *Account*, pp. 271, 278–90; *Proceedings*, pp. 63–9; and Hume, *Diary*, p. 135, recalling 'a long and learned discourse' from Fletcher, and noting particularly the reference to China.

the power of appointing the times of their meetings and adjournments, together with the nomination of committees to superintend the administration of the government during the intervals of parliament: all which, if it were necessary, might be proved by a great number of publick acts. So that if I demonstrate the use and necessity of the first article, there will remain no great difficulty concerning the rest.

My Lord Chancellor,

The condition of a people, however unhappy, if they not only know the cause of their misery, but have also the remedy in their power, and yet should refuse to apply it, one would think, were not to be pitied. And though the condition of good men, who are concluded and oppressed by a majority of the bad, is much to be lamented; yet Christianity teaches us to shew a greater measure of compassion to those who are knowingly and voluntarily obstinate to ruin both themselves and others. But the regret of every wise and good man must needs be extraordinary, when he sees the liberty and happiness of his country not only obstructed, but utterly extinguished by the private and transitory interest of self-designing men, who indeed very often meet their own ruin, but most certainly bring destruction upon their posterity by such courses. Sure if a man who is intrusted by others, should for his own private advantage betray that trust, to the perpetual and irrecoverable ruin of those who trusted him, the liveliest sense and deepest remorse for so great guilt, will undoubtedly seize and terrify the conscience of such a man, as often as the treacherous part he has acted shall recur to his thoughts; which will most frequently happen in the times of his distress, and the nearer he approaches to a life in which those remorses are perpetual. But I hope every man in this house has so well considered these things, as to preserve him from falling into such terrible circumstances: and (as all men are subject to great failings) if any person placed in this most eminent trust, is conscious to himself of having ever been wanting in duty to his country, I doubt not he will this day, in this weighty matter, atone for all, and not blindly follow the opinion of other men, because he alone must account for his own actions to his great Lord and Master.

The limitation, to which I am about to speak, requires, that all places, offices, and pensions, which have been formerly given by our

kings, shall, after her Majesty and heirs of her body, be conferred by
parliament so long as we are under the same prince with England.
Without this limitation, our poverty and subjection to the court of
England will every day increase; and the question we have now
before us is, whether we will be freemen or slaves for ever? Whether
we will continue to depend, or break the yoke of our dependence?
And whether we will chuse to live poor and miserable, or rich, free,
and happy? Let no man think to object, that this limitation takes
away the whole power of the prince. For the same condition of
government is found in one of the most absolute monarchies of the
world. I have very good authority for what I say, from all the best
authors that have treated of the government of China; but shall only
cite the words of an able minister of state, who had very well
considered whatever had been written on that subject; I mean Sir
William Temple, who says,

> That for the government, 'tis absolute monarchy, there being
> no other laws in China, but the King's orders and commands;
> and it is likewise hereditary, still descending to the next of
> blood. But all orders and commands of the King proceed
> through his councils; and are made upon the recommendation
> or petition of the council proper and appointed for that affair:
> so that all matters are debated, determined, and concluded by
> the several councils; and then upon their advices and requests
> made to the King, they are ratified and signed by him, and so
> pass into laws. All great offices of state are likewise conferred
> by the King, upon the same recommendations or petitions of
> his several councils; so that none are preferred by the humour
> of the prince himself, nor by favour of any minister, by flattery
> or corruption, but by the force or appearance of merit, of learn-
> ing, and of virtue; which observed by the several councils, gain
> their recommendations or petitions to the King.[41]

These are the express words of that minister. And if under the
greatest absolute monarchy of the world, in a country where the
prince actually resides; if among heathens this be accounted a necessary part of government for the encouragement of virtue, shall it be

---

[41] Sir William Temple, 'Of Heroick Virtue', sect. ii, in *Miscellanea. The Second Part*
(5th edn, London, 1705), pp. 185–6. Fletcher himself owned the *Miscellanea*, in
the two-volume editions of London [1684], 1692, with the third volume, London,
1701.

denied to Christians living under a prince who resides in another nation? Shall it be denied to a people, who have a right to liberty, and yet are not capable of any in their present circumstances, without this limitation? But we have formed to ourselves such extravagant notions of government, that even in a limited monarchy nothing will please, which in the least deviates from the model of France, and every thing else must stand branded with the name of commonwealth. Yet a great and wise people found this very condition of government necessary to support even an absolute monarchy. If any man say, that the empire of China contains divers kingdoms; and that the care of the Emperor, and his knowledge of particular men cannot extend to all: I answer, the case is the same with us; and it seems as if that wise people designed this constitution for a remedy to the like inconveniences with those we labour under at this time.[42]

This limitation will undoubtedly inrich the nation, by stopping that perpetual issue of money to England, which has reduced this country to extreme poverty. This limitation does not flatter us with the hopes of riches by an uncertain project; does not require so much as the condition of our own industry; but by saving great sums to the country, will every year furnish a stock sufficient to carry on a considerable trade, or to establish some useful manufacture at home, with the highest probability of success: because our ministers by this rule of government, would be freed from the influence of English councils; and our trade be intirely in our own hands, and not under the power of the court, as it was in the affair of Darien. If we do not obtain this limitation, our attendance at London will continue to drain this nation of all those sums, which should be a stock for trade. Besides, by frequenting that court, we not only spend our money, but learn the expensive modes and ways of living, of a rich and luxurious nation: we lay out yearly great sums in furniture and equipage, to the unspeakable prejudice of the trade and manufactures of our own country. Not that I think it amiss to travel into England, in order to see and learn their industry

---

[42] Temple, 'Of Heroick Virtue', *Miscellanea*, Part II, pp. 171–2, had noted that the 'Empire' of China consisted of fifteen kingdoms, now governed as 'provinces' by their several 'viceroys'. There were also 145 capital cities in the empire. He further observed (p. 188) that through its system of councils 'the whole empire of China' was governed through the several kingdoms that composed it.

in trade and husbandry. But at court what can we learn, except a horrid corruption of manners, and an expensive way of living, that we may for ever after be both poor and profligate?[43]

This limitation will secure to us our freedom and independence. It has been often said in this house, that our princes are captives in England; and indeed one would not wonder if, when our interest happens to be different from that of England, our kings, who must be supported by the riches and power of that nation in all their undertakings, should prefer an English interest before that of this country. 'Tis yet less strange, that English ministers should advise and procure the advancement of such persons to the ministry of Scotland, as will comply with their measures and the King's orders; and to surmount the difficulties they may meet with from a true Scots interest, that places and pensions should be bestowed upon parliament-men and others: I say, these things are so far from wonder, that they are inevitable in the present state of our affairs. But I hope they likewise shew us, that we ought not to continue any longer in this condition. Now this limitation is advantageous to all. The prince will no more be put upon the hardship of deciding between an English and a Scots interest; or the difficulty of reconciling what he owes to each nation, in consequence of his coronation oath. Even English ministers will no longer lie under the temptation of meddling in Scots affairs: nor the ministers of this kingdom, together with all those who have places and pensions, be any more subject to the worst of all slavery. But if the influences I mentioned before shall still continue, what will any other limitation avail us? What shall we be the better for our act concerning the power of war and peace; since by the force of an English interest and influence, we cannot fail of being engaged in every war, and neglected in every peace?

By this limitation, our parliament will become the most uncorrupted senate of all Europe. No man will be tempted to vote against the interest of his country, when his country shall have all the bribes in her own hands; offices, places, pensions. 'Twill be no longer

---

[43] The distinction between the 'horrid corruption of manners' and 'expensive way of living' learnt at court, and merely travelling into England 'in order to see and learn their industry in trade and husbandry', is characteristically sharp; no doubt Fletcher's own frequenting of London's chocolate houses had only the second, improving purpose.

necessary to lose one half of the publick customs, that parliament-men may be made collectors.[44] We will not desire to exclude the officers of state from sitting in this house, when the country shall have the nomination of them; and our parliaments free from corruption, cannot fail to redress all our grievances. We shall then have no cause to fear a refusal of the royal assent to our acts; for we shall have no evil counsellor, nor enemy of his country to advise it. When this condition of government shall take place, the royal assent will be the ornament of the prince, and never be refused to the desires of the people. A general unanimity will be found in this house; in every part of the government, and among all ranks and conditions of men. The distinctions of court and country-party shall no more be heard in this nation; nor shall the prince and people any longer have a different interest. Rewards and punishments will be in the hands of those who live among us, and consequently best know the merit of men; by which means virtue will be recompensed and vice discouraged, and the reign and government of the prince will flourish in peace and justice.

I should never make an end, if I would prosecute all the great advantages of this limitation; which, like a divine influence, turns all to good, as the want of it has hitherto poisoned every thing, and brought all to ruin. I shall therefore only add one particular more, in which it will be of the highest advantage to this nation. We all know, that the only way of enslaving a people is by keeping up a standing army; that by standing forces all limited monarchies have been destroyed, without them none; that so long as any standing forces are allowed in a nation, pretexts will never be wanting to increase them; that princes have never suffered militias to be put upon any good foot, lest standing forces should appear unnecessary. We also know that a good and well regulated militia is of so great importance to a nation, as to be the principal part of the constitution of any free government. Now by this limitation, the nation will have a sufficient power to render their militia good and effectual, by the nomination of officers: and if we would send a certain proportion of our militia abroad yearly, and relieve them from time to time, we may make them as good as those of Switzerland are; and much

---

[44] An allusion to the practice, previously denounced by Fletcher at the beginning of the *First Discourse of Scotland* (above p. 35) of using the customs as a source of political patronage, at the expense of the public revenue.

more able to defend the country, than any unactive standing forces can be. We may save every year great sums of money, which are now expended to maintain a standing army; and which is yet more, run no hazard of losing our liberty by them. We may employ a greater number of officers in those detachments, than we do at present in all our forces both at home and abroad; and make better conditions for them in those countries that need their assistance. For being freed from the influences of English councils, we shall certainly look better than we have hitherto done to the terms on which we may send them into the armies either of England or Holland; and not permit them to be abused so many different ways, as to the great reproach of the nation they have been, in their rank, pay, clothing, arrears, levy-money, quarters, transport ships, and gratuities.

Having thus shewn some of the great advantages this limitation will bring to the nation (to which every one of you will be able to add many more) that 'tis not only consistent with monarchy, but even with an absolute monarchy; having demonstrated the necessity of such a condition in all empires, which contain several kingdoms; and that without it we must for ever continue in a dependence upon the court of England; in the name of God, what hinders us from embracing so great a blessing? Is it because her Majesty will refuse the royal assent to this act? If she do, sure I am, such a refusal must proceed from the advice of English counsellors; and will not that be a demonstration to us, that after her Majesty and heirs of her body, we must not, cannot any longer continue under the same prince with England? Shall we be wanting to ourselves? Can her Majesty give her assent to this limitation upon a successor before you offer it to her? Is she at liberty to give us satisfaction in this point, till we have declared to England by a vote of this house, that unless we obtain this condition, we will not name the same successor with them? And then will not her Majesty, even by English advice, be persuaded to give her assent; unless her counsellors shall think fit to incur the heavy imputation, and run the dangerous risque of dividing these nations for ever? If therefore either reason, honour, or conscience have any influence upon us; if we have any regard either to ourselves or posterity; if there be any such thing as virtue, happiness or reputation in this world, or felicity in a future state, let me adjure you by all these, not to draw upon your heads everlasting infamy, attended with the eternal reproaches and anguish of an evil conscience, by making your selves and your posterity miserable.[45]

XV

My Lord Chancellor,[46]

This is an act for repealing a law made in the year 1700, which prohibits the importation of French wines.[47] We were then in peace with France, and are now in a declared war against them. The prohibition was made in time of peace, because the French laid greater impositions upon our trade than they did upon other nations: and yet 'tis desired, that French wines may be imported in time of war; though not only the same, but new burdens are laid upon our merchandise in France. 'Tis pretended that we shall not trade to France directly, but may buy French wines from certain nations, who trade to that country with our goods. I will allow all this, though it be false; but where is the necessity we should take French wines from those nations for our commodities? Have they not copper, iron, pitch, tar, hemp, flax, and timber for building of ships and other uses, which we need? Or if our consumption of these things will not answer the value of those goods they take of us, may we not export the overplus to other parts? Since therefore the same, or greater impositions continue still upon our merchandise in France, so as we cannot get of those neutral nations so high a price for our goods, as if the impositions in France were taken

---

[45] In the crescendo of Fletcher's rhetoric at the end of this speech, it should be remembered that these were his last words (at least, his last recorded, printed words) of the session: the speeches which follow were delivered before this one.

[46] The Act to allow the import of all foreign wines was also introduced and voted upon on 13 September; Fletcher joined the duke of Hamilton, the marquess of Montrose and others in registering a formal protest. This speech may have been delivered then or on 14 September, when consideration of the Act was continued.

    The Act was the bizarre finale to a chaotic parliament. Despite being at war with France, the Crown wished to repeal the ban on imports of French wine in order to raise customs revenue; their country opponents were anxious to block any form of supply, and made the most of the Act's endorsement of trade with the enemy. The Act none the less passed as the 13th and final Act of the session, receiving royal assent on 16 September: *APS XI*, p. 112.

[47] Act discharging Wine, Brandy and all other Liquors of the Growth of France: 1 William 8, no. 11, 31 January 1701, *APS X*, pp. 278–9.

off, the reason of the law made in 1700 still remains. And if we had sufficient cause to prohibit the importation of French wines by our own ships in time of peace, shall we purchase French wines from other nations in time of war? The French would not receive our goods in time of peace, upon equal terms with those of other nations, which obliged us to forbid their wines: shall we now take them at a double value in time of war? Or are we become greater friends to France now in a time of open war, than we were before in time of peace? Something might be said, if no wines were to be found in Portugal or Italy. But it seems no wine will please us, but that of a country, against which we are in actual war, and which uses us ill both in peace and war. One would have thought that the past services of a nation, which has more than once saved that base people from ruin, might have obliged them to a more favourable usage of us. But the world will say, we are yet a baser people than they, if whilst they continue to suppress our trade, we repeal a law, for which we have now more and better reasons than when we made it. To repeal such a law in time of war, will sound admirably well in England and Holland: since 'tis no less than a direct breach of our alliance with those nations; a formal renunciation of any advantages we may pretend in a treaty of peace, and exactly calculated to inform the world of the inclinations of our ministers. If we would trade to Portugal and Italy, we should have the benefit of English and Dutch convoys. We might trade in our own ships, not in Swedes, Danes, and Hamburghers, to the ruin of our navigation. For if they drive our trade for us, we may indeed burn our ships and plow our towns, as has been told us. And therefore I move that this act, as prejudicial to our trade and navigation, and highly injurious to the honour of the nation, may be thrown out.

XVI

My Lord Chancellor,[48]

One would think that of all men lawgivers should be of the most undoubted probity, and that selfish ends and disingenuity should

---

[48] Delivered on 14 September, when various additional clauses to the Wines Act were considered and rejected, and the Act was approved: Hume, *Diary*, p. 134; *APS XI*, p. 103.

have no place in their assemblies. For if those who give laws to other men, have not the good of the nations they govern in view, but are ready to sacrifice every thing to their own private interest, such a scandalous conduct must be of the last consequence to a government, by alienating the affections of the people from those who shall be found guilty of such practices. My Lord, no man in this house can be ignorant, that this act will not only open a trade and correspondence with France, contrary to the declaration of war, and our own standing laws; but that the design of those who promote the passing of this act is to have a trade directly with France. 'Tis known that Scots ships are already loading wines at Bourdeaux for this kingdom; and that a French factor is already arrived in this city. Besides, 'tis notorious, that a ship belonging to this port, and freighted with wines from France, is now lying in Queensferry-road, not eight miles from this place. She pretends indeed to be a Dane, because she came last from Norway; whither she was sent for no other reason than that she came too soon upon this coast.[49] This ship has an officer and divers seamen on board, sent from one of our frigates for her guard, who have absolutely refused to permit the persons that were impowered by the admiralty to examine her, unless they should produce an order from the captain of the frigate, or from your lordship. And as if our act for the prohibition of French wines were already repealed, and our collectors, no less than our former kings, might dispense with the laws; another ship loaden with the wines of that country has been brought into the Clyde, and her lading into the city of Glasgow, during this session, in contempt of the law and the authority of the parliament. All this, and much more of the same kind, is well known to those who are in the administration, and seem not to think it their business to take notice of such practices. But I hope this house will not overlook these gross mismanagements; and since the executive part of the government is arrived to that state, that hardly any law is put in execution, the parliament, according to the many precedents we have in our acts, will give order for a better administration in time to come, and take effectual care that those who are placed in the highest trusts, shall see the laws duly executed; especially your lordship, who during the intervals of parliament, as the principal person

---

[49] Norway was then within the Kingdom of Denmark.

in the government, ought to be answerable to the nation for their due execution. Now the great argument which is used for allowing the importation of French wines is, that we shall certainly have the wines of that country, though very bad and very dear, if the prohibition be continued. Which is only to say, we have no government among us. Two good laws were made in the year 1700. One against the exportation of our wool, the other against the importation of French wines; the first to give a being to a woollen manufacture in this kingdom, the latter to vindicate our trade against the impositions of France. We have already rendered the one ineffectual, to the ruin of our woollen manufacture; shall we now repeal the other? Shall we send them our wool, and buy their wines, and oblige them doubly for burdening and oppressing us in our trade? 'Tis pretended that the customs arising from the importation of French wines must serve to pay the civil list, because the former duties are fallen one half of the usual value. A very cogent argument indeed! When we know that the customs have been taken from the farmers, only in order to bestow the collectors' places upon parliament-men. Shall we make good such funds as are exhausted, by bribing men to betray our liberty? If any justice were to be found in this nation, the advisers of these things had long since been brought to a scaffold. But as there is no crime under heaven more enormous, more treacherous, and more destructive to the very nature of our government, than that of bribing parliaments; so there is nothing more common and barefaced: and I think this session should have been opened by purging the house from such corrupted members; which if we had done, we had not met with so many difficulties and obstructions of the publick service. But I hope we shall not be so remiss for the future. And for the present, my Lord Chancellor, I move, that this act for taking off the prohibition of French wines, as a design of the blackest nature, hurtful and ignominious to the nation, and highly reflecting on our ministers and administration, may be thrown out.

XVII

My Lord Chancellor,[50]

Yesterday a cause was brought into this house by a protestation for remeid of law: upon which a debate arose, whether a lord of session, who is also a member of this house for some shire or burrough, could sit again as a judge of the same cause. I was then of opinion he might; because the house had declared they would not confine themselves to decide this matter by what had been already alledged and proved before the lords of session; but would receive new proof and matter, if any had been discovered since the passing of the decrete. And indeed in that case I was of opinion, those lords of session might and ought to judge again, because new proof and new matter might induce them to alter their former judgment. But since no new matter or proof appears, and that the vote is stated. 'Adhere to the decrete of the lords of session, or sustain the protestation'; which is only and simply to determine the cause by what was alledged and proved before that bench; I cannot consent that any of those lords, though members of this house, should again be judges of the same cause. Nor indeed, till the house had over-ruled my opinion, could I think that we ought to decide any cause brought before us by protestation for remeid of law, otherwise than by the proofs and matters alledged and proved before the lords of session. Certainly 'twas never designed, by allowing these protestations, to bring all civil causes before our parliaments. For if we should judge of matters originally in this house, or go about to redress and relieve men against their adversaries upon new proof after the decrete of the ordinary judges, all the civil causes of the nation might under one pretext or another be brought before us. In these cases we are only to relieve the people by reversing the unjust sentences of the lords of session. And the privilege of the people to protest for remeid of law, was principally designed to be a check upon the ordinary judges, and oblige them to do justice: which if they should

---

[50] The case which prompted this speech, on 17 June, was an action for Remeed (remedy) of Law by Thomas Fothringhame, Laird of Powrie, against Patrick, Lord Gray, a lord of session. It concerned the purchase of fishing rights by David Fothringhame, father of Thomas, and was settled in Lord Gray's favour. Fletcher objected to lords of session sitting in judgement a second time on their own cases. *APS XI*, pp. 52–61 (14, 17 June); also Hume, *Diary*, pp. 106–9.

not do, and were convicted of bribery or other gross injustice, the parliament might remove them from their offices, or otherwise punish them in life or estate. So that these lords of session, who have formerly determined this cause, cannot, I think, reasonably pretend to judge the same again, though they are members of the house; because no man can be judge of any thing by which he may receive damage or profit. If the decrete now under consideration shall be found grosly unjust, I hope no man will say the judges may not be punished. And the judgment to be given by the parliament is to be confined to this; whether the lords of session have pronounced a just or unjust sentence. In the giving of which judgment, no lord of session can be present as judge; unless we will say that an unjust judge may be absolved by his own vote. But to all this a very easy remedy is to be found; I mean, that no lord of session should be a member of parliament, which would be highly advantageous to the nation on many accounts, and principally that our parliaments might no longer interrupt or disturb the common course of justice.

These speeches are published to prevent mistakes in the affairs to which they relate.

An ACCOUNT of
A CONVERSATION
CONCERNING
A RIGHT REGULATION
OF
GOVERNMENTS
For the common Good of Mankind.

I N

A LETTER to the Marquiss of
MONTROSE, the Earls of ROTHES,
ROXBURG and HADDINGTON

From London the first of December,
1703,

Edinburgh;
Printed in the Year MDCCIV.

My Lords,

You desire to know the sentiments of some considerable persons of the English nation, touching our affairs, and the common interest of both kingdoms. And I think I cannot give you more satisfaction in these particulars than by an account of a conversation I lately had with the Earl of Cr-m-rty, Sir Ed. S-m-r, and Sir Chr. M-sgr-ve; in which if the defence I made for you do not give you satisfaction, I shall be glad to hear a better from yourselves.[1] If you ask how I had the fortune to meet with men of sentiments so different from my own, that was partly owing to chance, and partly to the frank and courteous way which is so natural to the Earl of Cr-m-rty. For some days ago, walking slowly and alone in the Mell, the Earl and Sir Chr-st-ph-r overtook me:[2] and though during the whole time I was last in Scotland, I had not waited on the Earl, he with a very obliging air said to me, that if I expected not other company, they would be glad of mine; asking me withal if I was acquainted with Sir Chr. I said I had formerly the honour of some small acquaintance with him, which I should be very willing to renew. And after some compliments passed on all sides, finding I was not engaged, he invited

---

[1] The pamphlet is addressed to four young Scottish peers, all in their early twenties, who had supported Fletcher in the turbulent parliamentary session of the summer of 1703 (for their biographical details, see the Biographical Notes). It offers a defence of their conduct before the three elder statesmen (all in their seventies) who are participants in the conversation, along with Fletcher himself (who was now fifty). Whether a conversation between the four took place at this time, in anything like the manner described, is not known; but the participants could hardly have been better chosen to discuss the issues. The earl of Cromarty was a Scots peer who had held government office in every reign since the Restoration; an Episcopalian, he was an early and intelligent advocate of incorporating union. Sir Christopher Musgrave was a Country Party Tory MP from the north-west of England, with a record of protecting English economic interests from Irish competition. Sir Edward Seymour was by now the elder statesman of the Tory Party: devoted to the Church of England and the House of Commons, of which he had been speaker, he supported the Revolution but hated the Whigs; from a west country constituency, he too had a record of supporting protection against Irish imports. (Again, see Biographical Notes.)

The ingenuousness with which Fletcher describes the circumstances of the meeting, as well as the realism of the conversation itself, with its abrupt shifts between topics, suggest that it may well have been based on an actual encounter; but realistic dialogue was very much a humanist genre, and there is, as I have suggested in the Introduction, good reason to think that Fletcher's account of the conversation is carefully and artfully controlled.

[2] In 1703 the Mall ran down through open fields towards Buckingham House, then under construction to replace the demolished Arlington House.

me to dine with him, telling me he would give me the opportunity of doing as I desired; and therefore we should pass the time together till the hour of dinner. So we presently went to his lodgings in Whitehall, and entring into a room from whence we had a full view of the Thames and city of London, You have here, Gentlemen, said the Earl, two of the noblest objects that can entertain the eye, the finest river, and the greatest city in the world. Where natural things are in the greatest perfection, they never fail to produce most wonderful effects. This most gentle and navigable river, with the excellent genius and industrious inclination of the English people, have raised this glorious city to such a height, that if all things be rightly considered, we shall find it very far to surpass any other. Besides the beauty and conveniences of the river, the situation of this city is such, that I am persuaded if the wisest men of the nation had been many years employed to chuse the most advantageous, they could not have found a better: and as the prosperity of a country depends in a great measure upon the situation of the capital city, the good fortune of this nation in that particular, has chiefly contributed to the great riches and power they now have.[3] My lord, said Sir Chr-, you are so fully in the right, that notwithstanding the extent, and particularly the great length of the buildings; yet should they be removed but one half-mile either east or west, such an alteration would be disadvantageous. For to the eastward some rows of buildings do in a streight line cross the fields, and meet the river again at Blackwall; and to the westward the buildings run along a rising ground which overlooks Hide-park, and the adjacent fields. The whole town lies upon a shelving situation, descending easily, and as it were in the form of a theatre towards the south and river, covered from the north, northeast and northwest winds: so that in very cold and stormy weather, by means of the buildings of the city and on the bridge, 'tis both warm and calm upon the river; which being as it were the string to the bow, affords the great conveniency of a cheap and speedy conveyance from one part to the other. The shelving situation of the city is not only most fitted to receive the kind influences of the sun, but to carry off by common-shores and other ways the snow and dirt of the streets into the river, which is

---

[3] This account of the advantages of London's situation could have been intended to echo More's description of Amaurot in *Utopia*: Thomas More, *Utopia*, ed. G. M. Logan and R. M. Adams (Cambridge, 1989), pp. 45–8.

cleansed by the tides twice every day. But above all, the ground on which the city stands being a gravel, renders the inhabitants healthful, and the adjacent country wholsome and beautiful. The county of Kent furnishes us with the choicest fruit; Hertfordshire and Cambridgeshire with corn; Lincolnshire, Essex, and Surrey with beef, veal and mutton; Buckinghamshire with wood for fuel, and the river with all that the seas and the rest of the world affords. And this in so great plenty, that in times of peace, the common fuel, though brought two hundred miles by sea, is yet sold at a reasonable rate; and in so great variety, that we may find more sorts of wine in London than in the countries which produce the richest and the most. In a word, all the useful and superfluous things that nature produces, or the wit of man has invented, are to be found here, either made by our artificers, or imported by our merchants. That which is to be admired, said I, is the perfect peace and tranquillity in which the inhabitants live; proceeding either from their natural temper, or the good order and plenty of the place, and the security they enjoy from the attempts of any enemy by being situated in an island. So that this great city without walls or guards is as accessible at all hours of the night as the most inconsiderable village. But that which charms me most is the liberty and rights they are possessed of in matters civil and religious. To these advantages I might add many things which render this city great, convenient, and agreeable; such are, the important transactions of a parliament; the judgments in Westminster Hall; the business of the Exchange, navigation and commerce; the affairs and diversions of the court, together with the recreations and pleasures of the town. These last words have spoiled all, said Sir Chr. and unluckily revived in me the image of that corruption of manners which reigns in this place, has infected the whole nation, and must at length bring both the city and nation to ruin. And if one may judge by the greatness of the corruption, this fatal period is not far off. For no regulations of government are sufficient to restrain or correct the manners of so great a number of people living in one place, and exposed to so many temptations from the bad example they give to one another. And the frequency of ill example, which can never fail to be where so great numbers live together, authorizes the corruption, and will always be too strong and powerful for any magistracy to controul. For though every man may have his own scheme to reform and regulate these disorders, yet experience has taught us that no human prudence can preserve the manners of men living in great cities from extraordinary corruption; and that where great power, riches, and numbers of men are brought together, they not only introduce an universal depravation of manners, but destroy all good government, and bring ruin and desolation upon a people.[4] What great corruptions do you find in this place, so obstinate and incorrigible? said the Earl. No laws or regulations, replied Sir Chr-, are sufficient to restrain the luxury of women, to banish so many thousands of common prostitutes, or to prevent a far greater number of that sex from being debauched by the innumerable occasions and opportunities which so vast a city affords, where by means of a masque, a hackney-coach, a tavern, and a play-house, they are at liberty to do what they please. Even the poorer sort of both sexes are daily tempted to all manner of lewdness by infamous ballads sung in every corner of the streets. One would think, said the Earl, this last were of no great consequence. I said, I knew a very wise man so much of Sir Chr-'s sentiment, that he believed if a man were permitted to make all the ballads, he need not care who should make the laws of a nation. And we find that most of the antient legislators thought they could not well reform the manners of any city without the help of a lyrick, and sometimes of a dramatick poet.[5] But in this city the dramatick poet no less than the ballad-maker has been almost wholly employed to corrupt the people, in which they have had most unspeakable and deplorable success. Then Sir Chr- continuing his discourse, said, in this city gamesters, stockjobbers, jockies and wagerers make now the most considerable figure, and in few years have attained to such a degree of perfection in their several ways, that in comparison to many of the nobility, gentry and merchants of England, those in Newgate are mere ignorants, and

---

[4] Musgrave's lament for the corruption of the city may be read as a classic expression of the 'country' outlook, which combined a traditional, puritan apprehension of the immorality of city life with a more urgent fear of the growth of new financial devices, in particular public credit. But it may also have been intended to voice the complaints of the London Society for the Reformation of Manners, founded in 1691, which had begun a vigorous programme of prosecutions for drunkenness, prostitution, gaming and profanation of the Sabbath.

[5] The aside on the importance of ballad-makers is perhaps Fletcher's most-quoted observation. The obvious example of a legislator using lyric poetry to assist his reforms was Solon of Athens, whose proposals for a democratic constitution (*c.* 594 BC) were justified in his own poems.

wretches of no experience. In the summer they infest all the places of diversion throughout England, and may be justly called the missioners of this city. Sure, said the Earl, remedies may be found for many of these abuses. The too expensive apparel of women might be restrained, masques might be prohibited; vintners forbidden to receive women in their houses, and all stockjobbing, gaming and wagering suppressed. But who, said Sir Chr-, is to do this? For though these things might be easily done in a small city, yet in this place I am confident that the authority of the Queen and parliament would not be found sufficient for such a performance. I am fully persuaded of her Majesty's sincere intentions to discourage vice; yet some wise counsellor will not fail to tell her that it would be of dangerous consequence to forbid gaming, which consumes so much of the time, and takes up the thoughts of a great number of men, who, if they had not that diversion, might probably employ their leisure in thinking too much upon affairs of state. Might not we, said the Earl, play, like the Turks, only to pass the time? No, replied Sir Chr-, you have to do with Christians, who have a Christian liberty to play for money, provided they do not abuse it; though all men know, that if the thing be allowed, the abuse is inevitable. And yet this is not the worst; for the infection of bad manners has so thoroughly corrupted this place, that many even of those who ought by wholsome laws to reform others, are themselves infected by the contagion; so that when the country has sent persons to represent them in parliament, they in a short time seem rather to be only the representatives of this corrupt city, and artfully betray the nation, under the fairest pretences to good principles, contrary to their known duty, and the important trust reposed in them. I said, Sir Chr-'s observations were very impartial, and that I wished all those who were guilty of such practices, would impartially apply so just a censure to themselves. Sir Chr- continuing, said; all abuses, when introduced among great multitudes, become not only more enormous, but more incorrigible. The justices of London and Westminster will inform you of a thousand evils and incorrigible practices, which wholly proceed from the great number of the inhabitants and vast extent of our buildings, where all manner of crimes are easily concealed. Besides, the poor and indigent are so numerous in this place, that the ill practices to which men are tempted by poverty, are but too frequent: and the luxury of all other ranks and orders of men makes every one hasten to grow rich; and consequently leads them to betray all kind of trust reposed in them. In a word, this city abounds with all manner of temptations to evil; extreme poverty, excessive riches, great pleasures, infinite bad examples, especially of unpunished and successful crimes. Here Sir Chr- was interrupted by a servant, who acquainted us that Sir Ed. S--m-r was coming upstairs. He is welcome, said the Earl; and the more because he comes so early, for I expected him not 'till the hour of dinner. Upon this Sir Edw-rd S-m-r entered the room, and after he had saluted the Earl and Sir Chr-, the Earl presented me as his countryman and old acquaintance to Sir Edw-rd; and when we had placed ourselves in the chairs that were brought for us, said with a smile, that I was one of those who in the late session of the Scots parliament had opposed the interest of the court. My Lord, said I, does that character recommend me to Sir Ed-- S--m-r? Sir, says Sir Ed--, 'tis to me a great recommendation of my Lord's good nature, to allow you to wait upon him: but it seems you are one who signalized yourself in the late session of your parliament, by framing Utopias and new models of government, under the name of limitations; in which you had the honour to be seconded and assisted by several men of quality, of about two or three and twenty years of age, whose long experience and consummate prudence in publick affairs could not but produce wonderful schemes of govern-ment.[6] This rough and sudden attack made me take the freedom to ask him, if he thought that men wanted any more than the knowl-edge and the will to govern themselves rightly. To which, continu-ing in his former strain, he answered, that young men were always ignorant, confident, and of insupportable arrogance. Yet, said I, do you not think that young men in parliament are much more capable to resist corruption, and oppose ill men, than they would be in a court, where by temptations arising from vanity and pleasure, they are in hazard of being corrupted themselves? Whereas in parliament meeting with no temptation but bribery, which that age abhors, or the ambition of getting a place by arts they are unacquainted with,

---

[6] Seymour attacks the same young peers to whom the *Account of a Conversation* is addressed, providing Fletcher with the opportunity to defend their and his own conduct in terms calculated to confirm their support. At another level, however, the passage which follows is effectively a 'dialogue of counsel', of a recognisably humanist character, concerned particularly with the age of political wisdom.

the concern and assiduity of youth in their first applications, is of great moment and highly useful, especially in men of quality, whose example and early virtue is of the greatest influence. And if with these qualifications they have also the talent of speaking well, 'tis not to be imagined how much their pleading for justice, with that sincerity and unaffected eloquence so natural to youth, does inflame the minds of men to all kind of virtue. You begin to declaim, as if they overheard you, said the old gentleman; but you must not think such stuff will have any influence upon me, or that I am so credulous to believe that boys of those years can have any right notion of government: an art which demands the longest experience and greatest practice. This kind of dialect I knew to be the usual way of Sir Edw-rd S--m-r, and therefore without the least shew of resentment contented myself to say, that I was indeed of opinion, that to oppose the ill designs of inveterate knaves, is a work of great difficulty for young men to undertake; and that the common method of all governments now received in the world, to allow almost everything that tends to the corruption of manners, and then to restrain those corruptions, does not only require the longest experience and greatest prudence, but is far beyond the power of both. Yet to say that young men cannot understand the nature of government, and such regulations as are most conducing to the happiness of mankind, when at the same time they are thought capable of mathematicks, natural philosophy, the art of reasoning, and metaphysical speculations, which contain things more difficult to conceive than any in the art of government, seems absurd. But by the present manner of education, the minds of young men are for many years debauched from all that duty and business to which they are born; and in the place of moral and civil knowledge and virtue, addict themselves to mathematical, natural and metaphysical speculations, from which many are never able to withdraw their thoughts.[7] For the interest of some governments requiring that men should know little of publick affairs, the art of government has been looked upon as a kind of knowledge dangerous to be learned, except

---

[7] The argument here appears to run counter to that expressed in the *Proposals for the Reformation of Schools and Universities, in order to the better education of youth* (1704), a work which has been attributed to Fletcher. This strongly recommends the teaching of mathematics and natural philosophy (including motion, mechanics, hydrostatics, optics, astronomy and experimental philosophy) in the final two (of six) years of university.

by those who are advanced in years; and this only so far as the experience and practice of those corrupt constitutions and ways of living now in use among men will allow. Whereas young men have great advantages to find out what is right or amiss in government, by having never been engaged in the ill administration of affairs, nor habituated to bad customs and indirect practices, nor biassed by selfish ends, to entertain any other opinion of constitutions, laws and regulations, than what is just and right. And as their capacity for more abstracted sciences shews them sufficiently capable of understanding the art of government; and the innocence of their manners demonstrates that they are less biassed in judgment than other men; so in zeal and forwardness to put things in execution they are undoubtedly superior to all that are more advanced in years. The only difficulty in the education of youth, is to fix their application on things useful. And do you not think the young men you mentioned very happy, who instead of studying physicks and metaphysicks, have employed their thoughts in an active way to advance the interest and service of their country? Their relations have taken care to marry most of them young, in order to prevent innumerable inconveniences; and if they enter into a good œconomy of their private fortunes, they may certainly acquire greater riches than they can hope to have a venture for at court. And if they despise the ridiculous vanity of great titles, which is the peculiar folly of this age, of what use and ornament may they not be to their friends and country, the care of which has possessed them so early? 'Tis the experience of such men that will hereafter deserve to be valued, and not of those who from their youth have given themselves up to dissimulation and bad arts for worse ends, and are only skilled in the pernicious practices that tend to destroy the publick liberty. Still declaiming! said he, and the result of all is, that there are not two more proper qualities for government, than want of experience, joined to the violent disposition of youth. But, said I, when these are corrected by the advice, and controuled by the votes of men of riper years, do you think them still dangerous?

I do.

Would they not be more dangerous, if the old men had only the power of advising, and that, for example, in the senate of a commonwealth all things were to be determined by the votes of the young men?

Certainly.

Would there not be yet greater danger, if the young men had the disposal of all places and advantages, and that the old men, in order to obtain them, should be obliged to flatter, and give such advice as they knew would please, and at the same time be pernicious to the state?

Who can doubt it?

Now if the young men, by reason of frequent disputes, heats and factions among themselves, should chuse one of their own number, and invest him with an unlimited power, though he were younger by many years than the gentlemen in question: I say, if any people should be so governed, would you not look upon it as a mad kind of government?

Most surely.

And yet many nations think they can be no way secure under any other sort of government than that which often falls into this very inconveniency. You mean, said he, a young prince in an absolute monarchy. Pray, said I, what think you of a young prince in a limited monarchy, not accountable to any? Do you doubt of instruments to execute his will, and of the confusion things may be brought to before redress can be obtained? Do you not think such a one equally dangerous to the state as the young men we have mentioned? Ay! but, said the knight, they bring faction into the state. I confess, said I, the young prince does not, because he is uncontrouled; so far you are right.[8] But pray, Sir, what is it in those young noblemen, or in the proceedings of our parliament in general, that you think deserves so much blame? That they would talk, said he, of such limitations on a successor as tend to take away that dependence which your nation ought always to have upon us, as a much greater and more powerful people. I said, we are an independent nation, tho' very much declined in power and reputation since the union of the crowns, by neglecting to make such conditions with our kings, as were necessary to preserve both: that finding by experience the prejudice of this omission, we cannot be justly

---

[8] Though never a direct advocate of republicanism, Fletcher was fond of turning conventional wisdom against the idea of monarchy. In conversation with the learned Jacobite physician Archibald Pitcairne, he reportedly claimed to know a hereditary Professor of Divinity at Hamburg. Pitcairne scoffed, and Fletcher replied 'Yes Doctor, hereditary Professor of Divinity. What think you of an hereditary king?' G. W. T. Omond, *Fletcher of Saltoun* (Edinburgh, 1897), p. 95.

blamed for endeavouring to lay hold on the opportunity put into our hands, of enacting such conditions and limitations on a successor, upon the expiration of the present intail, as may secure the honour and sovereignty of our crown and kingdom, the freedom, frequency, and power of our parliaments, together with our religion, liberty and trade, from either English or foreign influence. Sir Edw-rd all in a fret; hey day, said he, here is a fine cant indeed, independent nation! honour of our crown! and what not? Do you consider what proportion you bear to England? – not one to forty in rents of land. Besides, our greatest riches arise from trade and manufactures, which you want. This was allowed by me: but I desired to inform him, that the trade of Scotland was considerable before the union of the crowns: that as the increase of the English trade had raised the value of their lands, so the loss of our trade had sunk the rents in Scotland, impoverished the tenant, and disabled him in most places from paying his landlord any otherwise than in corn; which practice has been attended with innumerable inconveniencies and great loss: that our trade was formerly in so flourishing a condition, that the shire of Fife alone had as many ships as now belong to the whole kingdom: that ten or twelve towns which lie on the south coast of that province, had at that time a very considerable trade, and in our days are little better than so many heaps of ruins: that our trade with France was very advantageous, by reason of the great privileges we enjoyed in that kingdom: that our commerce with Spain had been very considerable, and began during the wars between England and that nation; and that we drove a great trade in the Baltick with our fish, before the Dutch had wholly possessed themselves of that advantageous traffick.[9] Upon the union of the crowns not only all this went to decay; but our money was spent in England, and not among ourselves; the furniture of our houses, and the best of our clothes and equipage was bought at London: and though particular persons of the Scots nation had many great and profitable places at court, to

---

[9] The classic modern work on Scottish trade, T. C. Smout's *Scottish Trade on the Eve of the Union 1660–1707* (Edinburgh, 1963), contradicts Fletcher's belief that the decay of trade dated from the union of the crowns. While the seventeenth century did bring greater commercial dependence on England, the volume of Scottish trade was rising until 1688. It was only in the 1690s that crisis hit the Scottish economy. But Fletcher articulated what at the time was a widely held conviction.

the high displeasure of the English, yet that was no advantage to our country, which was totally neglected, like a farm managed by servants, and not under the eye of the master. The great business both of Scots and English ministers was, to extend the prerogative in Scotland, to the ruin of liberty, property and trade: and the disorders which were afterwards occasioned by the civil war, gave the last and finishing blow to the riches and power of the nation. Since that time we have had neither spirit, nor liberty, nor trade, nor money among us. And though during the time of the usurper Cromwel we imagined ourselves to be in a tolerable condition with respect to this last particular, by reason of that expence which was made in the nation by those forces that kept us in subjection; yet this was a deceitful substance, not unlike a plumpness in the natural body proceeding from a disease. The business of a Scots minister, is to get as much money as he can from our impoverished country, whilst he is in employment, well knowing that all regulations that may be established in order to inrich the nation, either by trade, manufactures, or husbandry, will require time before they can produce any considerable effect, and on that account will be of little advantage to him during his administration. I take all this freedom, said I, before the Earl of Cr-m-rty, though he be a Scots minister of state, because 'tis well known avarice is none of his faults, and that no person in our government is more ready to promote any new and solid project of improvement. I am obliged for the good character you give me, said the Earl; but very sorry I can promote none of your projects: they are I fear too great for our nation, and seem rather contrived to take place in a Platonick commonwealth than in the present corruption of things. My lord, said I, no man is more sensible how little is to be done in this age: but I think it the greatest of all follies to offer an expedient, which obtained will not answer the end, and to labour and toil for that which will not avail: such measures proceed in part from our ignorance of the ill condition we are in, and the means of recovery; but principally from a meanness of spirit, which hinders us always from applying the true remedies, if they are attended with the least appearance of difficulty or danger. And nothing does so much point out the want of sense and courage in particular men, or the degeneracy of an age and nation, than to content themselves to prosecute any considerable end by ineffectual and disproportionate means. Now the ill condition of Scotland proceeding from these causes; that our money is carried away and spent at court by those who attend there for places and pensions; that by the influence of English ministers upon our government, we are brought wholly to depend on that court; that by reason of the prince's absence, the laws are not put in execution: I say, these being the causes of our present ill condition, what other remedies can be found, than that the parliament of Scotland should for the time to come bestow all pensions and offices both civil and military; that our parliaments should be annual and not interrupted in their sessions, and have power to appoint committees for the administration of the government during the intervals of sitting? If these things are granted, said the Earl, I would know what power or authority is left to the prince. As great power, said I, as princes formerly enjoyed in most of the limited monarchies of Europe; their parliaments or diets were fixed, and at least annual: the chief officers of the crown and the counsellors of the prince were named by the states of most kingdoms; but the executive power of the government and the command of armies were vested in the prince, together with the prerogative of giving authority to the laws and currency to the coin, and a superiority in dignity and revenue, suitable to so high a station. But said the Earl, you diminish his power of administration, not only by refusing him the nomination of great officers, but even the inferior: you incroach upon his power as general, by taking from him the nomination of military officers; and you lessen the grandeur of his court, by refusing him the distribution of pensions. To this charge I made answer, that if princes might not appoint the principal officers of the crown, nor their own counsellors, the nomination of inferior officers seems to be below their care and dignity; that standing forces being pernicious to all governments, and national militias only safe and useful, 'tis but reasonable the people should have the choice of those who are to command them; that his lordship could not forget that the limitations in question were demanded for a kingdom, where the prince does not actually reside, as a remedy against the influence of a powerful court, on which otherwise we should be necessitated always to depend. And I think for a nation in these circumstances to have the power of conferring pensions, can no way lessen the grandeur of a court, where no court is. The Earl said, that no considerations whatever ought in such a degree to diminish the prince's power, which is the very essence of monarchical government; that no case could exist by which the essential part of any government could be so far lessened; and therefore such circumstances of affairs as I brought for reasons, being only accidents, could not be made use of to destroy the substance of a government. I told him I had always thought that princes were made for the good government of nations, and not the government of nations framed for the private advantage of princes. Right, said he, but then you must accommodate all monarchical government to the nature of princes, else you will make a heterogeneous body of the prince and state. I understand you not, said I, unless you mean that all limitations are contrary to the nature of princes, and that they will endure them no longer than necessity forces. And what hopes, said Sir Edw. S--r, can you have of enjoying them long, when your prince may be assisted by the power and riches of a far greater nation, which is highly concerned to take them away? I cannot think, replied I, that the people of England are obliged by their interest to oppose these limitations in Scotland, unless they think themselves concerned in interest to make us at all times their secret enemies, and ready to embrace every opportunity of declaring ourselves openly for such. For since we are not only become sensible of our present ill condition, but fully understand both the causes and the remedy; to oppose us in the prosecution of those means which are absolutely necessary to attain so just an end, would be no less than to declare open enmity against us. We shall run a great risque indeed, said Sir Edw-rd, in so doing! Sir, said I, no man is more fully persuaded than I am, of the great disproportion there is between the power of the one and the other nation, especially in the present way of making war. But you should consider, that by declaring yourselves in such a manner to be our enemies, you would drive us to the necessity of taking any power that will assist us, by the hand. And you can no way avoid so great danger, but by doing justice to your selves and us, in not opposing any conditions we may make with the successor to our crown. The Earl of Cr-m-rty said, that in his opinion there was an easy remedy to all these inconveniencies; which was an union of the two nations. I answered, I was sorry to differ so much from his lordship, as to think the union neither a thing easy to be effected, nor any project of that kind hitherto proposed, to be a remedy to our present bad condition: that the English nation had never since the union of the two crowns, shewn any great inclination to come to a nearer coalition with Scotland; and that I could not avoid making some remarks upon all the occasions that had given a rise to treat of this matter during my time. I have observed that a treaty of union has never been mentioned by the English, but with a design to amuse us when they apprehended any danger from our nation. And when their apprehensions were blown over, they have always shewn they had no such intention. In the year 1669, endeavours were used in Scotland to establish a good militia; which on account of a clause procured by the duke of Lauderdale to be inserted in the act, in order to make his court, so alarmed the English nation, that in the following year a treaty of union was proposed. But so soon as they perceived that our militia was ordered in such a manner as neither to be lasting nor formidable, they presently cooled, and the union vanished.[10] Upon the late revolution this treaty was again proposed: but when they saw we had chosen the same person for our king, and made the same intail of our crown they had done, the union, as a thing of no farther use to their affairs, was immediately dropped.[11] For the same reasons, I suppose, the late treaty was set on foot; and after they had nominated a successor without asking our opinion or concurrence, they thought this the only way to amuse us, and oblige us to take the same person.[12] Now as I have shewn how little the English nation has been really inclined to the union; so I must acknowledge that the Scots, however fond they have formerly been of such a

---

[10] Charles II had instructed the Scottish Privy Council in 1668 to raise a militia in Scotland, selected from areas in the country where royalist magnates were in a position to organise recruiting. Why the Scottish Militia Act should have alarmed the English is unclear: in the most recent account of the union negotiations during the 1670s, William Ferguson suggests that the key factors were anxieties over the English Navigation Acts, and Charles II's desire to cover his tracks while he negotiated the Treaty of Dover with the French King: *Scotland's Relations with England. A Survey to 1707* (Edinburgh, 1977), pp. 152–7.

[11] A union was proposed by the Scottish Convention of Estates in April 1689, following the overthrow and flight of James II and VII, but the English parliament showed no interest. On this occasion Fletcher himself had initially favoured union, writing to Andrew Russell in Rotterdam that 'For my owen part I thinck we can never come to any trew setlement but by uniting with England in parliaments, and traid.' Andrew Russell Papers, Scottish Record Office, RH15/106/690, no. 7: London, 8 Jan. 1689.

[12] The reference is to the union negotiations of 1702, which followed the unilateral English declaration of the Hanoverian succession in the Act of Settlement in 1701.

coalition, are now become much less concerned for the success of it, from a just sense they have that it would not only prove no remedy for our present ill condition, but increase the poverty of our country.

How, I pray, said the Earl?

I am of opinion, said I, that by an incorporating union, as they call it, of the two nations, Scotland will become more poor than ever.

Why so?

Because Scotsmen will then spend in England ten times more than now they do; which will soon exhaust the money of the nation. For besides the sums that members of parliament will every winter carry to London, all our countrymen who have plentiful estates will constantly reside there, no less than those of Ireland do at this time. No Scotsman who expects any publick employment, will ever set his foot in Scotland; and every man that makes his fortune in England, will purchase lands in that kingdom: our trade, which is the bait that covers the hook, will be only an inconsiderable retail, in a poor, remote and barren country, where the richest of our nobility and gentry will no longer reside: and though we should allow all the visionary suppositions of those who are so fond of this union; yet our trade cannot possibly increase on a sudden. Whereas the expences I mentioned will in a very short time exhaust us, and leave no stock for any kind of commerce. But, said the Earl, you do not distinguish right, nor consider where the fallacy of your reasoning lies. You talk of Scotland and Scots money, and do not reflect that we shall then be a part of Britain; England will be increased by the accession of Scotland, and both those names lost in that of Britain: so that you are to consider the good of that whole body, of which you then become a citizen, and will be much happier than you was, by being in all respects qualified to pretend to any office or employment in Britain, and may trade or purchase in any part of the island.[13] But, by your leave, my lord, let me distinguish plainly, and tell you, that if I make a bargain for the people that inhabit the

---

[13] The argument that a union would create a common 'British' interest was one which Cromarty urged repeatedly in his own pamphlet contributions to the union debate: see *Parainesis pacifica; or a perswasive to the Union of Britain* (Edinburgh, 1702, repr. London, 1702), and *A Letter from E.C. to E.W. concerning the Union* [Edinburgh, 1706].

northern part of this island, I ought principally to consider the interest of those who shall continue to live in that place, that they may find their account in the agreement, and be better provided for than they are. For if the advantages of getting employments, trading and purchasing in any part of the island, are the only things to be considered, all these may be as well obtained by any one who would change his country in the present state of things. And if in the union of several countries under one government, the prosperity and happiness of the different nations are not considered, as well as of the whole united body, those that are more remote from the seat of the government will be only made subservient to the interest of others, and their condition very miserable. On the other hand, besides our fishery, which God and nature has given us, together with the great privileges already granted to our African company, a distinct sovereignty does always enable a people to retain some riches, and leaves them without excuse if they do not rise to considerable wealth. So that if a sufficient provision be made to prevent the exhausting of our money by the attendance of Scotsmen at court, and to take away the influence of English ministers upon our affairs, no condition of men will be more happy. For we shall then be possessed of liberty; shall administer our own affairs, and be free from the corruptions of a court; we shall have the certain and constant alliance of a powerful nation, of the same language, religion and government, lying between us and all enemies both by sea and land, and obliged in interest to keep perpetual peace and amity with us. And this you cannot but allow to be a much happier condition, than any we ever could propose to ourselves by all the projects of union that have hitherto been formed. Here the Earl endeavoured by many arguments to shew that our country would be the place, where all manufactures, as well for the use of the whole island, as for exportation, would be made by reason of the cheapness of living, and the many hands that Scotland could furnish.[14] I said the contrary was not only most evident; but that the union would certainly destroy even those manufactures we now have. For example, the English are able to furnish us at an easier rate, with better cloth than we make in Scotland: and 'tis not to be supposed they will

---

[14] The argument that Scotland's low wages would give it a competitive advantage in a common market with England was another of which Cromarty made much in his own pamphlets, notably in *Parainesis Pacifica*.

destroy their own established manufactures to encourage ours.
Corn, and all manner of provisions are cheaper and more plentiful
in the six northern counties than in Scotland. The number of our
people was never so great as commonly imagined, and is now very
much diminished by the late famine; by extraordinary levies of soldiers; and chiefly by ill government, which having given no encouragement to industry of any kind, has necessitated great numbers of
men to abandon the country and settle themselves in other nations,
especially in Ireland. Besides, the natural pride of our commonalty,
and their indisposition to labour, are insuperable difficulties, which
the English have not to contend with in their people. But sure you
will allow, said the Earl, that a free commerce with England, and
the liberty of trading to their plantations, which cannot be expected
without an union, must be of incomparable advantage to the Scots
nation, unless you will disown one of your darling clauses in the act
of security. My lord, said I, the clause you mean, is placed there
without the condition of an union; and your lordship cannot forget,
was brought in by the court as an equivalent for all limitations, and
in order to throw out another clause, which declares that we would
not nominate the same successor with England, unless sufficient
limitations were first enacted. This was done to mislead the commissioners of burroughs, who for the most part are for any thing
that bears the name of trade, though but a sham, as this was. And
nothing could be more just than to turn it upon the court by adding
both clauses; which sunk your party in the house for a long time
after.[15] For my own part, I cannot see what advantage a free trade
to the English plantations would bring us, except a farther exhausting of our people, and the utter ruin of all our merchants, who

---

[15] The argument between Cromarty and Fletcher turns on different interpretations
of the decisions taken in the Scottish parliament in the previous summer. Cromarty seeks to side-line Fletcher's objections to free trade by pointing out that the
demand for free trade had been attached to the Act of Security voted by the
parliament: the Scots, in other words, had already made it one of the conditions
on which they would accept the same succession as the English. Fletcher counters
by pointing out that the Act of Security was not an offer of union (for which
Cromarty was now arguing), and that the demand for free trade had been introduced by the court in order to block a clause for limitations on the authority of
any future shared monarch; in the event, the parliament had frustrated the court
by adopting both clauses. Fletcher was on weaker ground in supposing that the
burgh representatives would fall for free trade: when the Treaty of Union was
negotiated in 1706 they gained significant protectionist concessions.

should vainly pretend to carry that trade from the English. The Earl, who knew the truth of these things, was unwilling to insist any longer upon this ungrateful subject; and therefore proceeding to another argument, said that when we shall be united to England, trade and riches will circulate to the utmost part of the island; and that I could not be ignorant of the wealth, which the remotest corners of the north and west of England possess. I answered, that the riches of those parts proceed from accidental causes. The lead and coal mines, which employ so much shipping, enrich the north. The western parts of England, besides mines of tin and lead, have many excellent harbours lying in the mouth of the channel, through which the greatest trade of the world is continually passing. I desired him to consider that Wales, the only country that ever had united with England, lying at a less distance from London, and consequently more commodiously to participate in the circulation of a great trade than we do, after three or four hundred years, is still the only place of that kingdom, which has no considerable commerce, though possessed of one of the best ports in the whole island; a sufficient demonstration that trade is not a necessary consequence of an union with England. I added, that trade is now become the golden ball, for which all nations of the world are contending, and the occasion of so great partialities, that not only every nation is endeavouring to possess the trade of the whole world, but every city to draw all to itself; and that the English are no less guilty of these partialities than any other trading nation. At these words Sir Chr- was pleased to ask me what were those partialities in point of trade, of which the English were guilty, and towards what nations: that for his part, he accounted them the frankest dealers, and the justest traders of the world. I said I would not insist upon the ill usage of the Scots nation in their late attempt to settle in Darien, nor enquire how far the late erected council of trade did in that affair second the partialities of a court engaged in mysterious interests with France; but desired to know his opinion of the usage their own colony in Ireland had received from them, and that he would excuse me, if I should let fall any expression about that matter which might seem hard; because in case he could give me satisfaction in this particular, I should very much incline to an incorporating union of the two nations. He answered, that he was very indifferent what course the Scots should take in the matter of an union, yet would not refuse to argue the point with me; and as to my question concerning Ireland, he said, he was of opinion, that a good measure of strictness and severity is absolutely necessary to keep them from the thoughts of setting up for themselves, and pretending to depend no longer upon England. I said that some late writers had undertaken to prove by authentick records, that the relation of that country to England was founded rather upon a very strict union than a conquest. But certainly, though the native Irish were conquered, your own colony was not; which yet you favoured no longer than till you saw them begin to flourish and grow rich.[16] And to shew what we are to expect, if ever we begin to thrive, though never so long after our union, I shall give some instance of your conduct towards Ireland in relation to trade. A law was made that no tobacco should be planted either in England or Ireland; and another, that no person, except of England or Ireland, might trade to the English plantations. Yet in the time of King Charles the second, great hardships and impediments were laid upon all those who should trade from Ireland to the English plantations, though they were still obliged to observe the law against planting tobacco in Ireland. And till the time of the late King no law was made in England for encouraging the woollen manufacture, but the like encouragements were given to the people of Ireland. Yet during that reign a law was made, which prohibits the exportation of all woollen manufactures from Ireland to foreign parts, and lays so high a duty upon all that shall be imported from thence into England, as amounts to a prohibition.[17] I forbear to mention any other hardships put upon those of that country, and chiefly the Scots who are settled in the northern

---

[16] Almost certainly a reference to the most important contemporary statement of the Anglo-Irish position, William Molyneux's *The Case of Ireland's being bound by Acts of Parliament in England, stated* (Dublin, 1698). Molyneux vigorously denied that the English king ruled Ireland by a simple right of conquest; in so far as there had been a conquest, it had been of the native (and Catholic) Irish only, and gave the Crown no right over the descendants of the English who had participated in the conquest. See further, Jacqueline Hill, 'Ireland without Union: Molyneux and his legacy', in Robertson (ed.), *A Union for Empire.*

[17] The 1671 Navigation Act forbade the direct importation of produce from the English colonies in America to Ireland, so that tobacco had to come through England; and the ban was re-imposed in 1685. It is unlikely, however, that the ban on planting tobacco in Ireland itself was of great significance. The Irish woollen manufactures were the target of a more recent bill of 1697, and the prohibitive duties had been enacted in 1699.

parts, though that colony still increases, to our loss and your advantage.[18] You speak of a conquered nation, said Sir Chr-, who have no sovereign rights belonging to them. I speak of a nation, said I, who affirm you have no shadow of right to make laws for them; that the power which the King's council has assumed was gotten by surprize; and that their first submission was founded on a treaty of union, which now on account of some rebellions suppressed, is called a conquest.[19] But sure, as I said before, you never conquered your own colony, and therefore ought to do them justice. Now if after an union with us the least commotion should happen in Scotland, suppose on account of church government; might we not expect that the suppression of this would likewise be called a conquest, and we or our posterity be treated as a conquered people? But can there be a more certain indication of what we may expect in point of trade from an union, than the usage of the postnati, who settled in England and the plantations, upon the faith of rights declared and ratified by both houses of parliament, confirmed by the decisions of all your courts, and affirmed by the Lord chief Justice Coke in the most hyperbolical terms, to be according to common and all law, which yet have been wholly violated and taken away, even to the prejudice of the English nation by the loss of such a number of people?[20] These things seem indispensably to require a guaranty, when the two parliaments come to be united, where we may possibly have fifty votes to five hundred, in a house already abounding so much in partialities, that the members who serve for one part of the kingdom, are frequently found in opposition to the

[18] Scots had settled in Ulster in large numbers in the early seventeenth century, in what was known as 'the Plantation of Ulster'.

[19] Fletcher refers to Poynings' Law (1494), under which all legislation proposed in the Irish parliament was supposed to have been approved by the privy council in England, and to the variant of the conquest argument which held that the Irish had forfeited any rights they once held as a result of their participation in later rebellions, notably those of 1641 and 1689. He dismisses both these claims.

[20] The 'Post-nati' were Scots born after James VI's accession to the throne of England in 1603. By the judgement in 'Calvin's Case' in 1608, they had been declared able to purchase land and to bring actions under English law, as if they were subjects of the King of England. None had been more emphatic in confirming this doctrine than the great English common lawyer Sir Edward Coke. Fletcher's point is that the rights of such Scots had since been violated by measures like the Navigation Acts, which had barred the Scots (like the Irish) from trading directly with English colonies. In practice Scots in the Americas had observed the Acts in the breach.

representatives of another, for the sake only of the particular interest of their own countries. Indeed, replied Sir Chr-, if your diffidence be so great, there can be no union. Sir, said I, if the matters of fact I mention are true, as I think they are undeniable, I am contented to make you judge of what we may expect from the nature of the thing, and genius of your people. In the first place, what security can a lesser nation, which unites to a greater, have, that all the conditions of union shall be duly observed, unless a third be admitted for guaranty of the agreement? And I suppose you would rather chuse to hear no more of an union, than that Holland or France should be the guarantees. True, said he; but guarantees are only proper in treaties of peace between nations not united: unions of nations, especially incorporating unions, of which we are speaking, suppose no breach of conditions; and we do not find that the nations which were so united to the republick of Rome had any guarantees for their security. Sir, said I, the union of those nations, and their admission to the rights and privileges of the city of Rome, could have no guarantees, because they were noble conditions given by that wise and generous state to nations they had conquered, and had in their power to use as they pleased: and if Ireland be yours by conquest, why do you not use them as well?[21] 'Twill certainly be our interest, said Sir Chr-, to observe the conditions on which we unite with Scotland. Do you think, replied I, that you always follow your interest? I must acknowledge, said he, not always. Then, said I, if at any time you should depart from your true interest in this matter, we shall want a guarantee and find none. On the other hand, if the temper, conduct and inclinations of your people be considered, 'twill appear that, except the union with Wales, which is still attended with great imperfections and inconveniences, they have never shewn the least disposition to unite with any other

---

[21] The Privernates, referred to by Fletcher in Speech no. IV (above p. 142) are an example of what Fletcher had in mind: conquered by Rome, they were then offered citizenship. Fletcher's response to Musgrave was also, however, an implicit comment on the passage in Grotius' *De Iure Belli ac Pacis* (1625), Book II, ch. ix, sect. 9, in which Grotius characterised the Romans' union with the Sabines as a full communication of rights between the two. The passage would repeatedly be invoked by advocates of incorporating union, including William Seton, John Clerk and Daniel Defoe, as demonstrating that parties to an incorporating union were necessarily equal. For Fletcher that communication of rights had been (as Grotius had himself acknowledged) a concession following conquest.

nation, though such as either stood upon equal terms with them, or such as they conquered, or even planted. How your colonies in America are treated, is well known to all men. You never could unite with Normandy, which had conquered you, nor with any part of France that you had conquered. But your oppressions in both were the principal cause of your expulsion from those countries. You could not unite with the states of Holland, when England was likewise a republick. And since the time of the late revolution, which was effected by the assistance of the states, and saved these nations from utter ruin, you can hardly endure the name of a Dutchman; and have treated them on all occasions with such scurrilous expressions, as are peculiar to the generality of your people. And if I should but touch upon the usage we continually meet with from this nation, I should not be believed, if all Europe were not sufficiently informed of their hatred to all strangers, and inveterate malice against the Scots. I know very well, that men of gravity and good breeding among you are not guilty of scurrilous reflections on any nation. But when we are to consider the case in question, we must have a just regard to the temper and general disposition of the people. At these words Sir Edw-rd, all in a flame, cries out, What a pother is here about an union with Scotland, of which all the advantage we shall have, will be no more than what a man gets by marrying a beggar, a louse for her portion? Upon this I turned to the Earl and Sir Chr-, and said, that if Sir Edw-rd had spoken these words in the house of commons,[22] I might not take notice of them, or question his freedom of speech in that place; but since he is pleased to express himself after this manner in a private conversation, I shall likewise take the liberty to say, that I wonder he is not afraid such language should make us suspect him not to be descended of the noble family whose name he bears. Sir Edw-rd going on with great passion; What account, said he, should we make of Scotland, so often trampled under foot by our armies? Did not protector Seymor at the battle of Muscleborough give you such a rout as destroyed the best part of your nobility and gentry?[23] And

---

[22] He had indeed spoken the words in the House of Commons, in opposing King William's suggestion of a union in 1700.
[23] Seymour invokes his ancestor, Edward Seymour, duke of Somerset and lord protector during the minority of Edward VI, who invaded Scotland and defeated the Scots army at the Battle of Pinkie (or Musselburgh) in September 1547.

of late years did not the very scum of our nation conquer you? Yes, said I, after they had with our assistance conquered the King and the nobility and gentry of England: and yet that which you call a conquest, was a dispute between parties, and not a national quarrel.[24] 'Twas, said he, inseparable from the fortune of our Edwards to triumph over your nation. Do you mean Edward of Carnarvan, said I, and his victory at Bannockburn? No, replied he, I mean Edward the first and third, whose heroic actions no princes have ever equalled. Sure, said I, you do not mean the honour of the first, or the humanity of the third so signally manifested at Berwick: nor the murder of Wallis by the first Edward, or the poisoning of Randolph earl of Murray by the third, after they had both refused to give battle to those heroes.[25] Sir Chr-, whose temper and gravity could not bear this upbraiding each other with old stories, interrupted these sallies, and desired I would farther explain myself touching an union between England and Ireland. The better conditions you give them, said I, the greater wisdom you will shew. But you do not consider, said Sir Chr-, that Ireland lies more commodiously situated for trade, and has better harbours than England; and if they had the same freedom and privileges, might carry the trade from us. Ay, said I, there 'tis: trade is the constant stumbling block, and ball of contention. But do you think, that if Ireland, by a just and equal union with England, should encrease in riches, such an encrease would prove so prejudicial to England, where the seat of the government is?

Certainly.

Then, said I, 'twere better to exclude Ireland wholly from trade; for in that case the trade of England would increase by so much as

---

[24] The 'scum of the nation' is the Cavalier Seymour's description of Cromwell's army, which had routed the Scots at Dunbar (1650) and Worcester (1651). In reply Fletcher points out that the Scots had previously assisted the English parliamentarians in defeating the forces of the king, and argues on this basis that Cromwell's victories had not amounted to a conquest, but were a continuation of the previous party conflict.

[25] Seymour's Edwards, both of whom won victories over the Scots, were Edward I (1272–1307) and III (1327–77). Fletcher responds with Edward II (1307–27), so decisively defeated by the Scots at Bannockburn in 1314. The 'honour' of Edward I was displayed in his treatment of captured Scots as if they were traitorous rebels, exemplified in the ritual execution of William Wallace in 1304. Edward III's 'humanity' is illustrated by his (supposed) involvement in the death of Thomas Randolph, earl of Moray and regent of Scotland, in 1332.

Ireland now possesses; and the power and riches of England confined at home would be no longer in danger of passing into any other nation.

I believe you may be in the right.

You will certainly find me to be so, said I, if in order to manage this new accession of trade, all the people of Ireland should be brought over to England; for in this case the value of England would increase much more than can be expected to accrue from Ireland in the present circumstances of things, that country being frequently not only unprofitable, but burdensome to England.[26]

I agree with you.

But, said I, if Ireland should be left without inhabitants, I fear the French King would take hold of the occasion, and possess himself of the whole country. That would only weaken him, said he, who grasping at the possession of the Spanish monarchy, has no number of people to spare. But, said I, a port in the province of Munster so near the entry of the channel, and over-against Brest, might be of use to him, require no great number of men to maintain, and be of the most dangerous consequence to us. So that for argument sake

---

[26] In this and the following paragraph Fletcher develops a variant of Sir William Petty's proposal in *The Political Arithmetick* (probably written 1671–6, but only published in 1690) to transplant the population of Ireland and the Highlands of Scotland into England. Petty had introduced his proposal in the following terms:

> And here I beg leave (among the several matters which I intend for serious) to interpose a jocular, and perhaps ridiculous digression, and which I desire men to look upon, rather as a Dream or Revery, than a rational proposition; the which is, that if all the moveables and People of Ireland, and of the Highlands of Scotland, were transported into the rest of Great Britain; that then the King and his Subjects, would thereby become more rich and strong, both offensively and defensively, than now they are. (*The Economic Writings of Sir William Petty*, ed. C. H. Hull, 2 vols. (Cambridge, 1899), I, p. 285.)

Petty used the suggestion virtually as a counter-factual, to demonstrate that the land of England should be able to maintain a far higher population than it was doing, with the greater part of the added population employed in manufactures. He did, however, follow this argument with the suggestion that the three kingdoms should be united into one, and equally represented in one parliament.

Fletcher, by contrast, uses the idea as an argument against union, by taking it still further towards a *reductio ad absurdum*: while omitting the Scottish Highlands, he extends the logic of transplantation to northern England and Wales, until all the wealth and population of England are concentrated around London. This will enable him to bring the conversation back to its starting-point, the danger posed by that great city.

we must suppose Ireland sunk in the sea; and then you will cease to fear either that they may set up for themselves, or carry away the trade from England. And being possessed of all their people and riches, you will be no longer liable to the expence of defending that kingdom. From these suppositions, said he, the consequence is just. Do you not think, continued I, that for the same reasons it might be the interest of England to bring the people of the six northern counties into the south, provided that country could also be sunk? For trade will certainly increase, and be more easily managed, when brought within a less compass. Besides, you would then have so broad a ditch to secure you against the Scots, that you would be rid of any trouble from them also. He could not but acknowledge the parity of reason, and said, that if nature had made such a ditch from the beginning, the happiness of England had been complete. I added, that Wales being a country inconsiderable either for soil or commerce, that people might be much more advantageously imployed in trading here than in keeping goats at home; and your union with them become much stricter by bringing them nearer London: and then I think that country might likewise be sunk with advantage. Though you banter, said he, yet the consequence will undeniably follow from your suppositions. And do you not think, said I, the same arguments would prove, that all the considerable trade of the world might be brought into one city, and all mankind to live within and about that place?

Perhaps.

For what end then, said I, did God create such vast tracts of land, capable of producing so great variety and abundance of all things necessary and useful to men? In order, I suppose, that these countries might not be inhabited, and that mankind might confine themselves to islands, strait, barren and unwholsome situations, and live upon trade. Can there be a greater disorder in human affairs? Besides, we know that such numbers of men did not meet together in morasses, and other inconvenient places out of choice; but were forced and driven by the violence of tyranny to shelter themselves in difficult and inaccessible situations, as is plain by the examples of Holland, Venice, Tyre and other cities: and when they were come together, they were necessitated, in order to subsist, to apply themselves to manufacture, navigation, and the like arts. But if the governments of the world were well regulated, and men might have the liberty of chusing, they would not be confined to such narrow, barren and unwholsome places, nor live so much at sea, or in the exercise of a sedentary and unmanly trade, to foment the luxury of a few; but would disperse themselves over the world in greater or lesser numbers, according to the goodness of the soil, and live in a more free and manly way, attended with a more equal distribution of riches than trade and commerce will allow. Trade is not the only thing to be considered in the government of nations: and justice is due, even in point of trade, from one nation to another. For every good government has always encouraged industry, because all mankind have a right to the fruits of their own labour. And on that account all governments which put discouragements on the industry of their subjects are not upon a right foot; but violent, and consequently unjust. Soft and fair, said Sir Chr-, the consequences of these maxims reach farther than perhaps you imagine. We must not rely too much upon our own speculations, or think the world can ever be rightly governed; but must take things as they are, and consider the interest of the society in which we live. And if any profitable trade be in the possession of our neighbours, we may endeavour to dispossess them of that advantage for the good of our own society.[27] Though this should be granted, said I, yet you ought not to deny to a people, who like Ireland live under your government, the fruits of their industry. This sure is great injustice.

Not at all, said he; for as I told you, they may break with us, and set up a distinct government in opposition to our right, and perhaps with the ruin of this nation. What can tempt and provoke them so much, said I, to do so, as unjust usage? But the surest way, replied he, is to put it out of their power to separate from us. If so, said I, you must own your way of governing that people to be an oppression; since your design is to keep them low and weak, and

[27] Musgrave assumes that international trade is a zero sum, in which one nation's gain is another's loss: England was doing no more than acting out of its own interest in taking steps to protect itself against any competitive advantage which the Irish might enjoy through lower costs (as in their wool manufactures). England would apply the same logic to the Scots. Musgrave's arguments are an epitome of those advanced in print by the English economic writers John Cary and Charles Davenant. On this context for the *Account of a Conversation*, see Istvan Hont, 'Free trade and the economic limits of modern politics: neo-Machiavellian political economy reconsidered', in John Dunn (ed.), *The Economic Limits to Modern Politics* (Cambridge, 1990).

not to encourage either virtue or industry. For the light of nature teaches, that men ought not to use one another unjustly on any account, much less under the specious pretext of government. But we have a right, answered he, to use them at discretion, because we have conquered them.

Then you have a right to do injustice.

'Tis not injustice, said he, because it is our right. And you do not consider that things just in themselves, are not always so in relation to government; that the condition of human affairs necessarily obliges those that govern, to attend the good and interest of the whole society, and not to be over scrupulous in doing exact justice to particular persons; especially if their interest should happen to be different from that of the community. And for this reason those countries which are most remote from the seat of the government, ought not to expect an equal participation of liberty and immunities with those that lie at less distance. For if they should enjoy the same privileges, the subjection of such nations could not be secured. You know that under the Roman government the liberties and privileges of those who lived in and about the city of Rome, were far greater than the rest of Italy enjoyed, which yet was possessed of many more than any of the provinces. I doubt not, said I, this order was very proper to retain the dominion of the world in the power of one city. But I think those nations might have lived more happily under another kind of regulation; and am fully persuaded, that all great governments, whether republicks or monarchies, not only disturb the world in their rise and fall; but by bringing together such numbers of men and immense riches into one city, inevitably corrupt all good manners, and make them uncapable of order and discipline, as you have already owned, and experience has but too well demonstrated. Rome, the greatest of all, incessantly disturbed her neighbours for seven hundred years; and after the conquest of almost all the known world, was corrupted by excess of riches and power, and spread the infection over all the parts of that empire, which at length brought in so many barbarous nations, and caused so many wars and so great effusion of blood, that the world suffered as much by the overthrow and destruction, as by the rise and continuance of that mighty power. Yet, said he, I think 'tis necessary that a considerable body of people should be united under one government, and by that means enabled to defend themselves against a powerful enemy, because by the successful ambition of some men, we frequently see great and formidable powers arise in the world, to the disturbance of all their neighbours. In that I perfectly agree with you, said I. Pray then, replied he, what numbers would you allow in such a body of men: or rather, what extent of territory would you think necessary to a right division of the world into several distinct governments, since you are so much an enemy to all great and over-grown powers? You seem willing, said I, to confer such an office upon me, that those who do not know my name, will take me for a second Phaleg.[28] Not to lay then too great a burden upon you at once, answered he, I desire you to acquaint us into what parts you would divide Europe, most commodiously to obtain the true ends of government. I replied, that God and nature seemed to have marked out certain portions of the world for several great societies of men; having divided them from each other by seas and mountains, or some remarkable difference of the soil and climate. The island of Britain and that of Ireland seem conveniently situated for one government: Spain and Portugal for another, because they lie together in one compact body, and are divided from the rest of Europe by the Pyrenean mountains. In like manner France is contained within the Alpes, Jura, the Voge, the Ardennes and the Pyrenees. Italy is separated from all other parts by the Alpes; and the three adjacent islands seem naturally to belong to that country. The seventeen Provinces, the circles of Westphalia and lower Saxony, with the archbishoprick of Cologn and kingdom of Denmark, seem commodiously placed to be united under one government. The rest of Germany, with the Swiss Cantons, and the provinces that lie between those countries and the Adriatick sea, might very well compose another. Norway, Sweden, Finland, Liefland, and the northern parts of European Muscovy, lying under the same climate, may be conveniently joined together. Poland, Prussia, Lithuania, and the southern parts of the European Muscovy, with the little Tartary, might likewise be properly united. The

---

[28] An allusion to Peleg, or Phalec, the son of Eber, of the line of Shem, son of Noah: Peleg was so named because in his days the earth was divided. (Genesis, 10: 25: 'And unto Eber were born two sons; the name of one was Peleg; for in his days was the earth divided'; also I Chronicles, 1: 19.) Peleg lived for a total of 239 years, but was comfortably outlived by his father Eber, who lasted another 430 years after he begat Peleg at the age of 34 (Genesis, 11: 16–19).

countries that lie to the north of Macedonia and Albania, and on
the south of the Carpathian mountains, from Austria, Stiria and
Carniola to the Euxin sea, might be a ninth distinct government,
and Macedonia, Albania, Thessaly, Epirus, Achaia, Morea, Negro-
pont, Candia, and the adjacent islands, a tenth. And now I think I
may rest, and take breath after so long a journey, leaving to any
other the liberty of making the like through the other three parts
of the world. What all this tends to I cannot imagine, said Sir Chr-
for by your division, our own government would continue to be of
as great extent as now. You shall know that, said I, before we part.
In the mean time, to justify in some measure the reasonableness of
this division, you may consider that almost every one of the ten
parts, into which I have divided Europe, speaks a language distinct
from all the rest, and that the people are generally of the same
temper and like dispositions. Sir Edw-rd, impatient to hear a discourse about so many things and places with which he is so little
acquainted, thought fit to interrupt us; and directing his words to
me; Sir, said he, are you undertaking to teach us geography? Else
what can you mean by such a division of Europe? Will you not
allow, said I, a private man to make an imaginary division of countries; when 'tis well known that a great king in the beginning of the
last age contrived one of the same nature?[29] And you do not yet
fully know what use I shall make of this division. You have led me
into such a maze, said the Earl, and raised so many new thoughts
in me, that without regard to our former reasoning, I must pursue
some of them. That which occurs to me first, is, that if governments
so equal in strength either on account of their riches or situation,
should come to be established, mankind might live in greater peace
than they do: especially if these governments were by mutual
alliances obliged to preserve the common tranquillity. But you are
to observe, said Sir Chr-, the imperfection of this project to preserve peace in the world. For though one or two of these governments might not dare to disturb and injure the rest, yet nothing can

[29] A reference, possibly, to the 'Grand Dessein' of Henry IV of France, by which
Europe would have been divided into fifteen dominions, comprising six hereditary
and five elective kingdoms, and four territorial republics: recorded in the *Mémoires
ou Œconomies Royales d'Estat Domestiques, Politiques et Militaires de Henry le
Grand*, par Maximilian de Bethune, duc de Sully, Tome IV (Paris, 1664), pp. 77–
89. Fletcher had a copy of the work in his library.

hinder one half of them from combining against the other. And as such wars would be managed by a far greater number of forces than the present, mankind must of consequence be made more miserable. The nature of human affairs is such, said I, that a perpetual peace is not to be preserved among men; yet certainly some constitutions of government are better fitted to maintain the publick tranquillity than others. And in place of the continual great and ruinous wars, which questions about the succession of princes, and their ambitious designs, have intailed upon the world, things might be brought to less frequent contentions, and the publick animosities either prevented from proceeding to open breaches; or if at some times wars could no way be avoided, they might be neither lasting nor bloody. If you can shew, said he, how so happy a state of things may be introduced into the world, you will do the greatest service imaginable to mankind. For matters are now brought to such a pass, that in every war almost all Europe and America, with a great part of Asia and Africa become engaged. You are in the right, said I; and these universal wars, as I may call them, which with little interruption have continued more than thirty years, have so distressed this part of the world, and occasioned such disorder in the affairs of men, that Europe is thought to be diminished a full fifth in value. For wars, besides that they are become universal, are now wholly managed by the force and power of money, and by that means most grievously oppress and afflict not only the places that are the theatres of action, but even the remotest village and most solitary cottage. And the French King having by the oppression of his subjects, and exact economy of his affairs, been able to keep such great numbers of troops on foot, has obliged the rest of Europe to a proportionable expence, and thereby made all wars by land at least twice as chargeable as formerly they were; and by sea to exceed all example. But to give you my opinion of this matter, I think mankind might be best preserved from such convulsions and misery, if instead of framing governments with regard only to a single society, as I believe all legislators have hitherto done, we should constitute such as would be no less advantageous to our neighbours than ourselves. You talk strangely, said Sir Chr-, as if our advantage were not frequently inconsistent with that of our neighbours. I am of opinion, replied I, that the true interest and good of any nation is the same with that of any other. I do not say that one society ought not to repel the injuries of another; but that no people ever did any injustice to a neighbouring nation, except by mistaking their own interest. You talk, said he, of injustice, but I speak of advantage. If you go about, said I, to take away by force any advantage that belongs to a neighbouring people, you not only do injustice to them, but injure yourself by the example. Whatever the example be, replied he, the advantage will accrue to my country. For the present, and in appearance, said I. But a citizen in the service of his country, said he, is not obliged to the same scruples as in his private affairs; and must be true to his publick trust, and take care that the commonwealth suffer no prejudice. Then, said I, no man can be a good citizen of a particular commonwealth, and a citizen of the world; no man can be a true friend to his country and to mankind at the same time. I confess, said he, this conclusion naturally follows: but we may not dispense with the interest of our country as with our own; and you know the precepts contained in the sermon on the mount relate to the actions of private men.[30] Do you think then, said I, that one nation cannot do injustice to another? Yes, answered he, when that which is done is to the prejudice of both. And do you not also think, said I, that one nation may make an unjust war against another?

Yes.

Then if your country should make such a war with success, they would have accomplished an unjust design. True, said he; but if thereby any advantage accrue to the nation, this becomes an acquired right to the people, and ought to be defended by all those who are intrusted with the publick affairs. Now if afterwards it should happen, said I, that such a neighbouring nation should renew the war, in order to recover what they had lost, would that war be unjust on their part?

I think not.

Then you lay a foundation as well for your neighbours to make a just war against you, as for your own nation to make an advantageous war (which you say is not unjust) against them. This sure is far from the design of abolishing wars so far as may be possible. By what other means then, said he, may we hope to obtain this good end? The most effectual way, replied I, is, that all such

---

[30] In the Sermon on the Mount (Matthew, 5–7) Jesus enjoined the love of one's neighbour and turning the other cheek; the sermon ends with the Lord's Prayer.

governments as are of a sufficient force to defend themselves, should be rendered either uncapable or unfit to make conquests. For the ambitious desires of men to encrease their dominions, have always been the principal cause of disturbing the peace of the world. 'Tis impossible, said Sir Edw-rd S--m-r, to take away that natural and generous inclination which is found in the best of men, to extend the empire of their country; especially among us, who have such great examples in our history to encourage us, and so noble and populous a city; which by being situated near the south-east point of the island, lies as conveniently to command the north of France and all the Low Countries, as the three kingdoms. But Sir, said I, do you approve what Sir Chr- has said, that wars are to be abolished by all possible means? Suppose I do, said he; yet how can so strong an inclination, found not only in particular men, but sometimes in the whole body of a people, be altered? If the dominions of a state, said I, might not be encreased by conquest.

How is that possible?

If, for example, said I, every one of those ten portions of Europe, I mentioned before, had ten or twelve sovereign cities well fortified within its territories, each of them possessing and governing the adjacent district: such a government strengthened with forts in passes, and other convenient places, might be very capable to defend itself, and yet altogether unfit for conquest.

Why so?

Because, said I, a conquest divided into twelve parts would be of little account, they could not be made adjacent to the several cities to which they ought to belong. But, said he, such conquered places might be governed in common to the advantage of the whole union. That, replied I, would be like a possession in common, for which no man has any particular affection, and on that account lies always neglected. But you talk, said Sir Edw-rd, of sovereign cities; I fancy you mean republicks; which is nothing to us, who live under the benign influence of monarchy. You may suppose those cities, said I, to be the capitals of sovereign and independent kingdoms or countries. For of such sovereignties united under one monarch we have many examples.[31] And the prince may either keep his court in

---

[31] Which examples Fletcher had in mind is not immediately clear. Since he was concerned to deny that his scheme was valid only for republics, the examples of the United Provinces and the League of Swiss Cantons, neither of which acknowledged a monarch, would not have satisfied Seymour. He may simply have meant

each of them successively; or, which is better, reside in the country, and permit no more buildings about his palaces than are absolutely necessary for his domesticks, and the dispatch of publick business, and not to harbour a crew of lazy, profligate and vicious wretches, fit only to render his court a mere sink of corruption, and a seminary to propagate all manner of vice through the whole nation. So that we may proceed to reason concerning the excellency of those governments, which consist of divers sovereignties united for their common defence, whether cities or kingdoms; whether independent already, or to be made so in order to put such a design in execution; whether governed by a prince, or by a great council of delegates. But certainly, said he, if these distinct sovereignties were incorporated under one head and city, such a government would be of greater force. If you mean, said I, to disturb their own peace, and that of their neighbours, I grant your assertion.

How so?

You must acknowledge, said I, that a great city is more tumultuous and disorderly, and therefore more capable of disturbing its own peace than small ones, and much more violently inclined to conquer other countries, because better able to retain the conquest. But sure, said he, if divers small sovereignties were united under one prince, his authority would better preserve peace among them, than if they were governed by a council of delegates, which in my opinion is only proper to set them together by the ears. I am very glad, said I, that you think such united governments more suitable

to remind Seymour (and his readers) that most of the great monarchies of Europe, including the Spanish, the Austrian Habsburg and the British, were already composites of formally sovereign states.

The idea of unions of equal sovereign states had been formalised by the jurists Grotius and, in more detail, Samuel Pufendorf: see the latter's discussion of 'systems of states' in *Of the Law of Nature and Nations* (originally published in Latin, 1672, transl., London, 1703), Book VII, ch. v, sections 16–21, expanded in the dissertation *De Systematibus Civitatum*, in Samuel Pufendorf, *Politica Inculpata* (Lund, 1679). (Fletcher owned editions of both these works.) Under the heading 'systems of states' Pufendorf had included both unions of states under a single monarch (as the British kingdoms) and strict confederations (such as the United Provinces).

The crucial difference of Fletcher's scheme, as he goes on to explain, is that in it the monarch would not be allowed to establish a permanent court in any one of his cities or territories: enormous capital cities, and the courts which resided in them, were what Fletcher's plan was designed to render impossible, so that the benefits of city life might be much more widely diffused.

to monarchies than to commonwealths; for if that be true, there will be greater hopes of introducing them into the world. And indeed a prince seems much more fitted to be at the head of such a league, than a council, as to the military part, in which principally such an union has occasion to exert its power. So that I have nothing more to do than to prove that such governments are of all others the best to preserve mankind, as well from great and destructive wars, as from corruption of manners, and most proper to give to every part of the world that just share in the government of themselves which is due to them. If you can prove, said Sir Chr-, what you undertake, I shall have no more to say. 'Tis indeed, said I, a most surprising thing to me, that not only all those who have ever actually formed governments, but even those who have written on that subject, and contrived schemes of constitutions, have, as I think, always framed them with respect only to particular nations, for whom they were designed, and without any regard to the rest of mankind. Since, as they could not but know that every society, as well as every private man, has a natural inclination to exceed in every thing, and draw all advantages to itself, they might also have seen the necessity of curbing that exorbitant inclination, and obliging them to consider the general good and interest of mankind, on which that of every distinct society does in a great measure depend. And one would think that politicians, who ought to be the best of all moral philosophers, should have considered what a citizen of the world is. 'Tis true, something like a consideration of the common good of mankind, appeared in the constitution of the Achaian league; and if any of the antients ever had a right view in this affair, the founders of that government were the men. But the mighty power of the Roman commonwealth oppressed them in the very infancy of their establishment, and so deprived posterity of a perfect knowledge of the tendency of that constitution.[32] Most governments have been

---

[32] The Achaian League was an alliance of cities in the northern Peloponnese, along the Gulf of Corinth. First formed for religious purposes, it was reformed in 280 BC to resist the expansion of the Macedonian monarchy. It lasted for the remainder of the third century BC before allying with Rome in 198 BC; and after an unsuccessful revolt against Roman authority it was finally dissolved in 146 BC. The fullest account of the League was that of Polybius, one of its last leaders: *Histories*, esp. Book II.37–70. It was taken by Machiavelli, *Discourses*, II.iv, to have been the Greek equivalent of the ancient Etruscan League in northern Italy (of which the modern equivalent, in Machiavelli's day, was the Swiss League). According to Machiavelli

framed for conquests; that is, to disturb the peace of mankind: though I know that some were less fitted for conquest than others, as the aristocratical. But there was nothing even in those constitutions that could sufficiently restrain the desire of enlarging their dominions, though no way formed to that end; which has frequently brought great calamities upon many of those governments, as the examples of Venice and Sparta demonstrate.[33] In the last of which the wise legislator having formed the manners of the people for war, and the constitution altogether unfit to retain conquests, I would willingly persuade myself, that he designed these two things should balance each other, in order to keep that people always exercised to arms, and yet not give them the occasion of rising to such a height, as would inevitably precipitate them into ruin. And this, I think, should have been obvious to all legislators, that whoever contrives to make a people very rich and great, lays the foundation of their misery and destruction, which in a short time will necessarily overtake them. For such vicissitudes of human affairs are as certain as those of heat and cold in the revolution of the year; and no condition of men, or publick societies, is durable and lasting, except such as are established in mediocrity. Now in small governments laws may be duly executed, and the manners of men in a great measure preserved from corruption: but because such governments are not of force sufficient to defend themselves, a considerable number of them should be united together for the common safety; by which union and league they will be enabled to resist a powerful invasion, and yet remain uncapable of conquest. The three kingdoms of Scotland, England and Ireland, may serve for an example of this: which, though situated on islands, are yet in their present condition exposed to the fate of a single battle, if a great army of enemies

these were leagues of equal 'republics', whose constitutions required the member-cities to deliberate together in a council, and which were as a result ill-adapted for expansion and empire. To Machiavelli they represented a second-best form of rule over extended territory, the Roman model of imperial rule being the best; in Fletcher's eyes, however, it was precisely the inbuilt reluctance to expand which made such leagues a plausible alternative to great empires. Machiavelli's discussion of their merits was almost certainly the most important single inspiration of Fletcher's own scheme.

[33] The observation that the aristocratic governments of ancient Sparta and modern Venice had been inimical to conquest was Machiavelli's: *Discourses*, I.v–vi. But even Sparta and Venice, Machiavelli noted, had eventually succumbed to the temptation.

could be landed near London. But if good forts were erected in the most considerable passes; and twelve cities with all the sea-ports well fortified, the loss of many battles would not determine the matter. And considering that our naval force might in a great measure intercept the supplies of the enemy, we might defend ourselves against all our neighbours. And as such a constitution would be altogether unfit to molest them, so it would give them little encouragement to disturb our peace. At this rate, said Sir Chr-, if we should continue long in peace, and unaccustomed to war, we might become a prey to the first invader. I answered, that I did not think we ought to be wholly unconcerned in the affairs of the continent; but that such a constitution would certainly keep us from the danger of making conquests abroad, which in the present state of things any ambitious prince may attempt. Our militias might be usefully and honourably imployed in assisting our neighbours to form the like leagues on the Continent;[34] and a gradual propagation of such excellent governments would become easy, when mankind should be convinced of the great happiness and security they would enjoy by living under them. And though these leagues might possibly at some time make wars upon one another on occasion of a sudden pique, or to take revenge for some un-neighbourly action; yet such wars could not be lasting, because nothing but hopes of making acquisitions and conquests can make them so. And as to the advantage of having twelve cities governing themselves happily and virtuously, instead of one great vicious and ungovernable city, I leave it to your consideration, who have so judiciously shewn, that great cities do not only corrupt the manners of their own inhabitants, but those of whole nations, and destroy all good government. Cities of a moderate extent are easily governed, and the example and authority of one virtuous man is often sufficient to keep up good order and discipline; of which we have divers instances in the history of the Grecian republicks:[35] whereas great multitudes of men are always deaf to all remonstrances, and the frequency of ill example

---

[34] Cf. *A Discourse of Government*, above p. 28. The structure of the militia proposed there, with its several camps throughout the British Isles, was broadly compatible with the decentralisation of government advocated here.

[35] Obvious examples of such reformers included the Athenians Solon (early fifth century BC) and Demosthenes (mid-fourth century BC); the maintenance and renewal of 'order' in a city was also a theme of Machiavelli's: *Discourses*, I.xviii, III.i.

is more powerful than laws. But, said Sir Chr-, to reduce London within the compass of the old walls, seems a thing impracticable. This difficulty will be removed, replied I, when this city shall be only the capital of the neighbouring counties. 'Twill be thought injustice, said he, to remove the seat of the government from a place which has been so long possessed of that great advantage. The injustice, said I, has been greater, that one place has so long enjoyed those profits which ought to have been divided among the considerable cities of the nation. I am afraid, said he, that all endeavours to disturb the affairs of so great a body of people, only out of a remote prospect of bettering their condition by a new regulation, may fall under the imputation of folly: and that men would think it hard to be plunged into such difficulties, as so great a change would necessarily occasion. Sir, said I, if a French King, when he is in peace with other nations, should suddenly attack us with his whole power, how can we resist him in our present condition; having no fortified cities, and the great seat of all our riches and power exposed to the very first insult of the invader? One would think such a people were predestinated to ruin. You talk of the folly and hardship of putting men into some difficulties by a new regulation of their affairs, and seem not to consider how much more cruel a thing it would be to suffer these nations to be inslaved by a foreign invasion, or inevitably lose their liberty by that corruption of manners which this vicious and profligate city diffuses into every part. I did not foresee, said Sir Chr-, what use you would make of my complaint against the depravation of manners that reigns in this town, but acknowledge the consequence you draw to be just; and that if we design to diminish the corruption, we must lessen the city. What visions have we here, said Sir Edw-rd? Destroy the greatest and most glorious city of the world to prosecute a whimsical project! Sir, replied I, you have heard what I have answered to Sir Chr-; and besides, do you not think the remoter parts of England injured by being obliged to have recourse to London for almost every thing, and particularly for justice? Do you not think them wronged, in that almost all the treasure of England is yearly laid out in this place, and by that means the substance of the other parts exhausted, and their rents and revenues diminished? This, said he, is of little importance to the nation, so long as they continue to rise in the counties that lie nearest to the capital. I do not know that, replied I, but am of

opinion, that if instead of one, we had twelve cities in these kingdoms possessed of equal advantages, so many centers of men, riches
and power, would be much more advantageous than one. For this
vast city is like the head of a ricketty child, which by drawing to
itself the nourishment that should be distributed in due proportions
to the rest of the languishing body, becomes so over-charged, that
frenzy and death unavoidably ensue. And if the number of people
and their riches would be far greater in twelve cities than now in
one, which I think no man will dispute; and that these cities were
such as are situated in convenient distances from each other, the
relief and advantages they would bring to every part of these kingdoms would be unspeakable. For example, if the people of York-
shire or Devonshire were not obliged to go farther than York or
Exeter to obtain justice, and consequently had no occasion to spend
money out of those counties, how soon should we see another face
of things in both? How soon would they double and treble their
present value? That London should draw the riches and government of the three kingdoms to the south-east corner of this island,
is in some degree as unnatural, as for one city to possess the riches
and government of the world. And, as I said before, that men ought
to be dispersed over all countries in greater or lesser numbers
according to the fertility of the soil; so no doubt justice should be
administred to all in the most convenient manner that may be, and
no man be obliged to seek it at an inconvenient distance. And if
the other parts of government are not also communicated to every
considerable body of men; but that some of them must be forced to
depend upon others, and be governed by those who reside far from
them, and little value any interest except their own, studying rather
how to weaken them in order to make sure of their subjection; I
say, all such governments are violent, unjust and unnatural. I shall
add, that so many different seats of government will highly encourage virtue. For all the same offices that belong to a great kingdom,
must be in each of them; with this difference, that the offices of
such a kingdom being always burdened with more business than
any one man can rightly execute, most things are abandoned to the
rapacity of servants; and the extravagant profits of all great officers
plunge them into all manner of luxury, and debauch them from
doing good: whereas the offices of these lesser governments
extending only over a moderate number of people, will be duly

executed, and many men have occasions put into their hands of doing good to their fellow citizens. So many different seats of government will highly tend to the improvement of all arts and sciences; and afford great variety of entertainment to all foreigners and others of a curious and inquisitive genius, as the ancient cities of Greece did. I perceive now, said Sir Edw-rd, the tendency of all this discourse. On my conscience he has contrived the whole scheme to no other end than to set his own country on an equal foot with England and the rest of the world. To tell you the truth, said I; the insuperable difficulty I found of making my country happy by any other way, led me insensibly to the discovery of these things; which, if I mistake not, have no other tendency than to render, not only my own country, but all mankind as happy as the imperfections of human nature will admit. For I considered that in a state of separation from England, my country would be perpetually involved in bloody and destructive wars. And if we should be united to that kingdom in any other manner, we must of necessity fall under the miserable and languishing condition of all places that depend upon a remote seat of government. And pray where lies the prejudice, if the three kingdoms were united on so equal a foot, as for ever to take away all suspicion and jealousy of separation? That virtue and industry might be universally incouraged, and every part contribute chearfully and in due proportion to the security and defence of this union, which will preserve us so effectually from those two great calamities, war and corruption of manners. This is the only just and rational kind of union. All other coalitions are but the unjust subjection of one people to another. Here I stopped; but after some pause finding the rest of the company silent, I continued to say, that I would not pretend to determine whether each of the portions into which I had divided Europe, should be confined to the precise number of twelve cities: though possibly if there were more, they might be subject to some confusion; and if not so many, would not answer the end: that I would not determine whether they should altogether consist of cities that are already considerable, as in these islands are London, Bristol, Exeter, Chester, Norwich, York, Sterling, Inverness, Dublin, Cork, Galloway, Londonderry; or whether some other places more conveniently situated for strength, and more capable of fortification, might not rather be of the number. But this easy division of territory I think indispensably necessary, that to every city all the next adjacent country should belong. I was going on to open many things concerning these leagued governments, when a servant came to acquaint us that dinner was set on the table. We were nobly entertained, and after dinner I took leave of the company, and returned to my lodgings, having promised to meet them again at another time to discourse farther on the same subject.

My lords, I shall add nothing to this account, being persuaded that so long a narration has already sufficiently tired you.

I am,

Your most humble servant.

FINIS.

List of variants

Changes of substance between the 1732 edition of *The Political Works* and the separate pamphlet editions of the works as they were published in Fletcher's lifetime are given below. Also included are the changes made in manuscript to David Fletcher's copy of the *Discourses*. (On these editions see the Note on the Text, above, pp. xlix–l.) Variations of spelling and punctuation are not included.

As there are no changes (other than in spelling and punctuation) between the pamphlet editions of the *Speeches by a Member of the Parliament which began at Edinburgh the 6th of May, 1703* (1703) and the *Account of a Conversation concerning a Right Regulation of Governments* (1704), and the versions published in the *Political Works*, these have not been included in the List.

The left-hand column gives the page and line number(s) and wording of the present text; the right-hand column gives the variant and the date of the edition of the pamphlet from which it is taken. A manuscript emendation in David Fletcher's copy is indicated by: *DF ms.*

A Discourse of Government with relation to Militias

The 1732 text reproduced that of the pamphlet of 1698 with only minor variants of spelling, which have not been listed. There are, however, major variants from the first, 1697, edition of the work, which had a different title; there are also several manuscript alterations in David Fletcher's copy.

1. *A Discourse of Government with relation to Militia's*

A Discourse concerning Militia's and Standing Armies, with relation to the Past and Present Governments of Europe, and of England in particular.

Res est periculi plena, summam Rei Publicae hominibus mercenariis, sine re, sine spe, quid vis ob pecuniam ausuris, committere; quorum profundam avaritiam incendat ad nova molienda occasio, & fortuna secum fidem circumagat. Thuan. *Hist.* (*London, 1697*)

2.07 by such men — *omitted* (*1697*)

2.09 means and — *omitted* (*1697*)

2.10 enslaved — brought into it (*1697*)

2.10 For though mankind — *insert before* 'For': But besides these changes that are introduced by the contrivance of designing men there are others no less fatal to liberty, qch [which] are produced by divers unforseen accidents concurring to make great alteration in the way of living. (*DF ms*)

2.20 soon — *omitted* (*1697*)

2.35 this — these (*DF ms*)

2.39 And 'tis worth observation, that though this change was fatal to their liberty, yet it was not introduced by the contrivance of ill-designing men; — *deleted* (*DF ms*)

3.02 nor were — no nor were (*DF ms*)

3.38 And — But (*1697*)

4.17 in the first place is, — is first of all (*1697*)

4.30 remote — *deleted (DF ms)*

5.15 that vicious appetite — their vicious appetites (*1697*)

5.17 to improve — to bring to perfection and

	which indeed severall ages before began to be in some measure cultivate (*DF ms*)
7.07 state, after the loss	state, even after the loss (*DF ms*)
7.12–9.02 Some princes with much impatience . . . they will maintain themselves under any.	*paragraph omitted* (*1697*)
9.04 and some raised by the edicts of princes	*omitted* (*1697*)
9.07 There were likewise mercenary troops sometimes entertained by princes who aimed at arbitrary power, . . . which this change has fix'd upon Europe to her affliction and ruin.	*omitted* (*1697*)
9.15 Britain	England (*1697*)
9.20 made	introduced (*1697*)
9.24–11.13 Neither could the frontier towards Scotland . . . that he will not burden his people by any tax or imposition for their maintenance.	*omitted* (*1697*)
11.14 King of England,	*omitted* (*1697*)
11.15 sooner, and understood better	*omitted* (*1697*)
11.15 before-mentioned, than any	before-mentioned, more than any (*1697*)
11.17 his successors	the succeeding princes (*1697*)
11.20 King James, who succeeded her, was a stranger in England,	King James the First was a stranger in England, (*1697*)
11.26 guards	troops (*1697*)
11.32 guards	forces (*1697*)
12.06 Britain	England (*1697*)
12.08 was favourable,	was favourable to the nation, (*1697*)

12.09 these kingdoms	the Crown (*1697*)
12.11 and England by means of her former riches	and by means of our former riches (*1697*)
12.25 Britain	England (*1697*)
12.26 British liberties	the liberties of England (*1697*)
12.28 standing armies	a standing army (*1697*)
13.01 both nations	a nation (*1697*)
13.05 Britain	England (*1697*)
13.10 these nations	England (*1697*)
13.12 Britain	England (*1697*)
13.14 as shall be proved hereafter	*omitted* (*1697*)
13.15 the nations	the nation (*1697*)
13.20 the parliaments of both nations	the parliament (*1697*)
13.25 Britain	England (*1697*)
13.32 The French King is old and diseased, and	*omitted* (*DF ms*)
14.14 a very united and formidable party in a nation.	*adds*: But the undertakers for a standing army will say; will you turn so many gentlemen out to starve, who have faithfully served the government? The question I allow to be founded upon some reason. For it ought to be acknowledged in justice to our army, that on all occasions, and in all actions, both officers and souldiers have done their part. And therefore I think it may be reasonable, that all officers and souldiers of above forty years, in consideration of their unfitness to apply themselves at that age to any other employment, should be recommended to the bounty of the Parliament. (*1697*)
14.19–27 Venice or Holland	Carthage, after the first Roman

are neither of them examples to prove the contrary; . . . and at last subdued by the Romans.

War, found how dangerous they were: and Holland, in the year 1672, how useless to defend them. (*1697*)

15.13–16.02 If during the late war we had followed so wise a course as that of Rome, . . . fit only to lose forty strong places in forty days.

paragraph omitted (*1697*)

16.06 our armies

our army (*1697*)

16.13 and that likewise is for the most part very ill paid, in order to render them the more necessitous and depending; and yet they permit them

whom, notwithstanding, they permit (*1697*)

16.17 numberless frauds, oppressions and cruelties

numberless oppressions and cruelties (*1697*)

16.33 standing armies in Britain

a standing army in England (*1697*)

17.04 Britain

England (*1697*)

17.05–13 But the undertakers for a standing army will say; . . . should be recommended to the bounty of both parliaments.

paragraph omitted (*1697*) [but see variant to 14.14 above.]

17.15 in Scotland, England, or Ireland.

in England or elsewhere. (*1697*)

17.18–31 Scotland and England are nations that were formerly very jealous of liberty; . . . in that glorious enterprize for our deliverance.

paragraph omitted (*1697*)

18.05 in both kingdoms standing armies of mercenaries

a standing army of mercenaries (*1697*)

18.10 monarchies of Scotland, and England

monarchy of England (*1697*)

18.16 the parliament of England having

the parliament having (*1697*)

18.17–20 and that of Scotland having not only declared them

omitted (*1697*)

to be a grievance, but made the keeping of them up an article in the forfeiture of the late King James.

18.23–4 If these be limited and not absolute monarchies,

If this be a limited and not an absolute monarchy, (*1697*)

19.01 the fittest instruments to make a tyrant

adds: tho' not of so gracious a Prince as we now live under, yet, to be sure, of some of his successors. (*1697*)

19.08 these monarchies
the monarchy (*1697*)

19.10 and 11 government
constitution (*1697*)

19.24 well-regulated militias
a well-regulated militia (*1697*)

19.25 these nations
the nation (*1697*)

19.28 After the barons
'Tis well known, that after the barons (*1697*)

20.01 And though upon the dissolution of that antient militia under the barons, which made these nations so great and glorious, by setting up the militias generally through Europe,

'Tis well known that after the dissolution of that antient militia under the barons, which made this nation so great and glorious, tho' by setting up militias generally through Europe (*1697*)

20.06 Nevertheless
And (*DF ms*)

20.24 these nations
this nation (*1697*)

20.27 both kingdoms
England (*1697*)

20.29–37 This doubt will be fully resolved, by considering . . . the tenants and vassals of the family of Gordon.
passage omitted (*1697*)

20.37 The battle of Naseby will be a farther illustration of this matter,
The battle of Naseby will fully resolve this doubt. (*1697*)

21.05 either
either side (*1697*)

21.09 was that army
were they (*1697*)

21.28 or starve?
or starve, unless we are to suppose we are to have no fleet at all? (*1697*)

21.29–29.33 A good militia is
eight paragraphs omitted:

of such importance to a nation, . . . and great numbers of their forces diverted from opposing the armies of our allies abroad, to the defence of their own coasts.

instead: But to come to some of the capital errors committed by those that established the modern militia's, besides what has been already mentioned; one of the chief was, the discontinuing to exercise the whole people, for which there were many excellent and wholsome laws in this nation, and almost everywhere else. Another error was, the taking men without distinction, and, for the most part, the scum of the people into that small number which they listed and exercised. Whereas if a small number only was to be exercised, no man of quality or riches ought to be excused from that duty. Thus it was, that these militias' fell into contempt; and men of quality and estates having power to send any wretched servant in their place, became themselves abject and timorous, by being disused to handle arms. 'Tis well observed by a judicious author, that 'tis easier to exercise a greater number than a less; and consequently all that are able to bear arms in a nation, than a small number pickt out of a wide country; who must march far, and be from home several days at each exercise. And perhaps it might be found an unnecessary trouble and burden, to have certain numbers of men listed and formed into bodies in time of peace, if the whole people were exercised, and an easy method laid down, by which such numbers of men as shall be thought convenient, may always be drawn out, even upon the most sudden occasion. For by this means the choice will be greater, as it ought to be, that so trade, manufactures and husbandry may be as little disturbed as possible, since the impediments of the several conditions of men are so many and so various.

'Twill be said, that I insist much upon the errors of the present militia, and do not propose a new model by which they may be amended. I answer, a parliament only can do that. The people are to tell wherein they are agrieved, and what is amiss: it belongs only to the wise council to apply sutable remedies: which cannot be difficult when the causes of the disease are discovered. And there are many models of militia, both antient and modern, from which divers useful things may be taken.

Of the fleet I shall say little, having chiefly undertaken to speak of militia's and standing forces. But surely England cannot justly apprehend an invasion, if the fleet alone were in such order as it ought to be. And it can never be the interest of this nation to take any other share in preserving the balance of Europe, than what may be performed by our fleets. By which means our money will be spent amongst our selves, our trade preserved to support the charge of our navy; our enemies totally driven out of the sea, and great numbers of their forces diverted from opposing the armies of our allies abroad, to the defence of their own coasts. (*1697*)

24.16 and new,

and altogether new, (*DF ms*)

24.25

add to paragraph: This nation had passed more or less of the years mentioned without applying themselves to any military exercise. Such a course might be taken as ye [the] circumstances of the times or the dispositions of these persons according to their several ranks and ages should afford. (*DF ms*)

24.26 What I would offer is, that four camps be formed, one in Scotland, and three in England; into which all the young men of the respective countries should enter, on the first day of the two and twentieth year of their age; and remain there the space of two years, if they be of fortunes sufficient to maintain

What I would offer is, that Scotland being divided into 6 districts, England into 28, Ireland into 16, in each district there should be a camp; into which all the young men of the district should enter, on the first day of the 18th year of their age; and remain there the space of two months in that themselves; but if they are not, then to remain a year only, at the expence of the publick.

27.11 two

27.16–29 But certainly it were no hard matter, . . . every man of a certain estate being obliged to keep a horse fit for the war.

28.14 being given only for one year,

29.14 and virtue imbided in younger years would cast a flavour to the utmost periods of life.

30.01 But if we send any forces beyond the seas to join those of our allies, they ought to be part of our militia, as has been said, and not standing forces; otherwise, at the end of every war,

30.04–and 12 these nations

30.12 so long

30.14–21 that the Scots, who have for so many ages, with such resolution, defended their liberty . . . who possess a country, everywhere cultivated

time of summer quh [which] according to the several countreys shal be freest from any necessary labour and this every yr for 9 yrs. The next 9 yrs having entered into the 27 year of their age they shall be oblig'd to come and remain in the camp only the last month of ye 2 & for 9 years thereafter having entered into the 36 year of their age shall be oblig'd to remain in camp only the last half of the last month. (*DF ms*)

some (*DF ms*)

passage deleted (DF ms)

deleted (DF ms)

and virtue imbided in younger years might probably last during life. (*DF ms*)

But if we send mercenary forces beyond the seas to join those of our allies, then, at the end of every war, (*1697*)

the nation (*1697*)

for many ages (*1697*)

that a country, whose fields are everywhere well cultivated and improved by the industry of rich husbandmen; (*1697*)

and improved by the industry
of rich husbandmen;

30.22 where men of vast
estates live in secure possession
of them, and whose merchants
live in as great splendor as the
nobility of other nations: that
Scotland which has a gentry
born to excel in arts and arms:
that England which has a commonalty, not only surpassing all
those of that degree which the
world can now boast of,

30.33 that in their days the felicity and liberties of such
countries must come to a
period, if the parliaments do
not prevent it, and his majesty
be not prevailed upon to lay
aside the thoughts of mercenary armies, which, if once
established, will inevitably produce those fatal consequences

31.05 the ruin of the nobility
by their expences in court and
army,

31.08–18 Then shall we see the
gentry of Scotland, ignorant
through want of education, and
cowardly by being oppressed;
then shall we see the once
happy commonalty of England
become base and abject, by
being continually exposed to
the brutal insolence of the soldiers; the women debauched by
their lust; ugly and nasty

where men possessing vast
estates are not hated and
abhorred as in other countries,
but deservedly blessed, by the
poorer sort of people, and
whose commonalty not only
surpasses all those of that
degree which the world can
now boast of, (*1697*)

that in their days the felicity of
a country must come to a
period, if the parliament do not
prevent it, and his majesty be
not prevailed upon to lay aside
the thoughts of a mercenary
army, which, tho it may seem a
security in his time, yet by
being continued, as will inevitably come to pass, must produce, under his successors,
those fatal consequences (*1697*)
the ruin of the nobility and
gentry by their expences in
court and army, (*1697*)
Then shall we see our once
happy commonalty become
base and abject, by being continually exposed to the brutal
insolence of the soldiers; our
women debauched by their
lust; ugly and nasty through
poverty, and the want of things
necessary to preserve their
natural beauty. Then shall we
see that great city, the pride

through poverty, and the want of things necessary to preserve their natural beauty. Then shall we see that great city, the pride and glory, not only of our island, but of the world, subjected to the excessive impositions Paris now lies under, and reduced to a pedling trade, serving only to foment the luxury of a court. Then will Britain know what obligations she has to those who are for mercenary armies.

and glory, not only of our island, but of the world, subjected to the excessive impositions Paris now lies under, and reduced to a pedling trade, serving only to foment the luxury of a court. Then will England know what obligations she has to those who are for mercenary armies. (*1697*)

31.12 the women debauched by their lust; ugly and nasty through poverty, and the want of things necessary to preserve their natural beauty.

deleted (*DF ms*)

Two Discourses concerning the Affairs of Scotland

The text printed in 1732 follows that of the first edition of the work in 1698, with only minor variations in spelling and punctuation, which are not recorded here. However David Fletcher's copy of the *Discourse* contains a number of ms alterations, which are given below.

First Discourse

50.22 In a word, our forefathers had two securities for their liberties and properties, ... but also when there is no sufficient caution in the constitution that it may not be exercised tyrannically.

paragraph deleted (*DF ms*)

Second Discourse

60.11 And the liberty every idle and lazy person has of burdening the society in which he lives, with his maintenance, has increased the numbers to the weakening and impoverishing of it: for he needs only to say, that he cannot get work, and then he must be maintained by charity.

And the liberty idle and lazy persons have of burdening the societys in which they live, with their maintenance, has increased their numbers to the weakening and impoverishing of it: for they need only to say, that they cannot get work, and then they must be maintained by charity. (*DF ms*)

61.11 Shall the far greater part of the commonwealth be slaves,

Shall two thirds of the commonwealth be slaves, (*DF ms*)

70.24 ... to live quiet, innocent and virtuous lives.

... to live innocent and virtuous lives. (*DF ms*)

76.06–08 But to oblige a man of great estate in land to sell all, except perhaps two hundred pounds sterling a year (which he might cultivate by his servants) and to employ ...

But to oblige a man of great estate in land to sell all, except so much as he might cultivate by his servants and to employ ... (*DF ms*)

76.11 being a thing impracticable:

being what is impracticable: (*DF ms*)

76.11–14 and also to employ the small stocks of minors, widows, and other women unmarried, in trade or husbandry, a thing of too great hazard for them;

deleted (*DF ms*)

76.17–22 obliging all men that possess lands under the value of two hundred pounds sterling clear profits yearly, to cultivate them by servants, and pay yearly the half of the clear profits to such persons as cultivating land worth two hundred pounds sterling a year, or

obliging all men that possess lands to sell the half of the yearly rent wch may arise from ye sd land to some other person at 20 yrs purchase. (*DF ms*)

above, shall buy such rents of them at twenty years purchase.
76.24–26 All interest of money to be forbidden

number this and the following two paragraphs: 1., 2., 3. (*DF ms*)

76.26–29 Every man cultivating land under the value of two hundred pounds sterling clear profits a year, to pay yearly the half of the clear profits to some other man who shall buy that rent at twenty years purchase;

Every man posessing land wch may pay the third of the yearly rent arising from the said land to some other man who shall buy that rent at twenty years purchase; (*DF ms*)

76.31–36 No man to buy or possess those rents, . . . may buy or possess such rents, though they cultivate no lands.

two paragraphs deleted (*DF ms*)

77.20–25 By the other articles; that no man cultivating land under the value of two hundred pounds sterling clear profits yearly, can purchase rents upon land from any other man; but is obliged to pay yearly the half of the clear profits, to such persons as shall buy them at twenty years purchase; and that only those who cultivate land worth at least two hundred pounds sterling a year, can buy such rents;

By the third article; that every man posessing land is obliged to pay the half of the yrly rent qch may arise from the said land to such persons as shall buy that rent at twenty years purchase; (*DF ms*)

77.26–30 except so much as may yield two hundred pounds sterling yearly, or so much above that value as they shall think fit to cultivate, may secure, if they please, the whole money they receive for their lands, upon those rents which the lesser possessors are obliged to sell.

except so much as they shall think fit to cultivate by servants, may secure, if they please, the whole money they receive for their lands, upon those rents which all possessors are obliged to sell. (*DF ms*)

77.32–33 as well as the other three sorts of persons excepted from the general rule, and mentioned in the last article,

deleted (DF ms)

78.02 the said lesser possessors
78.03–09 The reason of excepting three sorts of persons before mentioned from the general rule, is evident; ... since they cannot inspect either.

the said possessors *(DF ms)*
replace with: I know it will be look'd on as an extravagancy to make a man of 5000 pd St.[erling] a yr, but posessing only a park & garden or the land on which his house were built to pay the half of the yearly rental to any other man. To which I shall only say that if by such a regulation[,] qch every possessor of land pays as well as they[,] that man in place of an ill-paid rent should have 5000 pd punctually and fully brought to him without any trouble, would not this be vastly to his advantage. *(DF ms)*

78.18-21 and to make a law, that all those who at present possess lands under the value of two hundred pounds sterling clear profits yearly, should cultivate them by servants,

and to make a law, that all those who at the time it ceases possess lands, should cultivate them by servants, *(DF ms)*

78.24–31 they should be obliged to sell such rents to any other persons qualified as above: and likewise to make another law, that whoever possesses lands at present to the value of two hundred pounds sterling clear profits yearly, or more, should at least take so much of them as may amount to that value, into their own

delete all up to and including: ... This being done, ...;
continues: The yearly falling of the interest of money will force some of those who have money at interest, to take land for it: *(DF ms)*

hands. This being done, the yearly falling of the interest of money would force some of those who might have money at interest, to take land for it:

78.35–37 of which many might probably be paid out of those very lands they themselves formerly possessed.

deleted (*DF ms*)

78.39

add to paragraph: Which is not so much a forbiding the interest of money as a securing that interest in a better foot than at present.

79.01– any small possessors

any possessors (*DF ms*)

79.20 I believe no man can shew.

insert the following: Besides the project might take place if these were not rectifyed tho' perhaps not so easily. (*DF ms*)

Discorso delle Cose di Spagna

The changes between the texts of 1732 and 1698 are again few, almost all of spelling and punctuation: they do not affect the translation. There are, however, a number of mss emendations in David Fletcher's copy of the *Discorso*, and these have been translated below, opposite the (translated) passage to which they apply.

Advertisement

84.02 I have written of the causes of the decline in the affairs of Spain, of the measures required for its recovery, of the interests of the princes who are pretenders to that crown,

I have undertaken to narrate the causes of the decline in the affairs of Spain, to consider the measures required for its recovery, to discuss the interests of the princes who are pretenders to that crown, (*DF ms*)

84.13 Following this line of reasoning it should be easy to show which are the best governments, which nourish the virtues and are of most benefit to mankind; as also to show how great an opportunity the subjects of the Spanish crown will have on the death of their King to gain those advantages, and to enjoy the benefits of peace, of liberty and of good government.

And to provide the subjects of the Spanish crown with the opportunity on the death of their King to enjoy the benefits of peace, of liberty and of good government. (*DF ms*)

Discourse

86.03 I have therefore undertaken to discuss the interests of the princes who are pretenders to the crown of Spain; the decline in the affairs of that country, and the means which will be necessary to revive it and fit it to acquire the empire of the world.

deleted (*DF ms*)

86.15 a state

this state (*DF ms*)

86.17 and to make myself still clearer

deleted (*DF ms*)

103.04 Berry [and subsequent mentions]

Anjou (*DF ms*)

108.23 and not only the Spaniards, but all other peoples would be opposed.

deleted (*DF ms*)

112.24 it does not seem to me necessary to prolong this discourse, by demonstrating

deleted (*DF ms*)

112.29 nevertheless, to fulfill my promise

deleted (*DF ms*)

A Speech upon the State of the Nation

Two versions of this work were published in 1701, in quarto (4to) and octavo (8vo); that printed in 1732 differs from both only in the wording of the title (from the quarto edition), and in spelling and punctuation. But there are a number of mss. emendations in David Fletcher's copy (the octavo), which are recorded below.

118.01 A Speech	*followed by*: supposed to be spoke in ye House of Com. (*DF ms*)
118.03 State of the Nation	Partition Treaty (*DF ms*)
118.04 In April 1701	*omitted* (*1701 4 edn*)
118.05 Gentlemen	Mr Speaker (*DF ms*)
118.06 you repeated in lines: 7–10	we (*DF ms*)
119.01 you repeated in lines: 2–6	us (*DF ms*)
119.02 your repeated in lines: 3, 6, 8	our (*DF ms*)
119.08 You were formerly convinced	The members of this house were formerly convinced (*DF ms*)
119.14 you	them (*DF ms*)
119.15 you	they (*DF ms*)
120.07 your suspicions	the suspicions (*DF ms*)
123.15 This treaty like an alarum-bell rung over all Europe: Pray God it may not prove to you a passing-bell.	*deleted* (*DF ms*)
127.34 propose	desire (*DF ms*)
128.04 as accession of strength is more advantageous than ruin.	*deleted* (*DF ms*)

Index

Cambridge Texts in the History of Political Thought

Titles published in the series thus far

Aristotle *The Politics* and *The Constitution of Athens* (edited by Stephen Everson)

Arnold *Culture and Anarchy and Other Writings* (edited by Stefan Collini)

Astell *Political Writings* (edited by Patricia Springborg)

Austin *The Province of Jurisprudence Determined* (edited by Wilfrid E. Rumble)

Bakunin *Statism and Anarchy* (edited by Marshall Shatz)

Baxter *A Holy Commonwealth* (edited by William Lamont)

Beccaria *On Crimes and Punishments and Other Writings* (edited by Richard Bellamy)

Bentham *A Fragment on Government* (introduction by Ross Harrison)

Bernstein *The Preconditions of Socialism* (edited by Henry Tudor)

Bodin *On Sovereignty* (edited by Julian H. Franklin)

Bolingbroke *Political Writings* (edited by David Armitage)

Bossuet *Politics Drawn from the Very Words of Holy Scripture* (edited by Patrick Riley)

The British Idealists (edited by David Boucher)

Burke *Pre-Revolutionary Writings* (edited by Ian Harris)

Christine de Pizan *The Book of the Body Politic* (edited by Kate Langdon Forhan)

Cicero *On Duties* (edited by M. T. Griffin and E. M. Atkins)

Conciliarism and Papalism (edited by J. H. Burns and Thomas M. Izbicki)

Constant *Political Writings* (edited by Biancamaria Fontana)

Dante *Monarchy* (edited by Prue Shaw)

Diderot *Political Writings* (edited by John Hope Mason and Robert Wokler)

The Dutch Revolt (edited by Martin van Gelderen)

Early Greek Political Thought from Homer to the Sophists (edited by Michael Gagarin and Paul Woodruff)

The Early Political Writings of the German Romantics (edited by Frederick C. Beiser)

Erasmus *The Education of a Christian Prince* (edited by Lisa Jardine)

Ferguson *An Essay on the History of Civil Society* (edited by Fania Oz-Salzberger)

Filmer *Patriarcha and Other Writings* (edited by Johann P. Sommerville)

Fletcher *Political Works* (edited by John Robertson)

Sir John Fortescue *On the Laws and Governance of England* (edited by Shelley Lockwood)

More *Utopia* (edited by George M. Logan and Robert M. Adams)
Morris *News from Nowhere* (edited by Krishan Kumar)
Nicholas of Cusa *The Catholic Concordance* (edited by Paul E. Sigmund)
Nietzsche *On the Genealogy of Morality* (edited by Keith Ansell-Pearson)
Paine *Political Writings* (edited by Bruce Kuklick)
Plato *Statesman* (edited by Julia Annas and Robin Waterfield)
Price *Political Writings* (edited by D. O. Thomas)
Priestley *Political Writings* (edited by Peter Miller)
Proudhon *What is Property?* (edited by Donald R. Kelley and Bonnie G. Smith)
Pufendorf *On the Duty of Man and Citizen According to Natural Law* (edited by James Tully)
The Radical Reformation (edited by Michael G. Baylor)
Rousseau *The Discourses and Other Early Political Writings* (edited by Victor Gourevitch)
Rousseau *The Social Contract and Other Later Political Writings* (edited by Victor Gourevitch)
Seneca *Moral and Political Essays* (edited by John Cooper and John Procope)
Sidney *Court Maxims* (edited by Hans W. Blom, Eco Haitsma Mulier and Ronald Janse)
Spencer *Man versus the State* and *The Proper Sphere of Government* (edited by John Offer)
Stirner *The Ego and its Own* (edited by David Leopold)
Thoreau *Political Writings* (edited by Nancy Rosenblum)
Utopias of the British Enlightenment (edited by Gregory Claeys)
Vitoria *Political Writings* (edited by Anthony Pagden and Jeremy Lawrance)
Voltaire *Political Writings* (edited by David Williams)
Weber *Political Writings* (edited by Peter Lassman and Ronald Speirs)
William of Ockham *A Short Discourse on Tyrannical Government* (edited by A. S. McGrade and John Kilcullen)
William of Ockham *A Letter to the Friars Minor and Other Writings* (edited by A. S. McGrade and John Kilcullen)
Wollstonecraft *A Vindication of the Rights of Men* and *A Vindication of the Rights of Woman* (edited by Sylvana Tomaselli)